MARTIN O'NEILL

MARTIN O'NEILL

The Biography

Alex Montgomery

This paperback edition first published
in Great Britain in 2007 by
Virgin Books Ltd
Thames Wharf Studios
Rainville Road
London
W6 9HA

ISBN 978-0-7535-1241-8

Typeset by TW Typesetting, Plymouth, Devon
Printed and bound in Great Britain by
Mackays of Chatham PLC

Dedication

For Anne, Helen, Katie, Cameron,
George, Daisy and Lucy

CONTENTS

INTRODUCTION

This is the story of a man's life and is not intended as a history of the clubs he has played for or managed, though they are intertwined, one dependent on the other. I have a journalist's mistrust of statistics – probably because when I compile them they have a habit of coming out wrong – so the book is therefore short of these in the actual copy, although John Russell has put together a comprehensive statistics section at the back. We did not ask for Martin O'Neill's help or approval for this project so my hope is the finished article doesn't grate with him. This is his life as others close to the action see him. It is about a player strangely undervalued, certainly meriting more public praise than he received from the late Brian Clough, a player who tiptoed into management at non-League Grantham and developed through another non-League side Shepshed into one of the most astute in the modern British game – hugely successful at Wycombe, Leicester and Celtic. The next phase of his exceptional career will be played out at Aston Villa, a club bristling with potential. If anybody can tap into their resources it is Martin O'Neill.

Alex Montgomery, October 2006

AUTHOR'S ACKNOWLEDGEMENTS

A special thanks to Daniel King whose meticulous research helped provide the base from which everything else grew. Also to Kevin Moseley, an old friend whose knowledge of Ireland and the Irish and his many contacts in the game was an invaluable source of information. There are many others I am indebted to; in Kilrea and Coleraine and Belfast; in Glasgow; and those connected with Martin O'Neill's club sides at Grantham, Wycombe, Shepshed, Nottingham, Leicester and London. Their help was freely given.

1. 'DEADLY'S' VILLA COUP – MARTIN'S BACK

Martin O'Neill's admiration for Aston Villa goes back to the days when he was winning titles and European Cups for Brian Clough at Nottingham Forest. The young Northern Irishman was helping make history, but there was no argument that Villa, despite Forest's success, was the premier club in the Midlands. Birmingham City, Villa's neighbours and closest rivals, Derby County, who achieved so much in the 1970s with Clough and then Dave Mackay, Leicester City, who always acted bigger than they were and Wolves, who have failed in recent decades to recapture a glorious past, might not accept that, but O'Neill most certainly did.

There was an aura about Villa Park and its then classic exterior that appealed to him. Birmingham was recognised as England's second city; Villa was identified as the city's top club and in so many ways grander than Forest. They were a force as a team, particularly in the latter days of O'Neill's playing career, an outstanding side which won what was then the Football League's First Division championship in 1981 and went on under the management of the late Tony Barton to emulate O'Neill's achievement with

Forest by winning the European Cup. If he cherished any thoughts of playing for Villa then it went no further than talk among his family and close friends. It never materialised.

O'Neill's high regard for Villa was a clue to his intentions if and when the time became right for him to make his managerial comeback. He had walked away from five years of success at Celtic to help care for his wife Geraldine, who was undergoing cancer treatment, clear-minded about his role as a carer for the woman who had stood by him throughout their partnership. She had protected him and now it was his turn to devote time to her.

When he left Celtic in May 2005 he had no idea how long his exile would be. He refused numerous tempting offers to make a comeback when approached at the family home outside London where they had returned to. O'Neill is secretive about revealing these ultra-private details but various Premiership clubs would have rushed through negotiations to have him as their manager if he had given them any encouragement: he was in demand.

Every time a job became available in the Premiership O'Neill's name was on the priority list because his appointment would come with a virtual guarantee of success. His managerial career may have begun less than promisingly in non-League football but picked up speed at Wycombe Wanderers, and took off at Leicester, before he emerged in Scotland to regain Celtic's status as Scotland's premier club.

If he acted like a crazy man on the touchline and a saint on the box then that was part of the charm. The man not only talked well but produced results and he did so on restricted budgets, restricted when compared to the cash available to José Mourinho at Chelsea through his oligarch owner/boss Roman Abramovich, or Sir Alex Ferguson at Manchester United, or Arsène Wenger at Arsenal, or Rafa Benitez at Liverpool.

It was Geraldine's health that concerned him, not how quickly he would make a comeback. He refused to be panicked into resuming his career. There were those who warned him that even the best managers have to manage and that to be off the front line for a year or longer could prove suicidal: he would be forgotten and eventually discarded as a serious operator.

During this period his name was frequently linked with vacancies. Villa were the least quoted but prominent in the background to emerge as the prime movers. It was a case of the right club, the right time and an endorsement from his family to accept the most suitable offer.

There were two questions to be answered: would Villa chairman/owner Herbert Douglas Ellis OBE, aka Deadly Doug, finally sell off his controlling interest and stand down and could he, an 82-year-old who has survived prostate cancer, a heart bypass and a reputation as an impatient curmudgeon, possibly persuade O'Neill to be Villa's longed for saviour?

Ellis is one of English football's most dominant characters. He can be endearing or devilish, very difficult to those who oppose him, but despite the flaws it is doubtful Villa would have continued as a major club of sorts without the business acumen that made him a very wealthy man – his travel company specialised in package holidays for the masses – when he was in his forties.

Despite his devotion to Villa, 'Deadly' was never trusted as a true fan of the club. The supporters remember how he had been on the board of city rivals Birmingham City as well as Derby and Wolves. How, they asked, could such a man consider himself devoted to their club? Many were disgusted when the board agreed to rename the Witton Lane Stand the Doug Ellis Stand. At a dinner where he was guest speaker Jimmy Greaves, the Chelsea, Spurs, West Ham and England striker of some forty years ago said with a gentle dig that a further new stand would be called 'The Other Doug Ellis Stand'. Ellis is not short on ego. He carries around a postcard which confirms not only his interest but participation as a young footballer for Chester as proof of his credentials. He had a salmon he caught stuffed, if that's what they do to fish, and hung over the directors' room at Villa Park. One of the thirteen managers he hired and dispensed with joked: 'When I remember the fish I always think it could have been much worse than it was for me.'

Ellis's actions were regarded as expedient, self-glorying. He had been appointed chairman on two occasions; from 1968 until 1975 and from 1982 to September 2006. In all of his time as chairman – a total of 31 years – there were moments of success but not the sustained success you would expect of a club established in the English game. And it is ironic that Ellis was not a member of the board in their most successful years when Villa won the championship and went on to win the European Cup in 1982.

The last few years have been particularly difficult for Ellis to cope with. The team struggled badly and made no progress under previous manager David O'Leary. It was a considerable disappointment. O'Leary's achievements at Leeds United suggested he was the man with the managerial technique to re-establish Villa as a challenger to Manchester United and Arsenal and then Chelsea for the big prizes.

The chairman took the blame from a sizeable minority of Villa fans who staged protests against him. It was undeniable that the majority had no confidence in his chairmanship; they had given up on him. There were protests demanding his resignation and protests when he was accused of not supplying the financial resources O'Leary constantly claimed he required. The two, the octogenarian and the Irishman, put up a unified front. Ellis backed O'Leary when he referred to him and the club's problems in public.

Behind the scenes the atmosphere was fermenting and ready to erupt. The pressure on Ellis was mounting but even so his health worries did not stop him taking as full a part in the running of the club as he could. There was plenty for him to consider. A series of takeover groups made genuine moves to oust him and all bar one saw O'Neill as their first choice of manager should their takeover be successful.

At the time Randy Lerner, the American billionaire who was to eventually win the battle for control, was one of the interested parties. Michael Neville, a local businessman, appeared as the most persistent suitor. In October 2005 he had offered to buy out Ellis with the financial backing of the Comer brothers, Luke and Brian, of the Comer Homes Group. That fell flat. Neville came back for more this time with a plan that included a place for Graham Taylor, the former England manager, who had worked reasonably successfully with Ellis as Villa manager and went back for more of the same when he quit international football. Neville could not convince the Villa board, i.e. Doug Ellis, that he could finance the deal, which was to be valued at just under £70 million. Sven Goran Eriksson, then England manager, talked indiscreetly about Villa being one club ripe for plucking when he was hoaxed by a reporter from the *News of the World* disguised as a sheik and it was not a surprise therefore when Athole Still, Eriksson's agent, was reported to front a group financed with money from the Middle East. There was a Scandinavian group, AVO6, headed by Nicholas Padfield QC and with Michael Laudrup and John Jensen, two of Denmark's most high-profile footballers, being lined up as a management team. That also came to nothing, as did the introduction of another American group.

Ellis had to cope with a disturbing and nationally reported revolt among the players. It centred on a letter printed on 14 July 2006 in a local Birmingham paper and was ostensibly written by players as an official statement. It was highly critical of Ellis and the way he ran the club. They were asked for proof that the statement actually existed. No acceptable proof was forthcoming. A three-man enquiry was set up by the club made up of operations director Steve Stride and nonexecutive directors David Owen and Steven Kind.

Lee Hendrie, one of Villa's top names who was loaned out to Stoke City later in the summer of 2006, backed the club's view that not all the players had been informed of the 'unrest'. Hendrie was specific; the players, or certainly the majority, did not know what had happened and confirmed they had then met en bloc to discover the source. He felt the incident had been blown out of all proportion. Whom was he accusing on behalf of the majority of the players? The statement was narrowed to a Villa Park insider who was either crassly trying to stimulate argument or at worse trying to provoke a mutiny. A rumour that O'Leary was behind the statement remains as just that, a rumour in no way substantiated. Ellis was on holiday at the time and while the incident subsided in importance the relationship between O'Leary and Ellis was scarred. O'Leary left Villa by mutual consent on 19 July, five days after the statement had appeared in print. O'Leary's position was untenable. They had finished the season in 16th place – in the final weeks of the season they were quoted as one of the three favourites doomed to relegation – with 42 points.

Ellis's hand had in fact been hovering above the panic button for over a year. The club's discontent was openly revealed to shareholders in the Aston Villa plc interim report up to November 2005. It stated less than reassuringly for O'Leary, 'Overall League results have been inconsistent and generally disappointing, particularly following the substantial investment in new players during the close season.'

The report tried to be optimistic when it went on to state, 'Results have not, however, been assisted by a long injury list to key players'. It then went on to highlight Aston Villa's poor performance in the Carling Cup when they were beaten by Doncaster Rovers.

With O'Leary gone the stage was ethically clear for Ellis to approach O'Neill and also consider the only takeover that seemed viable, the one from the American Lerner. There have been suggestions that O'Neill spoke to Lerner about his takeover plans before agreeing the deal overseen by Ellis and it is impossible to believe a man as shrewd as O'Neill would accept a contract without knowing the immediate plans of both Ellis and Lerner. He originally and cautiously accepted a one-year rolling contract.

No matter who else was involved in the negotiations it was the Old Boy who concluded them. It was his ball game, his appointment, and he was going to see it through. Ellis may not claim this to be his greatest moment – he was never short of them in his own mind – but in clinching the signature of Martin O'Neill he had secured the best possible manager for his club. The deal was notified to the stock exchange on 4 August 2006 followed by a press conference which went out on national television live through Sky TV.

Ellis was as puffed-up with pride as a man who has had major heart surgery dare. Not only had he beaten off opposition for O'Neill from a number of his Premiership friends but he had secured the man many felt should have been given charge of England. O'Neill had been summoned by the FA for an interview with the other names invited to 'apply'; Alan Curbishley, Sam Allardyce and Steve McClaren, who was to be entrusted with the job. Everything about the secret selection process was leaked, even the 'secret' where-abouts of the meetings which were comically reminiscent of scenes from a spy novel – so secret, press photographers were in place to take shots of the arrivals and departures.

One informed whisper claimed O'Neill had lost any chance of being appointed because he was less than convincing during his interview. It was even claimed that it was his single-mindedness, his refusal to guarantee a place for David Beckham, losing the then England captain's commercial value, which was the black mark against him.

O'Neill has said nothing substantial about the interview and nor has the FA publicly, but nobody with knowledge of O'Neill could possibly believe a man of his intelligence, a highly articulate man, a man capable of inspiring groups of millionaire footballers and 'selling' himself to top bosses at his various clubs, would stumble before an FA committee.

There is an argument for saying he meant to, that he had no intention of taking the job, or rather he would have faced an almighty dilemma if it had been offered to him. That dilemma could be his Irish nationality. He came from a republican family in the north; he had experienced living with the sectarian troubles that scarred Northern Ireland in his home town Kilrea then latterly in Belfast. There are republican Irishmen who would have seen his appointment as a betrayal and that would have hurt O'Neill.

It must have been evident to him that there would be a strong possibility the manager of England would not have been warmly welcomed by a section of the punters at Celtic should he return to the club even as a visitor.

It would not be outrageous to argue that O'Neill would have recognised that and perhaps reasoned the job was not for him. In a later chapter he is quoted as saying how the verbal abuse he as a Roman Catholic Northern Irishman had to cope with at Colchester was the worst he could recall. Colchester is a British Army garrison town. It should also be remembered that a sizeable minority of England fans still scream 'No Surrender to the IRA'. There is no perceivable link between O'Neill and that sort of Irish extremism but it is possible it was seen by O'Neill, and maybe even the FA, though never discussed, as a factor they and he could do without, an extra unacceptable pressure in a job where an enemy lurks behind every corner.

The FA's approach to O'Neill was the first indication to Premiership clubs looking for a new manager that he was probably ready to return to action. They would be caught flat-footed, apart from Aston Villa and Ellis. O'Neill's attraction to Villa is historical, but that on its own would not be enough to coax him back. Villa ticked all the boxes for O'Neill: they are a very big club, they have a large and extremely loyal fan base, they are glamorous enough to attract quality players, they can and have produced success-ful players from their own community, they are/were struggling to make any sort of impact on the game: O'Neill could make them better with the proper planning and a backroom staff in John Robertson and Steve Walford he had worked with for many years. With the exception of Newcastle United there were no other clubs available with Villa's potential not already occupied.

On a personal level joining Villa meant he did not have to disrupt his family. He could drive easily enough from home down the M40/M42/M6 to Villa Park or the club's training ground.

O'Neill would use the same formula that had brought him success from Wycombe to Celtic via Leicester. The preferred system is best identified as 4-5-1. His players had to be powerful, runners, aggressive and committed: think Alan Thompson, Neil Lennon, Bobo Balde and Didier Agathe whom he brought to Villa. There was no lack of skill in his Celtic or Leicester selections. John Hartson, now with West Bromwich Albion, had a natural quality and immense power. Henrik Larsson, whom O'Neill inherited at Celtic, possessed a master's touch as a goalscorer and was one of the first on O'Neill's list of prayed for new Villa signings from Barcelona. He signed instead for Manchester United on loan, to his former manager's considerable disappointment. The Bulgarian Stilian Petrov, aka Stan, had a gliding style, a precise use of the ball that could not be dismissed as brutish, far from it. It is not the purists' way, not the way they preferred their football at Celtic. They loved the victories, but a lot of Celtic's support felt uncomfortable with what they then watched, though not so uncomfortable they threatened a boycott.

By the time O'Neill had been installed by Ellis with his backroom team of Robertson and Walford – both had remained free after leaving Celtic with the boss – it was certain Randy Lerner would be the new owner.

Ellis had followed to the letter the rules of the London Stock Exchange in refusing to divulge information both about O'Neill's appointment and the Lerner takeover. Now everything was coming out into the open. The crucial dates were these: 24 July 2006 – the first official report that

Lerner intended buying Villa. The first problem reared up two days later when he withdrew after talks with Ellis had broken down. They did not stall for long. The £64 million bid was on but Villa had to wait until 14 August for confirmation that Ellis had agreed the Lerner takeover in exchange for £62.6 million. The LSE confirmed that Lerner had acquired nearly 60 per cent of the shares and that included Ellis's 39 per cent holding; the Ellis era was over, though he was to remain as Life President. On 25 August Lerner was nominated chairman of Villa. The old Villa board had stipulated that the sale of the club was conditional on 90 per cent shareholder acceptance but by the time of the 18 September, 1 p.m. deadline only 89.69 per cent had been accepted. Villa agreed to accept the lower figure and business was completed. Ellis resigned the next day with the rest of his board, which was replaced by chairman Lerner plus General Charles C Krulak, Bob Kain and Michael Martin as nonexecutive directors.

O'Neill had already given his opinion of the takeover – delight would sum it up. Talking of Lerner he revealed on 25 August they had a two-hour meeting four weeks previously. He added, 'I am pleased he is coming because he has decided Aston Villa are a club worth going for and worth pursuing. I have not spoken to him about the strength and weaknesses of the squad because there was no point until the takeover was done and dusted . . . I think he would like to develop the training ground and that will be terrific but essentially we want to try and strengthen the side with a bit of quality. That is something the owner will hopefully entrust in me and accept the fact I am in a (better) position to make those judgements than anyone else.'

The relationship between a manager and his board is vital for the team's success, which means the success or otherwise of the club. There was every reason to believe O'Neill, Lerner and his emissary in the Midlands, Krulak, would continue to speak much the same language when it came to progress and Aston Villa's future. O'Neill's interest in American football will also have been seen as a plus by

Lerner. O'Neill has been a follower of the game for a number of years. He watches it and will bet on the big games. When O'Neill homes in on something it can become all-engrossing and so it has been with American football. Now he has a chairman in Lerner who not only shares his passion for football on both sides of the Atlantic but owns the franchise to the NFL club Cleveland Browns which was bequeathed to him when his father Al died in October 2002.

The arrival of Lerner at Villa gave the club the financial resources O'Neill needed to strengthen his squad. The initial estimate was £20 million, the figure unofficially released by Villa some three months after the takeover: good but not exceptional when compared to the amounts of money Chelsea spend, or the £60 million United laid out on buying just two players – Rio Ferdinand and Wayne Rooney.

It was never going to be crazy spending and O'Neill knew that from the outset. He was never going to be lavished with an endless stream of money and he is aware he will have to provide a reason for each and every penny spent.

At the time of writing Lerner's commitment to a signing policy had not been properly tested. Lerner is one of America's richest men and at 42 that is an indication of his brilliance as a lawyer/businessman. It was while he spent a year (1983) reading at Clare College, Cambridge his interest in the beautiful game developed. His stay in England coincided with Villa winning the European Cup, but it was his success in business – he is chairman of MBNA, the global credit card organisation taken over by the Bank of America, and his ownership of The Browns that led him to Villa and the Premiership.

British clubs have in the past appointed 'celebrity' directors but none have quite the intrigue of Lerner's non-exec General Krulak. There is nothing stuffy or withdrawn about either, despite warnings from the States that Villa would have to learn to cope with a sterner Lerner. There were no signs of that as Lerner and his associates high-fived in the directors' box during Villa's September 2006 win against

Charlton. Krulak, 64, is one of America's most senior and decorated servicemen. The general was Commandant of the Marine Corps with a list of assignments and decorations including the Distinguished Service Medal, Purple Heart with gold star, a Combat Action Ribbon, Republic of Vietnam Cross of Gallantry and two Kuwait Liberation Medals. Perhaps Ellis found time to advise the general of the battle tactics he used to catch his salmon during the takeover negotiations.

O'Neill will carry the weight of expectation for team performances, results and progress, but he can have no complaints about the men backing him from the boardroom.

The start of the 2006/07 Premiership campaign was almost too good, too easy, with the inevitable crash at the end of October 2006 when Villa's unbeaten run of nine Premiership matches ended at Liverpool in a 3–1 defeat, more comprehensive than the score might suggest and confirmation, for those who had not been listening intently to O'Neill's forecast, of the extent of the rebuilding job ahead. It became clear come mid-January 2007 when Villa's 3–1 defeat at Manchester United stretched their run without a win to twelve matches. O'Neill realised new signings were essential to add depth to a shallow squad but that he would have to wait until the January 2007 transfer window opened to try to secure the right men. So many names were mentioned during his first few months in the job and some, like Robbie Keane of Tottenham, made sense. He had used his 4-5-1 system which suited when he had Luke Moore and Gabriel Agbonlahor as his wide men. It was adaptable. When he lost Moore through injury he switched to 4-4-2 with the Czech Milan Baros operating with Juan Pablo Angel in the front line. This system crashed against Liverpool to end the last unbeaten run in the Premiership, which somehow O'Neill had stretched to the tenth match. They conceded three goals in thirteen minutes at Anfield with Agbonlahor scoring what was hardly a consolation.

* * *

O'Neill's immediate impact on Villa was fully expected by players who have worked with him, know how he operates and who also believe, given time and freedom, he represents the outstanding chance for propelling Villa on to a new level.

John Hartson, who won three Scottish Premier League championships in five seasons with O'Neill at Celtic, is an admirer of the Irishman's management skill. There have been whispers that O'Neill rarely attended training sessions, leaving these in the charge of coach Walford and his manager's assistant Robertson. Hartson says otherwise, claiming O'Neill was a regular who oversaw every aspect of training and if for some reason he was not there in body then you would feel his presence. Steve Walford would start sessions, but after an hour O'Neill would arrive with Robbo to analyse the training. He would make points he felt were necessary but succinctly explained his philosophy on how he wanted his teams to play.

Hartson confirmed O'Neill liked strong players, towering players, and would wait until they became available; that he wants his centre halves to be able to head the ball, in both boxes, but would encourage them to come out and play as well. O'Neill likes his front men to hold the ball and keep it. The Wales international striker who scored ninety goals for O'Neill has described how he would be told never to have too many thoughts on his mind when the ball came to him. O'Neill's reasoning was simple; if you thought about what you were going to do then you would already have too much on your mind and the resulting indecision would too often gift the ball to an opponent.

Hartson recalls that though Walford had the authority to make decisions, O'Neill's teams played the manager's way. O'Neill wanted training to be lively and that helped players like Hartson, who self-admittedly was not a good trainer, if a willing one.

O'Neill could be strict. When Hartson told him in a rash moment to 'eff off' he was dressed down by an enraged O'Neill, who did not speak to him for five days before accepting Hartson's apology and then, and only then, continuing their professional relationship as if nothing had happened between them.

Hartson ridicules the perception that O'Neill rules by fear as a tactic he learned from his years with Clough. O'Neill is witty, treats his players like men and expects them to play like men. And again, though he respects Clough's success, his associates will say that he uses only the best of Clough's methods, not the ones he was humiliated by and are recorded in a later chapter. There are players who have felt the full force of O'Neill's anger when he has lost his temper in the dressing room but his skill is in working with his players, cajoling them. It is his job to get the best out of them even when there may not be a lot to exploit. The image of him being a super-disciplinarian is also a myth according to Hartson. It is a mark of the respect they have for him that most of the Bhoys he left behind at Celtic would be happy to renew the manager/player partnership at Villa Park. Martin O'Neill equally would have gladly welcomed a few more of his former Celtic players to Aston Villa to help him in his plan to revive another great club.

2. BITTER-SWEET TIMES IN SEVILLE

The expectation level among Aston Villa fans had been diluted by failure. Martin O'Neill's arrival transformed that depressed attitude overnight. Instead of worrying about Premiership survival the talk was about revival – and European competition. Of all O'Neill's domestic achievements the one other that gave him great, we cannot say the greatest, satisfaction was Celtic's appearance in a European final for the first time since their middle-aged fans were youths. Celtic's UEFA Cup final against Porto in Seville developed into the biggest sporting craic in memory – there are those who claim it as the greatest of all time – three days of riotous alfresco partying that attracted Celtic fans worldwide, but principally from Scotland and most specifically the Dear Green Place called Glasgow. What had gone before in the long build-up was extraordinary enough but in the final days the gathering transcended all known experience of fan loyalty and unquestioning support for a club side. European competition! A European final! This is what Villa and their supporters believe Martin O'Neill will reintroduce them to, given time.

Any visitor to Seville in the run-up to the 21 May 2003 final, say an American from the Midwest with no knowledge of football, would have been justifiably mystified by the sights and sounds that had transformed this magnificent Andalucian city into a Glaswegian outpost with all the excess of behaviour that would suggest.

Why were so many wearing green-and-white hooped outfits – men, women and children?

They all carried bottles, or nearly all of them did.

When they weren't staggering, they were dousing themselves in one of the city's elaborate fountains, or the river.

Was it a bizarre invading army?

No, though Seville has survived those in the past, but it was the complete, trouble-free and temporary takeover of one of the world's most famous and historically significant cities.

No one can be certain, but well-informed estimates suggest some 80,000 Celtic fans descended on this sweltering south-west area of Spain. That figure may be an exaggeration but not much of one according to those professional observers who witnessed the increasingly bizarre scenes, with thousands sleeping rough, laid out on the palm-lined streets, through either a shortage of cash, or the impossibility of finding hotel accommodation, or a lack of desire to squander whatever money they had on anything as wasteful as a room with a bed.

The fact that only a relatively small number were officially in possession of tickets for a final that concluded a season of supreme effort in a European club tournament second only to the Champions League in importance was as irrelevant as their own creature comfort. They were going to be there, ticket or no ticket, bed or no bed. Hadn't they waited over 30 years – since Jock Stein's team faced and were beaten by Feyenoord in the old-format European Cup Final of 1970 – to revel again in such an occasion?

It was to be a family affair for many: credit cards took a pounding, moneylenders offered deals with outrageous interest rates that were recklessly entered into, normal holiday arrangements were shelved.

All that mattered was the right when it was all over to say you were there, side by side as it happens with the club's easily recognisable fans such as Rod Stewart and Billy Connolly, plus many other members of Scotland's showbiz glitterati.

There is a fan culture among the Scots that feeds on optimism. In the past it has been wholly justified. Scotland international teams may not have won anything of note, but they were capable of lifting the soul with world-class, if frustratingly inconsistent, performances. For such a small country they have, until the late 1980s, produced talent exceptional enough to test the best of opponents. Celtic played a considerable part in that past and compounded their traditional position as a torch carrier for the game when they became the first British club to win the European Cup. When that confidence is boosted with a surge of Irish enthusiasm no peak is too high to attempt.

The arrival of O'Neill and the immediate success he brought to Celtic released all those connected with the club, including the support, from the domination of Rangers. The joy that came from domestic success was considerable, but success in European competition was a force that propelled O'Neill and a support anxious to make their mark outside the restrictions of the Scottish game.

O'Neill's season was to be condensed, cruelly as it was to turn out, into Celtic's two remaining matches – the final against the excellent Portuguese side Porto and then the Scottish Premier League championship deciders that had reached the stage where one goal separated them from Rangers. The title was open to both and would depend on the extent of Celtic's win against Kilmarnock or their championship rival's against Dunfermline at Ibrox.

There was so much drama to unravel before that D (for domestic) Day Sunday.

The advance party of Celtic fans had arrived in Seville the weekend before the match, but the bulk of them surged into the city from the Monday, three days before the final.

The organisers, UEFA, had worked out their figures on the 52,000 capacity of the Estadio Olimpico, not anticipating a substantial extra number turning up without tickets. The Foreign Office in Whitehall advised fans without tickets to stay well clear of Seville, confirming that accommodation was impossible to find. It was like asking King Canute to call it a day, pick up his chair and go home.

From the start of the 'invasion', it was clear that UEFA had vastly underestimated the demands made of Seville by Celtic's support. For all the kindness and understanding of the citizens there was no way the city could cope supplying food, drink and accommodation for so many 'customers', though it was through the goodwill of everyone – the locals, Celtic and Porto supporters – and the patience and under- standing of the police and security forces that it was carried off with a minimum of trouble and not one arrest reported. One newspaperman put it down to good Catholic teaching, a novel way of explaining the good behaviour of football fans.

It was respect that prompted such an unprecedented show of allegiance: respect for the club they have been born to support, respect for O'Neill and his players and what they had achieved in qualifying for the final and a belief that their energy, their enthusiasm could tip the scale in Celtic's favour. There is an unflinching belief that they the fans are an essential part of an occasion of this importance. For three days in Seville they were the show. If passion and the emotion of fans can be transmitted to the players and used as an incentive to drive them on, then they know they can supply it. If intimidation does unsettle the opposition, then they will supply that too. It has worked many times over the decades, so why should it not work in Seville?

O'Neill's mood was hard to discern as he prepared his players in the calm luxury of Jerez, well away from the stifling heat of early summer Seville. They had a good idea of what it was like in the madhouse atmosphere of the city, that tickets were selling on the black market for in excess of

£300 and that not even the Spanish allocation would go anywhere near satisfying the demand of 20,000-plus extra fans. As it was, 35,000 are estimated to have made it into the stadium and the rest were able to watch the drama on giant screens. It was a reasonable gesture by the authorities, but it didn't quite work as planned when one screen failed to operate and another was rendered useless as the setting sun shone directly on it.

O'Neill was contemplative: camouflage perhaps? There is no reason he should have been anything less than upbeat, though the nerves would have been taut when he considered the almost obscene importance to him and his players of two matches inside five days that would mean the difference between heaven and hell to him and them.

They were the underdogs against the Portuguese, as they had been after dropping into the UEFA Cup because of their failure to overcome FC Basle in the European Champions League qualifier. The Swiss were to go on and prove themselves a side of genuine quality, but at the time it seemed a disastrous and unnecessary defeat for Celtic, deflating and seriously bad for morale. How quickly would they eradicate the feeling that they had succumbed too easily?

They had to grasp the opportunity now available to them in the UEFA Cup and they managed to ease their way in against FK Suduva. The Lithuanians were the victims of a 10–1 aggregate rout in the opening round.

Blackburn Rovers, managed by former Rangers boss Graeme Souness, were next and this was the turning point, the moment Celtic began to believe in themselves. They were outplayed at Celtic Park, yet won 1–0. It was never going to be enough – or so the pundits said. They were wrong. O'Neill's tactics were impeccable for the return and Henrik Larsson, who scored the only goal of the first leg, scored again before Chris Sutton hit number two for a 3–0 aggregate victory.

The charge was on and Celta Vigo were next to fall, but it could not have been tighter. Celtic won the first leg at home, but lost the Vigo leg of the tie to survive on an away goal from John Hartson. European football was beginning to rediscover the magnificent passion that is generated from a Celtic home crowd, a passion that was to climax six months later in quite astonishing scenes that were relayed round the world with admiration from Seville.

It was looking good for O'Neill and his European ambition, but Celtic still had to find a way of making it to the final and once again they were regarded as underdogs when drawn against German side Stuttgart. A 3–1 win at home with goals from Paul Lambert, Shaun Maloney and Stilian Petrov set them up perfectly and away goals from Alan Thompson and Sutton saw them through despite a 3–2 defeat.

It is far too easy for English clubs, clubs whose profess-ionalism is honed on the demands of the Premiership, to look less than kindly at Scottish football. From a distance it does appear to be a sick patient but that would be to misjudge a Celtic team, a team of O'Neill's no less, backed by power and pace and a determination second to none. Having disposed of teams ranging from good to excellent – Blackburn, Celta Vigo and Stuttgart – it was now the turn of Liverpool. Celtic were a goal in front from a Henrik Larsson strike after two minutes, but that allowed Liverpool adequate time to recover, which they did with the first leg finishing all-square. It was another occasion of remarkable participation from the fans at Celtic Park, as they sang the Anfield hymn 'You'll never walk alone' (also a part of the Celtic repertoire) for some time. But 'one-one', was this to be the end of the road, were Celtic on their way out? The bond established between the two groups of supporters was tested by a moment of disgusting behaviour, when Liver-pool's African El-Hadji Diouf spat towards a group of Celtic fans five minutes from the end of the first leg. Liverpool made their excuses and left, eventually fining Diouf two weeks' wages (around £45,000), and making that amount available to one of Celtic's charities. The Senegalese player was also banned for two matches by UEFA for an offence that is as bad as it gets.

The fear was that such crass behaviour might destroy the goodwill that clearly exists between the supporters of both clubs. Thankfully, there was no trouble at Anfield and, if emotion was the dominant feature of the night, it was to be Celtic's celebration with a convincing 2–0 win ensured with goals from Alan Thompson and Hartson.

The semi-final draw against Portugal's Boavista looked good, too good perhaps for a team that had disposed of at least three, probably four, more fancied sides. They drew in Glasgow 1–1, a result which was a timely warning for the return. But in Portugal, Celtic exploited Boavista's apparent uncertainty, or was it lack of confidence, on how to approach the leg and it was Larsson, appropriately, whose goal – the only goal of the night – delivered the final for Celtic.

The supporters' armada had already been mobilised in anticipation of Celtic making it to Seville. Flights had long since been filled and supporters were frantically reserving what they could to other near or far destinations in order to catch connections for Spain. They travelled by coach, by train, by car and on foot, hitch-hiking their way south; they flew in from Australia, the United States and Canada – just about any place you care to mention – and they were confident Celtic would win. Even the loss of Hartson, the heaviest of blows to the team, or the acknowledgement of Porto's class could not shake their spirit.

Too often these finals can be an anticlimax, but this was to be the exception. It was frustrating, without doubt, and there was a cynicism about Porto that became more evident as the final moved into extra time. The time wasting and the play-acting was disturbing because it went virtually un-checked by Slovakian official Lubos Michel. It was not as bad as Martin O'Neill made out at the end, but it was a factor, an unjust one and something UEFA must address when officials are appointed to take charge of finals. What cannot, and should not, be denied is the quality of José Mourinho's Porto team. They took the lead crucially just before half-time through their Brazil forward Derlei. Celtic replied two minutes into the second half through Henrik Larsson with a header from a position few could have scored from. Dmitri Alenichev reclaimed Porto's lead, but again Celtic recovered quickly and again it was the incredible Larsson who pulled them back with another header from about eight yards.

The overall event was awesome, among the loudest ever staged, according to one reporter who would know. Like the city itself, the Estadio Olimpico seemed exclusively a green-and-white area. By now, Celtic knew they could win and felt they would win. Their chances alas evaporated or were certainly reduced when Bobo Balde was red-carded for a second yellow-card offence five minutes into extra time. It was too much for Celtic to withstand and five minutes from the end it was Derlei, with the hugely talented Deco, Porto's best players, who struck the winner with the assist of an unexpected and extremely unfortunate error from Celtic's Scotland goalkeeper Robert Douglas.

The despair that engulfed Martin O'Neill came from losing a European final he felt Celtic should have won. You could have anticipated his next action would be to criticise Porto for time wasting and the referee for allowing it. The fans were so incensed by the Portuguese gamesmanship that they drowned out the presentation ceremony, only to be reprimanded for their reaction by UEFA; a sour ending indeed. In fairness to O'Neill, the referee's inadequacy was eventually going to induce murderous thoughts, but when was it not expected as part of the European game at this level? It is hard to accept defeat after such a glorious campaign, but an objective view would have to be that Porto were the superior side.

It was even harder, as Celtic returned to Glasgow, that a season of so much promise could end without a single trophy, unless they managed to clinch the title at Kilmarnock by ripping it with much satisfaction from Rangers' grip. Celtic had put together a run of not always compelling but winning football at the very period Rangers had apparently lost the championship plot.

The competition would be decided at either Ibrox or Rugby Park. Only one goal separated the teams, in Rangers' favour. Both were certain their rival would win the match – but by how many? The tension could be described as unbearable, but the intensity of it had to be borne by O'Neill and Rangers manager McLeish and their players.

If they could not be parted then a date had been set aside for a play-off that only those with a warped mind would have relished.

Celtic beat Kilmarnock 4–0; an exceptional recovery after Seville, but not good enough as Rangers' advantage in a 6–1 win against Dunfermline won them the title and brought a sickening end to Celtic's season. Celtic's attitude in defeat was one of gutting disappointment, articulated, quite wrongly, by Chris Sutton. His manager had accused Porto of time wasting to win the UEFA Cup. Now the Englishman accused Dunfermline's players of lying down and presenting Rangers with the title. If O'Neill and Celtic had a justified case to argue in Seville, Sutton's outburst – it cost him a ban – was the equivalent of a verbal spit in the face of fellow professionals. A quick and fulsome apology may have diverted some of the criticism he brought on the head of his club, but what followed was hardly what was required. Sutton's agent said sorry for him, O'Neill made his apologies on behalf of the club but it was only after a too long gap that the player said his piece.

Celtic lost everything in a season dominated by Rangers' Treble success and that sadly includes the sympathy vote of the neutrals should it matter to them. Paranoia has by tradition offered an escape route when life and results conspire against Celtic. Dunfermline chairman John

Yorkston talked about the culture of conspiracy theories at Celtic where everything that goes against them does so because people are ganging up on them. Paranoia indeed.

3. CELTIC BEFORE O'NEILL – A CLUB IN TURMOIL

Martin O'Neill has been called the Messiah who led Celtic out of the wilderness. It's an extravagant way to describe the work of a football manager, however talented and successful, but it highlights the impact he has had on a major club that had been wandering aimlessly for so long, with the occasional respite, in the footsteps of their city neighbours Rangers.

The mystery is just why Celtic had driven themselves and their supporters to the very point of despair. They have support as big in numbers, as fiercely loyal, as emotional and as passionate as any in the world. They have a tradition of success. They were the first British team to win the European Cup at the beginning of the Jock Stein era when their superiority was such that they went on to triumph in nine successive championships. That should have been the base for a consistently successful future, but with astonishing incompetence they meekly handed the initiative to Rangers.

Rangers found the money to exploit the transfer market and bring big-name players to Ibrox during the revolution ignited by Graeme Souness, underwritten by the wealth of owner David Murray and sustained diligently by Walter Smith. Celtic appeared parsimonious in comparison, lacklustre, almost as if they were unwilling to participate in the big fight lest they end up with a bloody nose. They possessed a stubborn reluctance to change. Good old-fashioned financial husbandry has its place, but it did not meet the demands of a world game where the participants are prepared to gamble their own or the fortunes of others in the belief, if not the desire, that the pay-off will immortalise them.

There has always been a powerful Irish-linked dynasty within Celtic, good men for sure, but for the most part having neither the financial clout nor the vision required for a change of direction in the late twentieth century. It's different now, and if all the high-profile factions keep away from one another's throats, the future could be good enough to once again fulfil expectations, whoever the manager. To know this part of Celtic's history is essential to any understanding of the Martin O'Neill story, for without it and the different approach adopted inside Celtic Park it is doubtful if the club would at this moment be as healthy as it is, as forward thinking as it is, as prepared as it is for the long haul many believe – and their optimism is justifiable – will one day win them back their place at the top table.

It perhaps needed an autocrat such as Scots-Canadian multi-millionaire Fergus McCann to reinvigorate the club, though those who have crossed swords with him may disagree. McCann, who had been treasurer of the Croy Celtic Supporters Club in his teenage days, bought a controlling interest for £7 million, and from 1994 the wind of change swept through Celtic Park. If you had to provide a word to sum up chartered accountant McCann and his attitude to business, it would be 'ruthless'. Those who took the McCann shilling, who shared his confidence, who were unafraid of his bristling manner, saw a different, more benevolent side to him. You don't end up with enough in the kitty to buy Celtic and the sort of comfort only the wealthiest can consider without a high regard for your own ability, the sharpest of business minds and a controlled passion for the club. He arrived with a five-year plan and left exactly on time. In between, he and those he employed turned a shambles of a club into a viable enterprise. He had constructed a base for the future, and Celtic should be forever grateful to him for that. If he retired with a hefty profit from his investment, then in the long term it may come to be considered a profit shared.

The most eloquent memory of his stewardship was the 1997/98 championship under Wim Jansen that halted Rangers winning what would have been their tenth SPL title. Jansen, who had enticed the Swedish striker Henrik Larsson to follow him to Glasgow, was one of the highly talented stars who had played alongside Johan Cruyff in the Netherlands national teams of the 1970s. He had an excellent reputation as a coach, if a quirky one. Jansen, alas, flew in then out inside twelve months, leaving Larsson as an invaluable legacy.

McCann's revolution – and it was to become that – stayed low key until he employed Jock Brown as the club's general manager. Brown was well known as a television commentator and journalist, brother of the then Scotland boss Craig, and a solicitor who read law and graduated from Cambridge University. He was also a Protestant. That wasn't acceptable to some, a minority perhaps, and to them his actions were always suspicious. The feeling of animosity spread. Rumours circulated – Celtic has always been a breeding ground for tittle-tattle – about his interference with the playing side, that Jansen didn't have a working relationship with either him or McCann. It was divisive stuff; dangerous for Brown, a thorn in the side of McCann. But there's no question that the orders emanated from the very top – McCann. There was an accountant's efficiency about him – a demand for proper written reports on all matters. Jansen, his staff and the players became 'The Football Department'.

It seemed reasonable enough. Brown had taken over the legal and contractual side of Celtic, which was described by those who were acquainted with it as chaotic. He was under orders to find a coach who had to be foreign – an extraordinary demand, but again one thought out by McCann who wanted nothing to do with what had become expressed among football directors in the United Kingdom as the 'managers' culture' – the British managers' culture, to be exact. It works like this: high-profile manager has the sympathy of the supporters, puts pressure on the club to buy, buy, buy; clubs really want a manager who says, 'I will go with what I have got, we'll spend the money on youth development.' A twisted philosophy when you consider that managers stand or fall by results, are rarely given the time needed to develop young players and have in the past had to fight for compensation when sacked, as the vast majority will be.

Not everyone was in accord with McCann's foreign-only policy, but Brown was dispatched to find a man. Gérard Houllier was contacted but he had already pledged his future to Liverpool FC. There were other European high-fliers, unnamed and to this day unnameable. There was even a near signing, then Jansen was mentioned in dispatches and, to the surprise particularly of the Dutch, he agreed to Brown's overtures to succeed Tommy Burns as manager, who in turn had taken over from another Celtic favourite Lou Macari. Macari was never going to suit McCann's style; they'd quickly fallen out. Macari had been warned to 'be careful' in a discreet telephone call that informed him McCann had taken over and was on his way to meet him. It ended in acrimony with Macari going to court against McCann and Celtic. It was a case most felt Macari should have won, but he lost, though McCann, too, carried scars after being criticised by the judge.

Hopes rested on the shoulders of Jansen, but it soon became clear all was not well. There are differing versions, all centred on Murdo McLeod, the man who had been

appointed reserve-team coach but became Jansen's assistant. McLeod was a client of Brown's legal firm at the time,
although no longer it has to be said. Any relationship they
had deteriorated to the point of open hostility and
McLeod's eventual sacking. When the former Celtic player
heard that Brown, too, had quit, he was at a public
function. It did not stop him openly celebrating his adver-
sary's demise. But it wasn't as good as it seemed for
McLeod, as Brown's departure was voluntary. He couldn't
do the job any more, it had become unworkable.

What part did McLeod play in the departure of both
Brown and, more importantly to the supporters, Jansen?
You pays your money and you takes your pick. McLeod was
to some a clever manipulator – too clever. He drove a
wedge, we are told, between the coach, the accountant and
the general manager. Jansen, remember, was hand-picked
for the job because of his Brit-free approach to management.
He had started happy enough to work with what he had in
terms of playing staff, with recommended additions such as
the hugely successful Larsson and Reggie Blinker, who was
a disastrous signing. Nine players were signed by Celtic in
his time – the only two credited to Jansen were Larsson and
Blinker. There was a strong feeling among the administration at Celtic Park that McLeod was instilling in Jansen, his
boss, the British managerial creed, the very approach
McCann had specifically wanted Celtic not to have.

McCann supporters insist he and the board were very
ambitious, determined to spend money on new players but
not to waste money on new players. Everything would be
decided by what they could afford – which, it is said, was a
considerable pool by Scottish standards, though not in the
same league as Manchester United, Arsenal, Juventus, the
Milan clubs, Real Madrid and Barcelona. That is not how
it appeared in the media. There, the stories were that Jansen
was being denied the cash to buy. Jansen seemed OK with
that, agreeable to working within the parameters of 'we're
weak here . . . is it possible to buy such and such a player?'

McLeod was appointed basically because he was Scottish; he knew the Scottish scene and Wim Jansen would need that local knowledge. He was employed as reserve-team coach with another Celtic legend, David Hay, still on the payroll. The story goes that Jansen had to wear McLeod like a jersey – where the manager went, so did Murdo. They got on well and they became indivisible. So the other side of the story was that McLeod was simply doing his job as it should have been done: he was the boss's confidant, right-hand man, shoulder to cry on.

Anyway, it was to be them against the rest, the good people versus the administrators. It's the oldest story in football at this high level. If McLeod was a link between Jansen and the media, then that too was a vital role to be played. Of course it would concern the administrators who would feel that was part of their area, and no longer totally controlled by them. The bickering that turned into open warfare didn't stop Celtic winning the title and halting Rangers' record at nine in a row. It now stood equally shared between Scottish football's top two clubs. Jansen had saved Celtic's honour. It's totally unfair to say, as some have, that Celtic won the title because of Rangers manager Smith's declaration at the club's AGM that he would quit at the end of that 1997/98 season. If that news actually made Rangers players take their foot off the pedal, then more fool them. Larsson's goals separated the contestants, and he was Jansen's perceptive buy.

The rumours against Brown went on and on. Was he a closet Rangers fan? When he played football for Cambridge, did he train in a Rangers jersey? Nonsense stuff, but important to the diehards. If there was trouble reported from within, then he was going to be the reason, the one person to be blamed. The championship should have been the springboard for even greater achievements in the new season, but then Jansen made demands that were denied. Anger, frustration, resignation. He was off. McCann had wanted to sack both him and McLeod six months earlier because of their attitude, which he detested. The Dutchman returned home to the Netherlands in the summer of 1998 where he remained 'resting' until he re-emerged as a coach in Japan. The season that internally appeared to be crisis-ridden ended with a championship, a League Cup and a £7 million profit.

After a year under Venglos, it was all change in the summer of 1999: Alan McDonald took over and appointed Kenny Dalglish who appointed John Barnes as coach. Eyal Berkovic was signed. The Israeli was a talented footballer but a strange choice in that his away form at West Ham was less than committed – not the best recommendation for the dreich winter nights in the north. He had also been involved in the infamous televised kick received from John Hartson, and it didn't help that rumours abounded that he had signed a contract worth more than Henrik Larsson's. Larsson cost Celtic the title that season not because of any discontent over his salary but a broken leg. It was unfortunate for the Dalglish/Barnes axis that they had to complete a whole season without one of Europe's most prolific goal scorers.

There are undoubtedly roles for which Dalglish is eminently suited, and it is possible that general manager isn't one of them. It wasn't a comfortable time for the man considered to be Celtic's most talented footballer of the modern era. Nor for Barnes, who was forced to leave King Kenny on his own. There were big financial players now involved with Celtic, and they don't come much wealthier or better connected than Irishman Dermot Desmond. They moved for Martin O'Neill, who had shown brilliant proof of his ability to take a modest group of players (by international standards) and mould them into an intimidating force. Now he was being asked to stretch himself further and give unlimited success to the club he had adored as a youngster in Northern Ireland.

4. CELTIC – THE TREBLE AND BEYOND

Baird's Bar in Glasgow's East End would not be considered the ideal choice for a romantic evening. It's a working man's pub, and none the worse for that, though women are certainly welcome so long as they are prepared to talk about Celtic Football Club and aren't overly sensitive to industrial language. The large 'green and white' public bar, situated close to the Barrowlands market, known to Glaswegians more familiarly as the 'Barras', is recognised as one of the city's exclusively Celtic drinking establishments. The Brazen Head in the Gorbals is another, and there are a few more where the Bhoys meet, to celebrate or commiserate with one another depending on results and on where Celtic stand in the order of things. These establishments are shrines to Celtic, the club's achievements and the great names who have played for and managed them over the decades.

The arrival of Martin O'Neill has meant more glasses raised in victory than drams sunk in defeat, so if you want to see uninhibited joy then one of these bars is the place to be when Celtic win titles and/or cups, or should Rangers be the victims of the day. They have celebrated exceptional success in the past: Jock Stein, of course, produced a clean sweep of domestic honours plus the European Cup in his second full season as Celtic manager in 1967. But the celebrations when O'Neill emulated the domestic treble at the end of his first season, 2000/01, were every bit as welcome and enthusiastic, maybe even more so because that degree of success was not anticipated. For Jock, it was the start of Celtic's domination of the Scotland scene, a dominance that was to last for over a decade during which they won the title in nine successive seasons, plus just about everything else on offer. These were sensationally busy days for the traditional Celtic pubs, and there were high hopes for O'Neill and the impact he was capable of making after his success at Leicester. But *three* trophies in that first season was almost too good and far too unexpected to have been forecast, even by those who have devoted their lives to homage of the club and what it stands for.

To say it was remarkable hardly justifies the dramatic effect it had on Scottish football – more especially across the city and at the home of Rangers, now depressed and ready for change. Rangers had to try to head off what had the distinct appearance of being a long-running Celtic revival. It spelled the end of Dick Advocaat's tenure as manager at Ibrox and the instalment of Alex McLeish as his replacement, so it was an exceptional debut for O'Neill, whose Celts went on to lift the title again in his second season, though in the process they conceded both cups, the CIS and Scottish Cup, to Rangers, who were by now in full recovery mode under McLeish. These two successes were accepted as a declaration that Rangers, having experienced the humiliation that came with a clean sweep in favour of their great rivals, were fighting back.

Rangers, when managed by Walter Smith, frequently out-thought, though rarely out-skilled, Celtic. Smith was an astute tactician who sent out teams in those Old Firm affairs to subdue then execute the opposition. Advocaat had his moments, but by the time he came face to face with O'Neill's system he gave the impression of being a spent force, unwilling or unable to communicate his thoughts to his players. They were there for the taking, and O'Neill accomplished the job in his usual style – manic on the touchline, generally urbane, sophisticated and helpful in press conferences, often touchy, moody and unpredictable. His style could be a masterclass in schizophrenia; will the real Martin O'Neill please stand up? He can be charming or dismissive, helpful or obstructive, naive – well, maybe not: he has the mind of a first-class politician according to those who have worked closely with him. If he can't see round corners then there are times when it seems he can. He is a great communicator, rarely dull company. There are other occasions when the apparent self-belief would appear to be used as a shield. Above all he is ambitious, a man driven, his friends would say, as much by the fear of failure as the glory that comes from success. This is what Celtic received for their money. O'Neill had a method of play and the money to buy the players essential for that system, and he was single-minded enough to see it through. O'Neill is, in short, a winner.

If O'Neill had advantages, money being among the most important, he also had the knowledge, accumulated along the road he took, for it to pay off. Then there was his chief asset Henrik Larsson, the Swede he inherited and whose goals helped to win those two championships (not to mention Jansen's one), and whose absence because of a broken leg for most of a season probably cost Kenny Dalglish and John Barnes any chance they had of stopping Rangers – and surviving. It was vital that O'Neill formed an immediate bond with Larsson, essential that he impressed a player who no longer needed to be impressed by managers. The goals came naturally, then the titles and the cups. Larsson is one of those rare players who confuses the theory that one man does not make a team. Maybe so, but a Larsson or a Cantona, a Di Stefano, a Pele and a Maradona can make a team so much better – they inspire by their contribution. Lucky is the manager/coach who can depend on just such a man.

O'Neill's signings have certainly been of a type – powerful and proficient. Chris Sutton, Neil Lennon, Alan Thompson and Bobo Balde are muscular and successful examples, great men to have beside you in the trenches of an Old Firm clash, capable of intimidation by their presence, match after match. They have undoubtedly helped to transform Celtic into the strong side we see today, and the financial backing and confidence of the current board, backed by Irish entrepreneur Dermot Desmond, has been crucial, running in perfect harmony with that unique quality managers such as O'Neill possess. The ups and downs of Celtic's first seasons under O'Neill have been set out towards the end of this chapter, but the most compelling question must be answered here: why was O'Neill so successful in a job in which others have failed to shine, even failed utterly?

The best people to judge are those who follow Celtic's fortunes assiduously, who have been there, seen it and tried to make it work: Billy McNeill, captain of the Lisbon Lions and twice manager at Celtic Park; that great Scotland striker and former Hearts and Bristol City manager Joe Jordan, who was Liam Brady's coach; Lou Macari, who took over from Brady as manager in October 1993 only to be ousted by Fergus McCann; and a fan who has followed Celtic since he was kitted out in a green and white babygrow.

First, Billy NcNeill, whose opinions on the modern era at Celtic must be accepted without argument as those of someone who cares deeply about the club. As Stein's captain, as the first British footballer to lift the European Cup, his place in the history of the game, not merely in Scotland, is assured. His triumphs as a player domestically and in Europe, and the position of respect he enjoyed, are unlikely to be equalled in an age when loyalty to club and country seems increasingly less important. As a manager, too, McNeill tasted success during two spells in charge of Celtic. In the five years between 1978 and 1983 he won three League titles, one Scottish Cup and one League Cup. He left for England to manage Manchester City, then Aston

Villa, frustrated at the club's directors' shameful lack of response to his vision of Celtic's future. But the pull of the club was too great for him to resist, and he accepted an offer to return for the 1987/88 season. It was the club's centenary year, and under McNeill they went on to win the League and Cup double. His employment was terminated during his third year there.

If anyone knows the importance as a manager of people backing you, it's Billy McNeill. 'Having the right men beside him would have been at the centre of Martin's mind,' he said. 'The first, most important thing he had to deal with: to have people next to him he can rely on and knows he can trust implicitly not to let him down. If you can do that then you have a chance of being successful, not just surviving. Martin did that, to his credit. He brought in John Robertson and Steve Walford. Both of them come into the category of confidants who graft, who basically give him what he wants and what he thinks the players need. You can't argue with them, they've done the business.

'There is no one quality required from a Celtic manager, and it is the same for any coach or manager with any major club worldwide. You must have a diversity of qualities – experience, persuasion, that sort of thing. If you have seen it happen before then it stands to reason you have a better chance of combating something, at least understanding it when it crops up. So experience is crucial, knowing how to deal with recurring problems.

'When you have a board to handle, as he has with Celtic . . . then having a persuasive side is a big asset. He was able to persuade them to let him bring in players he felt were going to be key to a winning team, powerful players like Chris Sutton. In the modern game the money that bought Sutton may not be so big, but for Scotland it represented a fair investment, a far greater investment than anyone before had ever been able to approach. He has managed to have money made available to him for new signings that Celtic managers in the past have not had. He was prepared to pay for players he thought would do him a job. They have not let him down. The big plus at the present time is you have sufficient, not unlimited, but sufficient resources to keep you way in advance of anyone in Scotland.

'Celtic's support is the greatest asset. The fans produce a full house virtually every week. They are very passionate whatever they do and support the team right to the hilt. They put their money in, they turn up on Saturday, they are extremely vociferous and they make idols out of those they feel worthy of it. They are by far the biggest assets, and when you start talking about money, it is the supporters that put the money into the club.'

McNeill and his team-mates had all originated from within a 30-mile radius of Glasgow. Times and circumstances have changed, but McNeill believed one criticism that could be levelled at O'Neill's Celtic, and most of the teams in the Scottish Premier League for that matter, was that the team was overly reliant on non-Scottish players and therefore slightly detached from its roots.

'Sometimes you've got to look to your own ranks for players that are developing, and that's an area where people might have a little question mark. One of the problems in Scotland is that to bring players of any quality in you have to pay possibly far more than they are worth. That's the trouble – we are not always getting the top level up here. Henrik Larsson is an exception, though the others are maybe very good players. Graeme Souness was the last to bring the good English boys up because he bought England's captain and goalkeeper, but it was at a time when England weren't doing anything in Europe. It was also at a time when Rangers paid over the odds, but they have suffered, their financial structure is ridiculous. Celtic's structure means whoever is in charge will always have to be very careful.

'But I think Rangers and Celtic are investing heavily in youth development. And they must. We are aware they have been doing this for some time. We are aware Celtic believe in youth development and through the years have produced good talent which, unfortunately, they couldn't hold on to for whatever reason. The money certainly wasn't there for them, but it is there for good youngsters now and it would be nice to see them getting a run in the team. The money in the game today is extraordinary. The Celtic bonus when we won the European Cup meant we just crawled over £10,000 that year. Celtic's bonus when they won the treble was a quarter of a million for the players.'

McNeill was in no doubt about the value of one of Scottish football's imports, Henrik Larsson, and the way the Swede helped both Jansen and O'Neill to maintain certain Celtic traditions.

'Celtic have always been a team who played good football. I think Martin has a pattern, a perception at least of how he wants them to play. He made it difficult first of all for teams to come to Celtic Park and leave with anything. And of course he inherited a wonderful asset in Henrik Larsson. When he plays, the team is electrified. With Henrik in the team you must always give yourself a chance of winning, or at least scoring enough goals not to lose. You could put him in anywhere and he would do a great job for you. You often hear arguments about whether or not Henrik would fit in to such and such an era. Would he have been able to score the same number of goals thirty years ago? Would he be able to maintain his scoring rate in the English Premiership, for instance? Would he able to play like this, a free-scoring forward, in Italy's Serie A? You could never eliminate him, no matter what generation. I agree it would be interesting to see him play in England, but I believe he would be good in England. I would back Henrik to be a star in the Premiership not only as a goal scorer of remarkable consistency but as someone who links up well and works well in a team for the team. The man takes knocks and gives them.

'Wim Jansen brought him from Feyenoord and he's been an exceptional acquisition. The first season he came he struggled to adjust to the demands of the game, but to his credit and ability he coped, then conquered. Larsson would have fitted in anywhere in the world, and that cannot be denied him. Celtic has had the best years from one of the most potent strikers Scottish football has enjoyed.

'Taking the title from Rangers in his first season was such a boost, a brilliant accomplishment. The truth is, it's either Celtic or Rangers. They are more powerful than others, even more so now. They are virtually invincible. The surprise, and it was a pleasant one for all the people who are associated with the club, was that it all happened so quickly. Less than a year after he had accepted the job, Celtic were celebrating a treble.'

Having been part of the Stein team which was the first British side to win the European Cup, McNeill is better placed than almost anyone to appreciate the importance of success on the Continent to Celtic's past, present and future. It is this aspiration, almost expectation, which has both driven and frustrated Stein's successors and which, alongside the sectarian pressures unique to Glasgow, McNeill felt would determine how long O'Neill stayed at Celtic Park. 'The European thing is of paramount importance to any Celtic manager,' he said, 'because of what has gone before. I think the desire to return to the top of European football is the focus of attention.

'None of us is entirely sure how long Martin is going to be around. You couldn't be entirely sure because I would have thought he would have declared himself earlier than he has. He could also have been saying "my job has not even remotely got to halfway, my job is here". I don't know how he operated in England, but he plays with words. He is a political animal. My worry is, if he leaves, he will leave Celtic with an expensive team of players that the club cannot afford. When you spend £6 million on a player such as John Hartson and you don't play him as often as you would expect of such an expensive player on thirty grand a week, it could be a problem. It would be different if Celtic had £20 million from television as Premiership clubs do. In these financial circumstances you can afford to take a few more chances.

'Martin has protected his family. They have never been high profile up here and I think he has handled that very well. I have to be honest, I don't know if my family had problems, but they never expressed them if they did. They are the ones who feel the criticism; as the manager you can just walk on, but your family can't. My kids never had any problems and Liz handled it very well. I think nowadays managers are earning so much money they can put themselves into areas where they are not likely to be pestered.

'Has O'Neill been appreciated? Oh yes, at Celtic Park he is the idol, and understandably so. He won the treble in that first amazing season and then retained the title. The only disappointment has been not doing it in Europe. For me, I would like nothing better than for Martin to stay for another three years. There may be bigger opportunities with clubs in England – though maybe not, with the exception of one, and we know who they are – but there is nowhere in the world where you will be more adored if you satisfy demand than at Celtic. I was captain of a team that won the European Cup. It seems such a long time ago, yet every member of that squad is to this day treated with the utmost respect. He could be the beneficiary of a similar legacy.'

Joe Jordan was enticed to Celtic in the role of Liam Brady's assistant, but the early 1990s was not a good time to be in charge, or to be the right hand of the man who was. Still, for Jordan it was an irresistible challenge to work with a club that has been close to his thoughts since childhood. His own managerial career at Bristol City had been so successful that he was offered the chance to manage Aston Villa, only to turn it down and join Hearts instead. It was his success there and the reputation he had built for himself as an excellent coach that attracted Brady. They needed time to grow as a partnership, but there was not enough left for Brady and he quit towards the end of 1993, leaving

Jordan, man of principle that he is, to follow him out, though there was no pressure on him to do so. As a result of these experiences, he can well appreciate the magnitude of what O'Neill has done.

'You can't fault Martin O'Neill's achievements,' he said. 'He has turned it round so dramatically. I don't doubt it was a considerable gamble for him to leave English football, that was the game he knew. He was comfortable with it, but instead he headed into a different culture, where basically only two teams compete for the championship and second best isn't acceptable. I think most people, even those who are steeped in the game up there, wouldn't have been able to give him a real chance – not in his first season. But he did it and he came back for the big prize a second time, and maybe a hat-trick of titles if it goes well for him in 2003. That is admirable in any league anywhere, any time. There are those who will try to denigrate it, say that anybody can win up there if you have a half-decent team. But you can't use the other side, Rangers, and say they weren't so good – you can't use that. It is really unfair to Martin. If Rangers were in transition, that's not Celtic's problem. Anyway, Rangers had been so strong for so long in Scottish terms it needed a substantial effort to overtake them, especially with the ease his teams have done it. Big points margins are down to hard work on the day and hard graft in training. It's about listening to what the manager and his coaches say, taking it in and applying it to your game.'

As well as possessing a playing pedigree other footballers respect, the keys to O'Neill's success in Glasgow, Jordan believed, have been adding mental toughness to Celtic's traditional flair and deciding on a system then sticking to it.

'I must have played against Martin but I can't remember any of the games. I certainly didn't have a confrontation with him. There were no incidents. He was a Steady Eddie type: he filled a position, held the position and did the job. He was disciplined. He won the European Cup. I couldn't say much more than that.

'Martin had to find a way of producing a team as determined and as gutsy as the ones Rangers had had over the years. There is no point in playing good football then losing, and that was Celtic's pattern. With Martin, the team has always been set out the same and that has been developed certainly in the first two seasons with Celtic. Martin's teams are much the same: powerful, committed, 90-minute teams. I am not familiar with his Wycombe team, but Celtic are very similar in shape and organisation to Leicester City, and look how successful they were under his system. It's three at the back with two wide guys – winger types. The Germans will play three at the back and two full-backs pushing on, and they will play with a more physical player who is equipped to defend but can get crosses in. Martin goes for players like the boy Guppy who will take a man on.'

But like McNeill, Jordan recognised the importance of finding success outside the narrow confines of Scottish football.

'Well, the next step for the supporters, as well as keeping things going on the domestic front, is to go and try to be a force in Europe. I think you can produce a winning team in Scotland, but I don't think you can take it much further, not at the moment, and I am talking about getting into the second phase of the European Champions League. If you don't have a little bit of quality it can't happen – that applies to Rangers as well.

'Scotland have been awful in recent years. The national side, well, it's at a particularly low ebb. When you are away from it I think you look at it from a supporter's as well as a neutral point of view. You can see what is there, and I don't think your thoughts are clouded by patriotism or passion. I think you can look at it more objectively, look at it from the outside, and it isn't good, though you must always work and hope for improvement.'

No one offered more of himself as a player to Celtic FC than Lou Macari. He has always believed that Celtic's vast base of supporters will forgive a player's deficiencies, apart from one: lack of effort. And that was never an accusation levelled at Macari. The opportunity to manage them after the fall of Brady was too good to be true, but his time there was to end within eight months with the arrival of a certain Fergus McCann. It was a break that eventually had to be resolved in court, Macari citing breach of contract. He lost, many felt unjustly, especially as McCann was described by the presiding judge, Lady Cosgrove, as 'a rather devious individual'. Still, Macari's bitter disappointment over the decision would never dissolve his love of Celtic, and while he could not help but envy the resources placed at O'Neill's disposal, he was ungrudging in his praise of how he had used them to date.

'A manager can't operate at the top and maintain his position or improve without cash to buy the best players possible,' Macari asserted. 'You can have a lot of money and spend it badly, but when you spend big amounts and win trebles and follow that up with another championship there can be no complaints, only congratulations.

'It signals a change in policy at Celtic, and that can only be good for the club. I don't want to go on about the money some have and others didn't. Mind you, I was one of the unlucky ones. At the same time it was a privilege to manage Celtic because of the people who support it, and anyway I was told when I joined that I wouldn't have money to spend. I could possibly use some of the cash from any player I sold, I was told, and I managed to sell Gerry Creaney to Portsmouth for £700,000 and was allowed to use £500,000 of that to bring in three or four players. You expect that to happen at a Third, Second or possibly poor First Division club in England, but it shows you what things were like: that Celtic, former holders of the European Cup, didn't have cash.

'It was a bad time for them financially. Kevin Kelly was still in charge, Jack McGinn and Jimmy Farrell were all on the board, and there was a lot of in-fighting as I understood it. But probably the biggest thing of all, the support had deserted the club. They weren't attending matches, they were actually boycotting games, and were even outside the ground stopping people going in. There was a desire for new ownership, and that was obviously Fergus McCann and Brian Dempsey. I had three games against Rangers. The first at Ibrox we won 2–1, then we lost at Celtic 4–2. My last was at Ibrox when we drew 1–1. It was bizarre. We had no support. They had been banned from attending. Unthinkable. We were actually winning 1–0, but all our supporters were at Celtic Park watching a reserve game and listening to the Old Firm on radio. It was so very strange to play without support, and I didn't think it would happen to me as manager – certainly not as manager of Celtic.

'For the first time for a long time I felt the game up there had developed purely into a two-horse race. In the not-so-distant past there'd been a challenge from Aberdeen and Hibs; Hearts, too, always mounted a bit of a challenge, but no longer. It is Celtic or Rangers for the title year in year out, and of course the stronger they grow financially the wider the gap between them and the others becomes.

'It was always difficult at Celtic to get the better of Rangers, but when you have no clout, no new material to work with, it is very frustrating. Liam Brady, who was there before me, had some money and spent it. They felt that was the end of the cash and I'd have to make do with what I had. Tommy Burns tried, and then Kenny, and both of them had vast amounts of money. John Barnes had millions. Fergus made sure they had something to spend. I think Kenny spent £18 million, which was the very opposite end of the scale from what I had. With John Barnes there was money before and after, but I didn't have any.

'Martin has so far received support of a positive kind from the board, who rightly took the view that to get success they had to give him financial support. He had a good knowledge of players in England and abroad and knew where to go for them. Given time in the job, he's realised what is required. I think he has brought a great deal of power and strength into the team. Martin has always gone for dominating figures defensively. If you've got a decent goalkeeper and another couple, you're halfway there. He's brought in strong, experienced European players that are just too strong and too experienced for the rest of the teams in Scotland, and above all he has Henrik Larsson. He is the goal scorer managers dream about having in their team.'

But managers such as Martin O'Neill dream of more than Swedish strikers; they aspire to a level of greatness that cannot be reached inside Scottish football. Like McNeill and Jordan, Macari was in no doubt that O'Neill would find himself increasingly torn between staying at Celtic Park and taking up the new challenges that were regularly placed before him.

'You can only try to understand what went through Martin's mind when Leeds United wanted him. There are a number of reasons for ignoring the call: he wants to finish the job at Celtic, he wants to win the European Cup for Celtic, there was no money even for essential buys at Elland Road. Maybe he realised early on that he had a cushy number in Glasgow. Call it boredom, and that's what it is if you are winning something every year. Do you become fed up with facing the same teams week after week and not winning anything in Europe? That's what he has to come to terms with in Scotland. For me, he is the type of fellow who can't make up his mind what he wants to do. I think you can come up with all these reasons and excuses for delaying things, but simply, if Leeds show an interest you either go or you don't. You don't turn round and say you want another chance at European football, like the players nowadays at struggling clubs who say "unless I've got Champions League football I'm not happy". He's in there at Celtic and he's got the one team each year to get the better of. He's managed to do that for two years and he knows that will go on for the next few seasons. It's a great number. Does he want to go to Leeds with the chance of getting his reputation tarnished because he can't get them up and running? To be honest, for them to come up against Arsenal or Manchester United is going to be tough no matter who's in charge. He doesn't have that problem in Scotland. I think he realises how well off he is there, though he's not going to admit it. I wouldn't think moving was high on his priorities when Leeds were apparently knocking at the door.

'For an outsider, any country, and that includes Scotland, can be a strange environment to be in all the time. There are times when it can be so easy that everyone loses sight of the fact that in Europe it will be far more difficult to make an impact. And that's why they are shocked when Celtic don't do so well. The Scottish league programme can give you a false idea of how good you are. Celtic are superior to all bar Rangers at home, but the challenge is Europe where there are no also-rans. That is the test that confronts Martin – if he takes it on.'

It is right in a city where football is such an integral force in uniting and dividing the people that the final word on O'Neill and his achievements should go to a fan. And to a Celtic supporter who revelled in the self-respect O'Neill returned to Celtic Park, and who had firm ideas about what O'Neill had done, how he had done it and what he might do next. Anonymity in these circumstances may seem odd, but there are good reasons for it. The fan has been supporting the club as far back as he can remember, and there is nothing he doesn't know about Celtic. He suffered the ignominy of the bad years and enjoyed the good ones. Most importantly, he was not blinded by the belief that everything Celtic do is right, that everything everybody else does is a deliberate slight on his club. He was neither biased nor paranoid in his views, which were therefore invaluable, but because he is heavily involved in the game he felt it would be unacceptable to declare his passion for Celtic.

'Most fans,' he began, 'felt O'Neill would be right because he would understand what the job was all about, being a Northern Irishman. He would know about the Catholic–Protestant, Celtic–Rangers thing and how vitally important it was for his club to be the winning club. If you look at one of his predecessors, Tommy Burns, well, he was a great Celt but he was too passionate, almost too much of a fan to make the right decisions. O'Neill would have the cold objectivity to go out there and do it properly the way Jock Stein had done so successfully for so many years. He proved his point very quickly.

'There was always a slight doubt about the style of football he played. If you look at his Leicester City side, I mean, it wasn't like it was wrong, but it wasn't the style that Celtic enjoyed or have been credited with. From the fifties onwards Rangers were always considered, by Celtic fans anyway, to be the tough, strong side, and Celtic the ones who played football. O'Neill's tactics seemed to be principally to get the big men up there and hump the ball. That wasn't necessarily the tactics the supporters were looking for, but at the time I think any victory would have done. There was never any criticism of O'Neill, everyone looked on him as a good appointment; what we didn't know was just how brilliant it would be. He was seen as part of a new age, the sort of guy we would need, someone who'd get it done, who had proved he could do it at Leicester. If there was a question, it was, would he be big enough to do it at Celtic? There was always that doubt. Celtic fans think the club is one of the major ones worldwide, which it probably is, or potentially could be. Here, at last, was someone that had much more of a CV in managing a football club than a John Barnes or some of his predecessors.

'The start couldn't have been any better, with us beating Rangers 6–2. It looked so good after that. There was a real feeling that he had got it right and would be able to build on it. There was a fear among the supporters that after the brief success of Wim Jansen there was going to be another long period of relative mediocrity. It looked as if Rangers were set to go on. I don't think the financial crisis at Rangers was widely known then, so it was natural for the Celtic support to think, "Well, we are never going to spend any money and Rangers are going to spend lots." But after that 6–2 match everybody began saying, "We've got a man that can get the team playing."

'Most of the players were the ones that had done so little beforehand, underachieved even, as he hadn't yet brought in a huge number of players. There is no doubt he has been very, very impressive. Just like Jock Stein, he proved very quickly he could do it with the players that were there. He managed to get more out of the ones who hadn't been fulfilling their own ability. You couldn't point a finger at them and say they were complete failures because they had won a championship just a couple of years before. The Henrik Larssons, the Lamberts, the Boyds and the McNamaras. They were still there, but now O'Neill came in and made them beat Rangers and we thought they could go on and win the championship. They were now organised, which they hadn't been; in fact, the defence was a joke under Barnes. Jansen had made them solid and I think that was the thing the fans liked about him and his style – the organisation he imposed on the team. O'Neill did the same.

'He knew what he was buying, too. Some people weren't sure about Chris Sutton, they thought he might be a typical Martin O'Neill buy, but he was very effective. He scored in the first minute of the 6–2 game and did what Tor Andre Flo didn't do for Rangers, looked effective. Sutton scored consistently that first season, and even though Rangers beat us 5–1 in the very next Old Firm game we were down to ten men and it didn't erase the pleasure and the significance of that first win of O'Neill's against Rangers. He certainly bought himself time if he needed to do that. He had a great start, and the team kept winning.'

There was even success, albeit limited, outside Scotland.

'I think even the most ardent fan of Celtic, or Rangers for that matter, now realises just how important Europe is. It's all very well saying we won the treble and they won nothing, but if you don't do it in Europe it doesn't really matter. We've just come through a long period when Rangers were in the ascendancy and the one pleasure Celtic fans were able to take from that was the recognition that they'd never match us in Europe – that they'd never win the European Cup.

'We recovered some pride in Europe with a great victory against Ajax in O'Neill's second season, so that was them back to being a Celtic side that could do something in Europe. The fans could hold their heads up, not only in Scotland but in Europe too after beating the Dutch to qualify for the European Champions League proper, and we felt we were unlucky, or rather badly treated by the referee, when we played Juventus in the Champions League in Turin. O'Neill takes all the credit. He has restored the pride and the passion, he's got the players committed again and capable of beating Rangers, the very thing we seemed to have lost. When it came to anything physical pre-O'Neill we would chicken out of it and allow Rangers to win.'

Not that he and others were totally convinced by everything O'Neill did. Although the fans acknowledge that he shook many players out of a slough of underachievement, they also believe he inherited one or two key pieces in the puzzle and did not always spend his unprecedentedly high budget wisely.

'He bought Neil Lennon, and I personally don't like him. His way of playing, rather. On the other hand, he was buying another Northern Irish sort, so a large element of the fans would be attracted to that, because of his background and things. He's another one for whom they would be able to say, "He will understand what it is about to play for Celtic." That's all very well, but a lot of us aren't convinced about Lennon and maybe one or two others. Sutton, though, was a magnificent buy. He gave Celtic what

Rangers had in Mark Hateley, a strong front man. It was players like Hateley that meant we always lost when Rangers equalled our record of nine successive championships. You could see it coming in games where Celtic had matched Rangers, who would then do us on critical dead-ball situations. Sutton was a psychological high for Celtic and bad for Rangers, who seemed to lose the plot, the dressing room and the players to injury all at the same time.

'Larsson is the most outstanding of strikers. We like to think he's the best in Europe and one of the best in the world game. It was Jansen who brought him in through his Dutch connections, and the Swede has been nothing short of sensational. We've got our own song for him, and so we should: "King of Kings". Larsson was a masterstroke, and so was Paul Lambert, who came in at the same time. I think it was the club's former chief executive, Jock Brown, who was very much involved in signing Lambert. That's the word. That's why I'd say that Brown made a lot of good signings and maybe didn't get the credit for them.'

How long could the good times last?

'There are fears, concerns that O'Neill won't stay and that the board won't give him the money to make him stay. Is he as committed to Celtic as the fans would like him to be? He never said whether he was going to leave or not, but we are into his third season so if you look on the bright side you can say that actions speak louder than words and he is still there and he is still talking. The one difference between Martin O'Neill and all the recent managers at the club is that he keeps things very close to his chest and it is therefore very difficult to get near him. It used to be a bit of a joke among the fans that everything that happened at Celtic Park was in the papers before even the board knew. O'Neill keeps people at arm's length, even his employers. I haven't a view about his future. If negotiations are going on at the moment all that the fans can take in is what they are told. We know it can be updated at any time.

'We get the impression, at least a lot of us do, that if the application [by Celtic and Rangers] to join the English Premier League was accepted or even considered as a possibility in the near future he'd be strongly tempted to stay. We are told that is unlikely. But again, if Manchester United suddenly came up and said, "How about it, Martin, do you want the job here?" then most would bet on him saying yes – maybe wrongly. Jock Stein, we are told, turned down Manchester United at one stage, but he played for the club and he probably felt gratitude to Celtic for rescuing him from obscurity. For O'Neill, it is different. He was already making his way in football and there is a strong family desire there. It is often quoted that his father said to him that if he ever got the chance to go and play for Celtic he should be happy to walk to Glasgow. He maybe doesn't feel Celtic did him any favours, but he was doing them one. All you can deal in is the facts you know, and Martin O'Neill is idolised by the vast majority. Some of the more perceptive or tactically aware ones would be disappointed, but there are other tacticians about, and I think tactically he can be out-thought. His departure would have to be a disappointment from a Celtic point of view, but you wouldn't see it as the end of the world.'

MARTIN O'NEILL – FIVE DOMESTIC SEASONS PLUS ASTON VILLA

1 June 2000

O'Neill is presented as the new man in charge, replacing the disastrous John Barnes. He insists it is a role he could not turn down, having followed the club as a youngster. He is guaranteed full authority over the team and appoints John Robertson and Steve Walford as his assistant and coach. Kenny Dalglish stands down as director of football and severs connection with the club a short time later.

July

Celtic begin 2000/01 season with a 2–1 victory over Dundee United at Tannadice. A good start, but O'Neill's ultimate test will come against Rangers.

27 August

Celtic annihilate Rangers 6–2 in what is an extraordinary Old Firm debut for the new boss and Chris Sutton, his new £6 million signing, who scores twice. Henrik Larsson, Paul Lambert and Stilian Petrov are the other scorers.

September and October

Celtic continue at the top of the SPL unbeaten.

26 November

The winning run ends with a 5–1 thumping by Rangers at Ibrox, and Alan Thompson is sent off. Disappointing? Certainly, but in championship terms barely a blip for Celtic who remain twelve points clear. O'Neill's legend continues to grow with the vast Celtic Park support.

7 February 2001

The first of two games with Rangers in a week. Celtic eliminate them from the CIS Cup with a 3–1 win in the semi-final. Chris Sutton scores the opener, with Henrik Larsson scoring two.

The victory is marred by the dismissal of fans' favourite Lubo Moravcic, plus Rangers' Michael Mols and Claudio Reyna. Celtic to face Kilmarnock in the CIS Cup final. The treble is on schedule and Rangers are left wondering if Martin O'Neill can do any wrong.

11 February

Martin O'Neill is elevated to super-status with his second win over Rangers in a week. Alan Thompson scores the winning goal. This all but ends Dick Advocaat's title challenge. Rangers remain twelve points behind. O'Neill is publicly playing it down, but the Irishman is set to make history and win by a massive margin in his first season at the helm.

18 March

Celtic clinch the first honour of the season by beating Kilmarnock 3–0 at Hampden, and Henrik Larsson is again the star, scoring a hat-trick. O'Neill is jubilant, but credits all his players, as well as assistant John Robertson and coach Steve Walford. The treble draws ever closer.

April

Tommy Johnson scores the winning goal against St Mirren on the 7th, and the championship is Celtic's. Martin O'Neill can celebrate success at his first attempt. It is the quickest title win in 26 years. Celtic round off this perfect season with a 3–0 victory over Rangers at Ibrox on the 29th. Larsson nets his fiftieth goal of the season and O'Neill is hailed by the fans.

May

Celtic are unbeaten at home all season and finish with a record-breaking 97 points. They collect the championship trophy in front of 60,000 fans, all of them prepared to accord O'Neill legendary status. That is confirmed on the 26th when the treble is attained after Celtic's 3–0 win against Hibernian in the Scottish FA Cup final. Henrik Larsson scores two and Jackie McNamara the other. Martin O'Neill had been asked to finish no lower than second, presumably behind Rangers, but ends with three trophies and the adoration of all those who support Celtic.

August 2001

Europe is the target, but the domestic campaign looks pretty similar to last season, as Celtic Park proves an impossible place to get three points. Martin O'Neill's squad strengthened by the arrival of Bobo Balde, Momo Sylla, John Hartson (who had earlier failed a Rangers medical) and Steve Guppy.

30 September

Celtic continue to dominate Old Firm encounters, beating Rangers 2–0 at Ibrox. Advocaat comes under pressure from his fans in direct contrast to O'Neill, who has found Paradise, where else but in Paradise.

October

Excellent in Europe, dominant at home, but not all-conquering. Livingston manage a goalless draw with the champions, but it is still all clear at Celtic Park.

25 November

The second Rangers game of the season ends with another victory to Celtic: 2–1 to the champions. The result is overshadowed by the loss of Didier Agathe with knee ligament damage.

December

There is disappointment in Europe, but in the domestic arena Celtic are the front-runners. Some results have often been ground out in the last minutes of games, but O'Neill's men have a winning mentality. They are in pole position.

5 February 2002

In the first Old Firm encounter of 2002, O'Neill is shocked at the defeat of his team by Rangers in the CIS Cup final.

Bert Kontermann ends Celtic's Old Firm dominance under Martin O'Neill and hopes of a back-to-back treble by scoring the extra-time winner. Peter Lovenkrands had opened the scoring for Rangers, and Bobo Balde had scrambled the equaliser for Celtic.

10 March

Celtic are determined to avenge their cup defeat against Rangers but are forced to settle for a point from a 1–1 draw. Stilian Petrov scores for Celtic and an Arthur Numan stunner saves Rangers from a second home defeat. Celtic remain ten points clear of Rangers, and a League and cup double is still a possibility.

23 March

A Scottish Cup semi-final victory against Ayr United at Hampden Park means Celtic will face Rangers in the final.

6 April

Celtic win title for second successive season with a 5–1 home win against Livingston. It is the first time Celtic have won back-to-back titles for twenty years, and O'Neill is now being spoken of with reverence as the new Jock Stein. The Irishman insists it was more difficult this time round but all the sweeter for that.

21 April

The match against Rangers was supposed to go down in history for Celtic as the first time in their 114-year existence that they had finished a season with a one hundred per cent home record, but they can only manage a draw. Peter Lovenkrands puts the visitors ahead, Alan Thompson nets Celtic's equaliser. There is an amazing goalmouth bust-up among the players after a Mjallby shot is stopped. After the mêlée, involving nearly all the players, Mjallby and Hartson are sent off for Celtic, and Ricksen for Rangers.

4 May

Martin O'Neill so disappointed at defeat in the Scottish Cup final against Rangers. The treble has been reduced to just one triumph – but the most significant, the Scottish Premier League championship. O'Neill had injury problems for the Hampden final and gambled by playing an unfit trio of Chris Sutton, Paul Lambert and Bobo Balde, but it didn't pay off. The legions of Rangers fans have no complaints with Peter Lovenkrands, who scores twice, including the winner.

2002

Celtic were odds-on to dominate again but there were a couple of early warnings that Rangers, having had to bite the bullet since O'Neill's arrival, were ready to fight back. They drew 3–3 at Celtic Park in the first meeting of the season on 6 October and in their second SPL encounter went down 3–2 at Ibrox on 7 December.

2003

There was a recovery 1–0 win against Rangers on 8 March but the month was a disaster domestically. Celtic suffered when they were beaten yet again by Rangers on 16 March. This time it was by 2–1 in the Scottish League Cup. The agony went on as they slumped out of the Scottish FA Cup, humiliated in a 1–0 defeat by Inverness Caledonian Thistle on 23 March. It was in complete contrast to their stunning success in reaching the final of the UEFA Cup but as losers to Porto they had to face Kilmarnock on 25 May in their final league match. It was straightforward – they had to win and if Rangers won their final match then they needed a better goal difference. They beat Kilmarnock 4–0, a superb result after the collective trauma experienced against Porto, but Rangers topped it in the 6–1 defeat of Dunfermline to snatch the SPL title by one goal. It was an horrendous ending with no winning trophies to parade from a season which promised so much.

2004

A near perfect second half to the 2003/04 season after they had been knocked out of the Scottish League Cup 2–1 by Hibernian on 18 December. It was their last domestic stumble. Celtic went on to win the Premier League title by seventeen points from Rangers and clinched the classic double with a 3–1 win in the SFA Cup Final against Dunfermline on 22 May.

2005

Another dramatic end to the 2004/05 season and as so often it is a straight battle between Celtic and Rangers for the SPL title. Rangers had come back after their mauling in the previous season to eliminate Celtic from the League Cup, but O'Neill's team were favourites to stabilise and lift the championship. They threw it away on the last day at Motherwell on 22 May. They had dominated the match but had managed just one goal. They were two minutes from the title when Scott MacDonald, a self-professed Celtic fan, scored twice to hand the championship to Rangers.

2006 – Aston Villa

The start could not have been more promising, so much better than anticipated. After nine matches Villa were the only club in the Premiership unbeaten. The run began with a 1–1 draw against Arsenal at the new Emirates Stadium on 19 August. It was the first of six draws with West Ham, Watford, Chelsea, Tottenham and Fulham with wins at home against Reading and Newcastle, although they have stumbled since this impressive start.

MARTIN O'NEILL – FIVE SEASONS IN EUROPE

9 November 2000

Celtic exit the UEFA Cup after a 2–1 extra-time defeat against Bordeaux at Celtic Park.

9 August 2001

Celtic produce an excellent 3–1 victory against Ajax in Holland. O'Neill preaches caution, but qualification for the lucrative group stages looks a probability.

23 August

Celtic go through despite losing 1–0 at home in the return against Ajax and qualify for the Champions League proper. Keeper Rob Douglas is the hero.

18 September

O Neill's entry on to the major European stage begins with a thrilling performance in Turin. Juventus emerge 3–2 victors after a late penalty is controversially awarded to the home side for an Amoroso dive. O'Neill is incensed, and is sent to the stand for protesting. Trezeguet scores a double for Juventus, while Stilian Petrov and Henrik Larsson net for Celtic. O'Neill is proud of his players after what is generally accepted as a highly creditable performance.

25 September

Celtic 1 FC Porto 0. It is the perfect response to the frustration felt in Turin. Martin O'Neill has to watch the action from the stand, but is delighted to pick up three Champions League points thanks to Henrik Larssen.

10 October

Celtic 1 Rosenborg 0. Another three points sees Celtic top

their group in the Champions League. Martin O'Neill back in the dugout. Alan Thompson is the goal scorer.

17 October

Martin O'Neill insists his side is not yet what he wants it to be. As if to prove the point, they lose 3–0 to FC Porto. Progress into the second stage of the Champions League appears doubtful.

23 October

It gets worse. Celtic travel to Rosenborg and straight into another defeat, this time going down 2–0 to the Norwegians. Harald Brattbak, a former Celtic player, scores both goals.

31 October

Celtic fail to go through to the second phase of the Champions League, though they produce a wonderful performance to defeat Juventus 4–3 at Celtic Park. Goals come from Henrik Larsson, Joos Valgaeren and Chris Sutton (two). Lubo Moravcic is outstanding. Celtic have won all their home matches, but their away results are their undoing.

22 November

Celtic now transferred to UEFA Cup but lose to Valencia in Spain 1–0. It is tough on them. Chris Sutton is forced to pull out due to a family illness, and with just fifteen minutes remaining Celtic are beaten on the night by a Vicente goal.

6 December

Celtic are now out of the UEFA Cup after losing a penalty shoot-out, despite beating Valencia 1–0 on the night with another priceless goal from Larsson. Martin O'Neill can only watch in despair as his men crash 4–5 on spot-kicks. Valgaeren, Larsson and Petrov miss.

14 August 2002

Martin O'Neill is angry after conceding a home goal in a first-leg Champions League qualifier against FC Basle, which Celtic win 3–1.

28 August

Disaster for Celtic as they crash out to Basle 2–0 on the night and fail to make the lucrative stage of the Champions League. The Swiss go through on the away-goal that O'Neill had found so troubling, and Celtic are 'demoted' to the UEFA Cup.

19 September

Celtic have never had a much easier tie than their opening UEFA Cup clash with FK Suduva of Lithuania. They win 8–1, and Henrik Larsson scores three. Celtic Park enjoys every minute of the rout.

3 October

The return leg has to be completed despite the inevitability of the outcome. Celtic win 2–0, and 10–1 on aggregate.

31 October

The atmosphere at Celtic Park for Celtic's first-leg tie against Blackburn, sold as the Battle of Britain, is dramatic. Rovers manager Graeme Souness, formerly of Rangers, sees his team dominate the match only for Celtic to win through a Henrik Larsson goal.

14 November

Few give Celtic a chance at Ewood Park, but O'Neill outsmarts Souness with his tactics, and his players then outplay the English side, finishing them off with goals from Larsson and Sutton.

28 November

The Scots win the first leg of their next tie against Spanish team Celta Vigo by a goal to nil. Larsson is again the goal scorer, but O'Neill is red-carded and banished to a seat in the directors' box.

12 December

Celtic survive – just. They are beaten 2–1 but thanks to a John Hartson strike went through to meet Stuttgart on the away-goals ruling.

20 February 2003

Celtic are still the underdogs, but they clinically dismember the Germans to produce a convincing 3–1 lead with goals from Paul Lambert, Shaun Maloney and Stilian Petrov.

27 February

There were still those unbelievers who felt Celtic would struggle in Stuttgart. They are beaten, conceding three goals, but first-half strikes from Alan Thompson and Chris Sutton see them through to the quarter-finals, and deservedly so.

13 March

This was the Battle of Britain Part Two. The ease with which Celtic, inspired by O'Neill's masterly tactics, had disposed of Part One in the shape of Blackburn Rovers and their manager Graeme Souness increased the depth of confidence among the faithful. Yes, they could take out Liverpool. They draw the home leg 1–1 with Henrik Larsson scoring yet another vital goal. Surely it would be too difficult at Anfield?

20 March

England was preparing for Liverpool to sweep on to the semi-final spot; weren't they representing the Premiership? And hard working though the team might be that Martin O'Neill would select they could not possibly survive this test on Merseyside. Celtic win 2–0 (Alan Thompson again and John Hartson were the scorers), Monsieur Gerard Houllier is, like his troops, in shock. Celtic had made the semis.

10 April

This was the first occasion since the first round that Celtic were favourites, if only slightly. Boavista were, on all known information, the weakest of the semi-finalists. They were badly placed in the Portuguese league and could be described as 'imminently beatable'. Celtic struggles in Glasgow but manage a 1–1 draw thanks again to the goal presence of Henrik Larsson.

24 April

The return is hardly a classic, and is justifiably dismissed as a dull, dreary, tepid contest. Only winning semi-finalists are remembered, not how well or how badly they performed. Larsson strikes again in a 1–0 victory, and Celtic travel home with what they and their fans most wanted – a place in the Final.

21 May

Travelling may be better than arriving, but not for Martin O'Neill, his players and the greatest army of fans mobilised by a club for a European final outside their own country.

Porto were known to have the players good enough, experienced enough and cynical enough to win. They test Celtic's commitment, they are the better side, they win 3–2 (the phenomenal Larsson scoring both Celtic's goals) and but for their gamesmanship deserved every credit in victory.

2004

Seville was to be the pinnacle for O'Neill, while the club hoped for a long run in Europe's top club competition the Champions League. Celtic, despite their pedigree, were forced to qualify. They had disposed of FBK Kaunas and MTK Hungaria before the end of August. They went on to lose to Bayern Munich 2–1 in Germany (17 September), beat Lyon 2–0 at Celtic Park on 30 September, then lost 1–0 to Anderlecht in Belgium on 21 October. They won the return against the Belgians 3–1 (5 November) but could only finish their group ties with a goalless draw against Bayern (25 November) and a 3–2 loss in Lyon on 12 December. They failed to qualify for the final rounds but moved into the UEFA Cup as consolation. They had a wonderful 1–0 win against Barcelona in Glasgow (11 March) and confirmed their form in the Nou Camp return drawing 0–0 on 25 March. It was Spanish outsiders Villarreal who ended the campaign when they drew 1–1 at Celtic Park on 8 April and won the return 2–0 ten days later.

2005

Celtic conceded nine goals in the first three Champions League ties. They lost 3–1 at home to Barcelona on 14 September, 3–1 in Milan on 29 September and another devastating defeat, this time 3–0 against Shakhtar Donetsk on 20 October. They went on to beat Shakhtar 1–0 (2 November), draw 1–1 with Barcelona (24 November) and 0–0 with Milan in Glasgow on 7 December. It was not good enough to qualify for the UEFA Cup.

MARTIN O'NEILL – THE SIGNINGS

Alan Thompson, Chris Sutton, Neil Lennon, Magnus Hedman, Ulrik Laursen, Didier Agathe, John Hartson, Ramon Vega (till the end of the first season), Steve Guppy, Bobo Balde, Rab Douglas, Joos Valgaeren, Momo Sylla, David Fernandez.

There is no question that the launching pad for the success attained in O'Neill's first two incredible seasons was Celtic's 6–2 win over Rangers in his debut encounter with the enemy. Such a substantial victory, such a comprehensive dissection of the only club that stands between Celtic and the championship, had two great benefits for O'Neill: it improved the confidence of his own players and diluted the high morale of everyone involved with Rangers. Not even a comeback and a 5–1 win for Rangers in the next encounter was enough to reverse what was to become an unhindered march on the title, the League Cup and the Scottish Cup.

The professionals sensed a changeover of power during O'Neill's first Old Firm confrontation. Dixie Deans, a Celtic veteran of these matches, the most intensely fought in world domestic football, acknowledged the new mood, realising that his former club was back in control and that O'Neill had every chance of surpassing expectations. In an interview with the *Daily Mail*'s Brian Scott, Deans, one of Celtic's great strikers of the 1970s, was clearly convinced that O'Neill was exactly the new boss Celtic needed – an autocrat in the mould of a Jock Stein or a Brian Clough. Deans explained, 'I get the impression Martin is the no-nonsense type. If players don't perform for him there'll be no messing with them. They will be off. That's the way it was with the old school, men like Jock Stein, Brian Clough, Willie Waddell, Jock Wallace and Matt Busby. You just need to watch him on the touchline to see who's boss. He lets the players know it, and they'll respect him for it. This is something which Celtic Park hasn't had enough of in recent years. For too long there have been rifts in the camp. I'm not saying there were none in Big Jock's time, but nobody got to hear about them.'

Deans was enthusiastic about the scoring potential of O'Neill's new strike partnership of Chris Sutton, the £6 million replacement for Mark Viduka, and Henrik Larsson, back and fully fit again after injury, but also thought he could detect signs of arrogance in the Rangers set-up. 'Maybe the result highlighted that Rangers aren't quite as good as they think they are. There are still only two teams who can win the League and it is far too early yet to say which one of them will this time ... but just so long as Celtic don't get carried away by this one result and continue going about things the way they have been so far I think you could see me celebrating come the end of the season.'

It was a forecast that, of course, was to prove uncannily accurate; remarkably made, too, on the strength of one victory. It was the product of an instant belief in Martin O'Neill's powers of motivation and man management.

5. MOVING ON

The morning after the night before can be difficult. Apart from the pains in the head and the queasiness, there is the feeling that the brain has no connection with the body: then there is the paranoia and those moments when you ask, why me? Celtic supporters are well acquainted with self-inflicted conditions. The loss of the championship and living with that underachievement; the bitter disappointment of Seville and the enforced acceptance that Rangers had lifted all the prizes contributed to the malaise. But from the ashes of that failed campaign on every front arose another that was to recover damaged reputations. This was due principally to the confidence, forcefulness and ability of The Leader, O'Neill, to ensure whatever happened outside the camp, whatever was being talked about, not just on the sports desks in newspaper offices, but we can also be certain, among directors of certain English Premiership clubs, was not going to erode the spirit at Celtic Park – the winning football – nor rob them of the very impetus that was to propel the team to another domestic double.

There were good reasons to suppose it was going to be tough for Celtic, principally because of the uncertainty about O'Neill's future. The papers and the football grapevine in England continued to sustain the rumours about it. The conjecture surrounding which club he was going to join, informed or otherwise, was to prove costly for one newspaper, the *Scottish Daily Record*, despite such rumours, perhaps in more diluted form, being a long accustomed part of the game worldwide. It is no secret that a team's performance can be adversely affected by careless talk about the future departure of their manager. The British game is littered with club casualties after a manager either deliberately, or by mistake, or from information emanating from the boardroom, is revealed to be quitting the club. One example was at Southampton when the south-coast club slid down the English Premiership after it had been 'leaked' that manager Gordon Strachan would be leaving for personal reasons when league business had been concluded. It was not Strachan's indiscretion and he was furious that his plan had become headline news. The information had come from within the club and we can assume too high up the pecking order to end with the culprit being sacked. It cannot be mere coincidence that almost from the point when it was made public Southampton's form dipped. The Celtic situation was different. O'Neill had said nothing for public consumption; there was no question the club would have been devastated had he hinted he was going to leave anyway, but whether he or they liked it the persistence of the rumours continued to give legs to the belief that the coming season could be his last. It was incumbent on him, therefore, to counter any form of even seeping submission among his players and extract the maximum from them on a game-by-game basis. There was the equally depressing realisation among players and fans that the season would for certain be the great Larsson's final one as the supreme supplier of Celtic's goals. Put both together, O'Neill's predicted departure and Larsson's certain farewell, and it was enough psychologically for a squad already burdened by self-doubt to lose their focus after Rangers' clean sweep. They did not: their desire was beyond reproach and their reward the Scottish Premier League title and Scottish Football Association Cup double as testimony to O'Neill's management skills.

Rangers' previous season's success had suggested – but only to the uninformed – that they would be there again fighting to retain their title. They were on the way down. Pressured financially by wildly extravagant spending and bad buys – an unfortunate legacy left by former manager Dick Advocaat – they forced McLeish to be rid of quality players and struggle on, hopelessly as it was to prove, with what in terms of football quality was dross.

O'Neill will bristle at the thought, but unpalatable though it may be to him it is a fact which cannot be denied; there were times when Rangers looked incapable of beating the big drum in a flute band. When the new season began, Rangers, despite the treble, were emitting all the signs of a club in total disarray. That is not for Celtic to concern themselves about and, if championships are decided in Scotland these days by the outcome of the four Scottish Premier League clashes between the Old Firm, then they struck the first and most decisive blow. It came at Ibrox in October, only by one goal from John Hartson, but it gave Celtic number one positioning in the SPL: they were never to look back, only downwards, with a chuckle perhaps at floundering Rangers who would have to endure a further three SPL defeats from Celtic, four in total when you include Celtic's Scottish Cup quarter-final victory, throughout what was a humiliating season for them.

There was so much good to record in a march that became a yomp that had begun with a 5–1 victory against Livingston, went on to confirm the SPL title on a grey gloomy April date at Kilmarnock, clinched the cup with a decisive if slow-coming 3–1 win against Dunfermline and then ended with a fabulous goodbye party for Larsson on Wednesday 26 May in a friendly against Sevilla.

The end of the season was also to clear up, to Celtic's satisfaction, an unfortunate legal battle between them and

the *Scottish Daily Record*, a conflict of considerable importance that will take more than court settlements to sort out.
The rancour, Celtic's utter fury at the way they were being
treated by the *Scottish Daily Record*, had been ignited the
year before over stories surrounding the infamous Bhoys
Outing to Newcastle that ended with claims alleging
drunken and disorderly behaviour among O'Neill's players
who thought, wrongly as it turned out, they had escaped the
close attention of the press. I suppose, if you want to have
a party and your home base is Glasgow, then Newcastle is
as handy a place as any for the ribaldry, or is it bonding, to
take place. One question that has to be asked is what sort
of corporate naivety sanctioned the trip south for a Christmas drinks party thinking Celtic's finest would be anony-
mous on Tyneside? It was a little tour asking for trouble and
unfortunately it came.

There were reports of conflict between them and a press
photographer; Neil Lennon was isolated as a troublemaker
and subsequently proved innocent of all charges laid against
him by the media. One headline – THUGS AND THIEVES –
was so outrageously over the top, it is impossible to see how
Celtic could react in any way other than through a court of
law, or the steps outside the court, where matters of this
nature are often resolved between lawyers.

The next stage of what had become a professional
stand-off between Celtic, O'Neill and the *Record* came over
a story stating that Liverpool had not only made contact
with O'Neill to replace Gerard Houllier but also had a
pre-agreement in writing with the Celtic manager, even that
a residence for the O'Neills was being arranged. This was
virtually a repeat – a 'lift' in journalistic terms – of a story
aired on commercial radio, which basically only differed
from previous press speculation by stating an agreement had
been reached. It was a source of considerable embarrassment to O'Neill who was sensitive to accusations from the
Liverpool end and especially from Houllier who had been
baying for some time that the Irishman was after his job.

It was hardly the crime of the century in media terms, but it was either right or wrong, or rather it could either be proved right or the paper would have to suffer the consequences should O'Neill go for litigation. He chose the latter, which is his right, won his case and picked up costs and compensation. The harm done to the *Record* was far greater than a financial handout, infuriating though that would have been to their legal department. The strength of the fall-out and the by-products of that breach in the relationship between one of Europe's great clubs and Scotland's biggest selling newspaper contributed to the demise of editor Peter Cox, threatened the paper's circulation and cost them one major advertising account with the car dealership Phoenix Honda. The *Record* was also on the receiving end of constant criticism from Celtic's official 'newspaper', the *Celtic View*. The drip-drip criticism was devastating for the *Record* and it didn't stop in Glasgow. The effects were felt on Merseyside, too, where Liverpool's chief executive, Rick Parry, also contested the facts of the story and collected a considerable financial settlement.

There will be those who say the *Record* have quite correctly paid the price of inaccurate journalism. Celtic's attitude to what they see as an unwarranted and inaccurate slur against the club can be judged from the wording of the statement they issued after being advised that there would be no police action against Lennon or the other players mentioned in the original story.

STATEMENT FROM CELTIC FOOTBALL CLUB

Celtic Football Club welcomes the announcement today by Northumbria Police that no charges are to be brought against any Celtic player with respect to incidents alleged to have taken place in Newcastle last December.

Joos Valgaeren, Johan Mjallby and Bobby Petta who were pictured on the front page of the *Daily Record*

newspaper under the headline 'Thugs and Thieves'
always maintained their innocence and are delighted,
but not surprised, at this outcome.

The players are now taking legal advice concerning the
vicious personal attack launched upon them by the
Daily Record and by its editor, Peter Cox, who went on
national television to repeat in graphic detail what have
now been found to be grossly unjustified allegations.

The decision of Northumbria Police to take no action
against the players confirms that the *Daily Record*'s
claim of 'thuggery' was a completely unwarranted
description of events.

Once again Celtic Football Club finds the good name of
the club and its players used disparagingly simply to
boost a newspaper's failing circulation.

Without prejudicing possible legal action (by individual
players or the club) Celtic Football Club looks forward
with interest to see if the *Daily Record* and its editor
now adopt an honorable course of action.

We look with interest to see if they have any proposals
to apologise and attempt to put the 'record' straight.

We also look forward to seeing what action the *Daily
Record*'s local management plan to take against those
who wrongly attacked the club and its players.

We also look forward to seeing what the Trinity Mirror
Board in London, who ultimately control both the
Daily Record and *Sunday Mail* in Scotland, intend to
do with an organisation that seems to have their own
agenda when covering issues relating to Celtic Football
Club.

We clearly expect an equitable and effective end to this
unsavoury journalistic episode.

In happier times it would have been resolved, after some
huffing and puffing, less painfully than it had been this time.

There are also those who will predict that even the winners in these legal confrontations don't win in the long term. There has been an increasing attitude in football that newspapers no longer really matter, that television is the paymaster now and can be controlled. When you consider the sycophantic drivel that often smothers football coverage on the wee box then maybe they have a point. Is this really what football wants; having sanctioned massive changes to the game as it was played, it now wants the information flow controlled to the point at which newspapers will be restricted to the level of uselessness, neatly emasculated by legal process. This is no reflection on what has happened between Celtic FC and the *Scottish Daily Record*; that has been sorted out by the country's legal system and is accepted in its finality. Hopefully, though, it is worth illustrating how easily it can go wrong for newspapers in a distinctly different but not impossible situation. Consider this scenario: Club A feels their current manager has to be replaced. They look around for a suitable successor and settle on manager B. He is contacted in the strictest confidence with secrecy paramount to both. Experience over the years, though, tells us there is no such thing as a secret inside a football club. Newspaper C finds out about it and prints the story. Both A and B are stunned by the revelation of a fact that must never be confirmed. B sues C and, using A's denial, wins his case. Hypothetical? Naturally. A possibility? Only to the most cynical. What should be realised is that no newspaper, whether regional or national, wants to sever a respectable liaison with one of their two biggest football clubs. There has to be understanding, but on both sides.

TEMPTATION

O'Neill's name had been linked with a return to English football before the Liverpool 'connection' was headlined. As Celtic had come to expect, the name of their manager was first choice of those ambitious clubs looking for a new leader. O'Neill had been faced with a major decision in the summer of 2002 in only his second season at Celtic when Leeds United increased their interest in him. Yokohama was the venue, the World Cup final was the occasion. As he made his way across the foyer of Yokohama's most prestigious hotel he was entitled to a feeling of contentment.

It would have been unusual had he failed to notice the interest his presence had caused among the few wealthy Brits mingling with well-heeled Brazilian and German football fans gathered for the 2002 World Cup final in Japan, less than 24 hours away. The BBC had flown him in as part of its panel of experts to analyse the climax to the finals played for the first time in the Far East. It was to be a glorious end to an acclaimed tournament, the perfect finale to a competition that had satisfied most of the demands made of it by a worldwide audience (unless you were French, or Argentine, or English for that matter, and had watched your team say hello and goodbye too early). Even some abject refereeing couldn't detract from the entertainment on offer in South Korea and Japan. It was now down to the two most powerful and successful football nations to decide if the world championship was heading back to Europe or being returned to South America.

But if O'Neill appeared relaxed, then that disguised what for him was a considerable personal dilemma.

The Leeds United manager's job was his for the taking. It was an exciting prospect, and was planned as an immediate appointment. But how, just how, could he leave Celtic after leading them to back-to-back championships, the most recent – and the reason for his justified satisfaction – coming twelve months after winning the treble in his astoundingly successful debut season? He had subjugated city rivals Rangers and was regarded as saint and saviour, certainly among the 'punters'. It would be difficult to walk away from such a reverential status, even to a club where his salary would be vastly improved and where the Premiership challenge would come from half a dozen clubs not just one. Most importantly, would his family be happiest living back in the south? Questions, always questions.

His immediate future had to be decided and the media were pressing him for answers, though here on this mild oriental night he was with friends. The decision was made: he wanted to accept the offer. There is no doubt among those who knew him and knew him well that he considered any opportunity to succeed David O'Leary, another Irishman, as manager of the Yorkshire club too good to turn down.

There are differing reports from equally immaculate sources about Leeds' involvement in trying to entice O'Neill into the job. One says they were waiting on him to make his view public before revealing theirs. It was for him to say 'I want the job; I want to manage Leeds United'. In their minds they believed a show of public commitment would confirm his intentions. They weren't prepared to make the running up front, to risk the possibility – in O'Neill's case a slim one – of being cynically used by him to secure an even stronger position at Celtic. But they had walked down this road with O'Neill before. There were those in the Elland Road hierarchy who warned of the damage to the club's credibility if they declared an official interest and after a few days were left beached and helpless should he turn them down, as he had done when he was offered the chance to replace George Graham. Then, Leeds had been so acutely embarrassed when he said no and elected to remain with Leicester City that there were those within the club now who were opposed to his appointment, whether or not he declared his intentions. Some say there were no talks between O'Neill and Leeds United, but the facts as revealed by an unimpeachable source are different: there was at least one meeting with the club, a meeting the parties vowed should remain a secret.

The turmoil in O'Neill's mind was perfectly understandable. Here was a man, a favoured son of Ireland, brought up in the north, one of nine children in a family devoutly Catholic and political – meaning nationalist – who from his earliest years worshipped those who wore the green and white of Celtic. There was a bond between him and the great Glasgow club. To take charge of the team and to return them to success – well, some would say it was his destiny.

But the decision in his own mind was clear. He would have to leave; he had already accomplished far more than had been expected of him. There would be no debts unpaid, no reasons for recrimination.

The *Mail on Sunday* and its football editor the late Joe Melling, a former Sports Reporter of the Year, were convinced O'Neill would move to Leeds. The headline on Melling's back-page story on the morning of the World Cup final, 30 June, claimed O'NEILL READY TO JOIN LEEDS, and the sub-heading read 'Celtic Boss is Prepared to Move – and Ridsdale Wants Him'. Melling does not deal in 'fliers', that is, writing stories with only the flimsiest relationship with the truth. If his name was on it then there was no room for doubting the path O'Neill was prepared to follow. The story that followed was shared between Melling in Japan and Peter Fitton, a reporter back in the UK with close links to Elland Road. It read:

> Martin O'Neill is ready to quit Celtic to become Leeds United's new manager following the sacking of David O'Leary. O'Neill has not yet been officially approached for the job but Leeds chairman Peter Ridsdale plans to speak to Celtic within the next 48 hours. And O'Neill, who is in Yokohama with the BBC's World Cup team, will be ready to enter into contract negotiations.
>
> Leeds' decision to go for O'Neill will be confirmed at a conference-call gathering of Elland Road's directors this morning, when the Irishman they wanted to take charge four years ago will again emerge as the firm boardroom favourite. Last night Ridsdale said: 'It is not

a matter of rocket science in putting our managerial shortlist together. The major issue is how gettable are the principal candidates. There are not many quality people around, and even less who are available. I have half-a-dozen names in mind who are worth considering and one or two obviously fall into the priority category. My objective in talking with the other directors tomorrow is to gain a mandate from them to go for the preferred candidate, with a backstop option also named. By midweek I expect to make a formal move for the manager we want in place, and by the end of the week it should be fairly clear who we can realistically pursue. By then I hope to have permission to speak to the individuals involved. If possible, we want the situation resolved speedily.'

O'Neill is concerned that Celtic will not have the financial muscle for him to compete successfully in the Champions League next season. He fears he may have taken Scotland's leading club as far as he can. He will seek guarantees from Ridsdale over the funds available to bolster Leeds' challenge for a Champions League spot in the season after next before committing to the job. But the former Leicester manager accepts that Leeds have to sell Rio Ferdinand for a £35 million fee to satisfy the demands of the plc board. O'Neill can expect a contract with Leeds worth at least £2m a season. He also wants the Yorkshire club to pay full compensation on the remaining year of his Celtic contract.

Only if Leeds cannot persuade Celtic to let them talk to O'Neill will they chase their backup targets. Republic of Ireland boss Mick McCarthy is the likely second choice, although certain elements of the Leeds hierarchy are concerned about his lack of big-club experience. Leeds are also aware that England coach Steve McClaren, former national manager Terry Venables and Blackburn's Graeme Souness are all interested in taking over from the departed O'Leary, as is Dutchman Frank Rijkaard, who is keen to coach in the Premiership.

In a bizarre twist last night, it emerged that O'Leary would be a strong contender to take over at Celtic if O'Neill leaves. Despite his sacking by Leeds, O'Leary is close to, and still highly rated by, Celtic's majority shareowner, Dermot Desmond. Ironically, O'Leary was a leading target for the Celtic job before O'Neill was appointed two years ago.

O'Neill, who has a £2m stake in Celtic, earned praise from Manchester United's Sir Alex Ferguson for his transformation of the Glasgow giants.

The article was positive. Both reporters were utterly convinced that Leeds wanted O'Neill, that he wanted to join the club, and that it would be only a matter of time before the deal was confirmed officially and publicly. They were unsure if Leeds had at that point made contact with him either directly or through a third person, but it was certain O'Neill knew the job was his for the taking.

If further confirmation was needed, it came from the 'personalities' gathered in Yokohama. It is fair to say O'Neill's hotel was out of reach for all but the wealthy and the elite groups of TV pundits in town for the big event. Alan Hansen, Mark Lawrenson, Ron Atkinson, Andy Gray and Ian Wright were among those deposited as guests of television, and all of them would have bet on O'Neill having already decided to return to England and the Premiership. It seemed a simple enough decision when you stripped away the emotional ties.

The reality of the situation was this. With a well-controlled financial structure, O'Neill in two years had achieved at Celtic what would have been acceptable over a five-year span. Their success had demoralised Rangers, which is the priority for most Celtic fans at the start of every season, and had accelerated the demise of their Dutch coach, the 'Little Emperor' Dick Advocaat – sweet satisfaction that hadn't been enjoyed since the days when Jock Stein was in his pomp. The one failure was in European competition, but to attack that particular target, to emulate Stein's European Cup-winning team of 1967 and return the title to Celtic Park, would need either time to develop their own quality players or revenue far in excess of the club's resources. It was Stein's success and vision that had ensured there would be no limit to the club's future ambition, though in reality Scottish football could no longer produce enough talented players nor generate the vast amounts of money needed to buy the best and pay them upwards of £3 million a season. In England, the gold mined from television, for the moment at least, guarantees Premiership clubs £20 million a year – enough, if properly controlled, to give the decently run clubs a chance to compete at a high, if not the very highest, level.

O'Neill was anything but hyper in Yokohama, more earnest and reflective, a man who certainly knew he had a lot to consider, a major career decision to make. Then something happened to change the course of proposed events, and O'Neill went back to attend to his duties at Celtic. It was Terry Venables, the former England manager rated among the top coaches in world football, who moved to Elland Road. There was no official line from Leeds other than to say that El Tel had always been in their thoughts.

So why did O'Neill choose to stay with his Scottish champions? One Leeds source confirmed that O'Neill told them he wanted one more year tussling with the Juventuses, the Real Madrids, the Barcelonas and the Bayern Munichs in the European Champions League. That would also allow him to fulfil his contractual arrangement with Celtic, a three-year deal due to end in the summer of 2003. O'Neill had earned great credit from the League Managers Association in England when he'd refused to push to leave Leicester City when Leeds originally moved for him four years earlier. At the time, the LMA was trying to impress on clubs the legal rights of managers, and it would have made nonsense of its argument if such a high-profile move had taken place amid accusations of contract-breaking by one of its own members.

It is perfectly feasible that it was an accumulation of factors that ended Leeds' interest in O'Neill. Or was it O'Neill's loss of interest in moving to Leeds that halted formal negotiations? He had won all he could domestically with Celtic and could only repeat the honours. Boring. But in losing two cup finals to Rangers in his second season it was obvious Celtic's big rivals were successfully regrouping under their new young boss, Alex McLeish, and traditionally they had proved willing to gamble on strengthening their squad with owner David Murray's generous cash injections. O'Neill could have no complaints about the money released to finance his buys; it was much more than had been available to previous managers, including Dutchman Wim Jansen, who had stopped Rangers' march on a record tenth successive Scottish Premier League title with the help of goals from Henrik Larsson, the Swedish striker he brought to the club for £700,000. That buy must be ranked alongside Manchester United's cut-price purchase of Eric Cantona from Leeds as one of the most successful signings in the history of the British game: both were exceptional enough to win their clubs championships.

So much of what O'Neill had assumed would be put in place, such as improved training facilities, during the term of his contract hadn't even been started as he ruminated in Yokohama. One important project, perhaps *the* most important, was the proposed Celtic football academy. The Irishman knows the long-term value, indeed the absolute necessity, for any top club to run its own 'university', for that's what it is, a place where talent is nurtured and honed, where young minds are expanded. Rangers, on the other hand, spent as much as £20 million establishing their academy, and although it has undoubtedly helped to push them deeper into the red, it has to be seen as a gamble worth taking, one to which they had no reasonable alternative. O'Neill, no mean punter, would certainly agree to it as a 'must' investment.

Any investigation into Leeds' finances would have told him the unfortunate truth that the money at Elland Road had dried up. At that time, as he sat in his luxury hotel room, the full extent of Leeds' financial crisis was not quite clear, although the warnings were starting to filter through. They would have to sell England defender Rio Ferdinand to Manchester United, but what most didn't know was how serious their money problems were. The situation was compounded, as we know, by a Premier League placing below the qualification standard for the Champions League and its guarantee of huge cash returns; without that, unhappiness. Celtic had also put their foot on the spending brake, but if there were to be restrictions at Leeds and no more money, in fact less as it happens, to spend in the transfer market than there was at Celtic, what would be the point of moving on?

There was one other consideration: if he moved now he would be taking over a team in a relatively high Premiership position, but whose form had begun to wither alarmingly since February. This form would surely continue into the new season, and with little or no money to spend on new signings he would carry the blame for the slump. Let someone else take responsibility, and if things worked out, if the timing was appropriate, he could step in with a rescue plan. He had done it at his first club, Grantham, and at Wycombe, Leicester and Celtic.

O'Neill's behaviour during that period was exemplary; not a foot was misplaced, not a word spoken out of turn. No embarrassment, just on with the job. Unfortunately, his desire to challenge in the Champions League with Celtic ended in pre-league qualification defeat, not against one of the giants of the European game but against the Swiss side

FC Basle, who ordinarily should not have stood in the way of Scotland's champions.

From then onwards there was constant talk, incessant publicity, about O'Neill's future, particularly about how, where, when and whether he was going to extend his contract at Celtic, former boss Wim Jansen advising his successor to keep to himself exactly how the negotiations were progressing. Rangers manager McLeish insisted he wanted O'Neill to stay after O'Neill had stated, on the Leicester website of all places, 'Nothing is for ever. The days of someone staying at a club for ten years are few and far between. I was happy to honour my contract . . . I have been told when the time is right we will discuss my future.' The club wanted him to extend his contract far beyond the summer of 2003, which he finally did, but when for so long he side-stepped the issue, not always neatly and certainly initially in a way that suggested, correctly or incorrectly, it seemed he had no intention of signing, whatever the pressure from the club and the supporters.

O'Neill inspired a belief among Celtic fans, though not propagated by himself, that a new era of plenty could be theirs. He achieved that with more success than any manager since Jock Stein, who quit for Leeds United leaving so many challenges for his successors to meet and beat. Of them all, an auspicious list that includes the acknowledged successful but eventually disillusioned Billy McNeill, plus David Hay, Liam Brady, Lou Macari, Tommy Burns, Wim Jansen, Dr Josef Venglos, Kenny Dalglish, John Barnes, O'Neill and now Gordon Strachan, it was O'Neill who arrived with the right background and who delivered success quickly, with almost ridiculous ease in that first season. But at the club there was always the fear, not that he would break his contract, but that he would leave when it was completed. Three years was the length of contract signed, the very time a number of his associates said should be his limit in the job before returning to England and a major appointment in the Premiership. He has been linked with Manchester United, and, not surprisingly, that would be his choice.

When he joined Celtic from Leicester on 1 June 2000 one of the questions he was asked at his first press conference was, 'Is there any other club you would have left Leicester for?' His reply was so typical of him, honest and perhaps too indiscreet. 'There is one,' he explained, 'but the best manager in the world is there and he isn't giving up yet. I suppose Maidenhead crossed my mind but, honestly, this club, with its tradition and with these sixty thousand fans coming every week, was a lure I could not resist, even though I had been very happy at Leicester.' Aston Villa would not have been a consideration.

Leicester were as determined to keep him as Celtic were to extend his original deal. The East Midlands club had more or less cleared the decks and offered him a new contract that would have made him one of the highest-paid managers in the Premier League. Listing the exact amounts involved is speculation, but the offer was more than the £1.3 million a year Celtic pay him and less than the £3 to £3.5 million basic salary Sir Alex Ferguson earns at Old Trafford and Arsène Wenger receives from Arsenal. That sort of money is paid in return for the success managers have brought to their clubs and is just about as good as it gets. In the cases of Ferguson and Wenger it is their justifiable reward for winning major honours consistently. By comparison, O'Neill had only reached the foothills, but he had shown he possessed the promise to achieve greater success if he was offered the chance to join a bigger club. He had taken Leicester to three League Cup finals, led them into lucrative European competition and secured their respectability in the Premiership.

O'Neill had earlier expressed what he described as the lure to join Celtic. Managers usually talk up a job to impress their new supporters, but O'Neill's post-signing comments were so one hundred per cent believable. He told Ken Gallacher, a great friend of mine who died so suddenly in January 2003, but was then chief football writer of

Glasgow's *Herald* newspaper, 'I am not being patronising, nor am I being trite when I talk about the lure of Celtic Football Club and what it means to me. That is the way I feel about this club. I have felt that way ever since 1967 when they won the European Cup, and then from a night in 1974 when I came up here to see a match and climbed all the way up to the top of one of these giant terracings. There was something special about that. And, of course, Jock Stein's achievements were fantastic. He is immortal, and you would have to be mad to think you could do what he did. I remember being at Nottingham Forest when Tommy Gemmell came down and I said to him, and you know I was in awe of him, "That was some goal in the European Cup Final." He replied, "Which one, son?" (Gemmell played in two European Cup Finals for Celtic and scored in both.) And, you know, he was right.'

The pleasure O'Neill took from his appointment as Celtic manager, walking in the footsteps of his heroes, could be described as wide-eyed. If only his folks had been alive to enjoy the experience. His father adored sporting events for the atmosphere that was often made more intense by the few bob bet on the combatants, two- and four-legged. He had said to his son on more than one occasion that if he was offered the opportunity to play for or to manage Celtic FC, he should walk all the way to Glasgow from wherever he was at the time. Now here he was, ensconced at Parkhead, or 'The Park' as the players called it, and which is now more commonly known as Celtic Park. For O'Neill the dream had become reality. He later revealed his fear that the job was going to be snatched by Dutch coach Guus Hiddink, who subsequently flew to the Far East and eventually performed miracles on behalf of South Korea in the 2002 World Cup finals. O'Neill said, 'This is a great, great club, and that is why I have taken the job. I have to say that when I saw the stories of planeloads of people going over to talk to Guus Hiddink in Spain I thought I was going to miss this chance. It was all a bit fraught, but it does not matter to me if I was

his name is constantly linked with the job at Manchester United, a job that will only become available when Sir Alex Ferguson stands down; why Liverpool in the past was attracted to his style of management, despite denials, and also Newcastle United. Celtic accepted they had a manager in demand and that to keep him they would have to offer competitive contracts, find the cash to buy new players to challenge the best in Europe – Real Madrid, Barcelona, Juventus and the two Milan clubs – and finance new developments such as an academy and a training centre.

The truth is, that it is virtually impossible even for the biggest of fish in a small pool, and alas that's the situation in Scottish football. Potentially it possesses the peak of a pyramid in both Celtic and Rangers, but it has no base from which to elevate them. Entry to the European inner sanctum is restricted to those clubs in countries with far bigger populations than Scotland's five million. It is straightforward O-level economics. The big money comes from television; it is what has turned the English Premier League into the Profligate League. Revenue is gauged on the numbers of viewers the TV companies can attract; as an added incentive sponsorship and other hugely lucrative generators of cash go to those clubs who can attract the largest audiences through television.

All these issues would have been occupying the mind of O'Neill in Japan. Leeds are a far smaller club than Celtic both in average gates and worldwide interest, yet paradoxically, thanks to the Premiership TV contract, they could guarantee around £20 million per season without a ball being kicked. But at the very moment they were trying to entice a new manager they were being financially embarrassed by debts of more than £70 million due to a spending policy that gave them an excess of players in some positions but left them, if not bare, without competition in others. The failure of O'Leary to qualify them for the Champions League sealed one Irishman's fate and opened the door for another, only for an Englishman to walk through.

It is a matter of fact that Terry Venables was promised £15 million of the £40 million received from the sales of Ferdinand and Keane, Rio to Old Trafford, Robbie to Tottenham Hotspur. But before the transfer window closed in August 2002 Venables was only able, or rather allowed, to spend £2 million on Nick Barmby from Liverpool.

Celtic have often been criticised for being ridiculously cautious about spending money, and compared to Rangers in the past decade or so, that would be a fair conclusion. O'Neill made them loosen the purse strings to supply the millions needed to sign players such as John Hartson and Northern Ireland midfield player Neil Lennon from Leicester City. The club wanted to give O'Neill a salary commensurate with his position, close to the deals accepted by the Fergusons, the Wengers, the Houlliers and the Robsons in English football. It would have made him the highest-paid manager in Scotland, but the reaction was typically slow from O'Neill. There were many occasions when it was strongly hinted that a decision on his future was imminent only for there to be another delay. It was reported in Glasgow's *Daily Record* that O'Neill had definitely decided to quit at the end of his contract, but that was immediately denied by O'Neill, who said, 'It was news to me. There have been no discussions, none at all. I would imagine that anything I might have to say I will do first to the chairman. No one would know anything because I have discussed absolutely nothing yet with the board, or anyone else.'

Glasgow's green-and-white aficionados waited anxiously for the answer but became increasingly depressed as summer turned to autumn and then winter with O'Neill still having discussions, then making statements along the lines of 'It's going well, we need to sort this out as quickly as we can.' A typical statement read, 'I would say that something will happen in days rather than weeks, and certainly weeks rather than months ... I am sure things will go fairly amicably and favourably.' But for whom? And so it continued.

There are factors other than those involved in football that would have been uppermost in O'Neill's mind as he considered whatever contract Celtic would offer him. Those factors wouldn't necessarily be obvious to those without personal experience of the sectarianism that exists in Northern Ireland and Scotland, particularly in Glasgow. It can be intimidating, violent and deadly. There are forces from both sides of the religious divide capable of inflicting mental and physical abuse on each other. The two Glasgow clubs are at the very heart of this, and by definition the extremists see both Rangers and Celtic as the rallying point for their views. The managers and players are the focus, and it can be a constant worry and a strain, not perhaps so much for O'Neill, say, or the then Rangers manager Alex McLeish, but for their families. It didn't help when a large Union Jack was stuck into the ground on the O'Neills' front lawn after Rangers won an Old Firm clash. It was disturbing for O'Neill's wife, Geraldine, who telephoned her husband at the ground in a state of shock – not caused by the presence of the flag but by the idea that people determined enough to take such action knew exactly where they lived. Even by Glasgow standards a demonstration of that type, so personalised, is rare. It is the sort of incident that will have stayed with O'Neill as a warning of what could happen. It hadn't helped that a Scottish newspaper had printed pictures of what was then the new O'Neill home days after they had moved into it – an unfortunate breach of privacy given the circumstances. O'Neill warned then that it might change his plans for the future – and he meant it. He also pointed out that it was one of a number of incidents they had had to deal with, all sectarian linked. It was a prank, but a serious one, as the O'Neills' security as a family had been penetrated. There were suggestions that Geraldine actually wanted her husband to pack up and go there and then but, distressed as she was, she has been a football wife for a long time and has learned to cope.

Fierce criticism comes with the territory and is never far away. Sometimes, as in this case, it can be classified as deliberately intimidatory and, in law, criminal. How deeply it would affect O'Neill was the question Celtic were keen to have answered, and one he was being forced to ponder in the sumptuous surroundings of his Japanese retreat; a question that was answered at a press conference on 22 January 2003 as a result of the talks between O'Neill and Dermot Desmond, the club's major shareholder, that we now know were more productive than simply discussing the lush interior style of Desmond's newly refurbished Sandy Lane Hotel in Barbados. O'Neill agreed a one-year rolling contract which though welcome was not considered an insurmountable barrier for those clubs determined to entice the Irishman out of Celtic Park for, say, no more than the cost of a year's salary in compensation.

Players, too, have to bear the burden of their high-profile lifestyle and that can develop to frightening levels. Neil Lennon found himself in the front line of intimidating behaviour at its best, criminal at worst. The attacks on him were extremely worrying and not only because they were inexplicable, but also because they are seemingly never ending. Why him? The obvious answer is that he is Northern Irish and Catholic in a city where the religious divide exists as a way of life. There are obviously those few who still feel somehow justified in abusing Lennon in the street, or when he is trying to enjoy himself on a night out. It is disturbing and unacceptable and was justifiably de-scribed by Celtic chairman Brian Quinn as the 'reprehen-sible' work of 'morons'. Lennon has been the target for this apparent appalling behaviour since his arrival at Celtic from Leicester City. Even in his native country he has attracted verbal abuse bad enough for him to refuse to play for the national side, although they continue to try and persuade him back to the fold. But to wake up in the morning to find a death threat painted outside your home as he has done must be a shocking experience. It was the latest in a series of similar abuses so there must come a time when you would want to walk away from it all. Which brings us back to the question: why has Lennon been treated in this way?

He is not the first Northern Irish Catholic to play for Celtic, but he is certainly the first to be hounded without restraint over a long period. Those who know him say he is pleasant and amicable, approachable; a guy good to be around, so the shameful behaviour he had to endure was one of the very few black areas on what otherwise was a season of Celtic triumph. Maybe his attitude on the park, his showiness off it and his appearance were enough to antagonise those people determined to paint the warning 'You are a dead man Lennon' beside his home. Lennon took his time about declaring his future with Celtic, à la O'Neill, and the strong belief was that he was waiting to learn just what the boss's future plans were. It seemed inconceivable that Lennon would remain in Scotland if O'Neill were to leave, but in that climate, some felt that if he was so disturbed by the lunatic fringe, then his own career and peace of mind would be better served somewhere else, with or without O'Neill. Not for the first time Lennon's stoicism was strengthened by O'Neill's attitude to these matters and his previous experience in dealing with them when they have affected his own family.

Larsson's was a loss of a far greater magnitude and not just for Celtic but also for Scottish football. He has graced the Scottish game, confounded it indeed with the consistency of his goal scoring which above all else has been the main factor in Celtic's success since his arrival from Holland. Larsson is the greatest of the foreign players imported to Scotland not just because of his scoring record but also because he has maintained the highest of standards longer than any previous player, even Michael Laudrup, the Dane who reached iconic status at Rangers and who was generally respected for the class he introduced to the Scottish game.

O'Neill's search for the new Larsson continued, but he would be as well looking for El Dorado. The best O'Neill could hope for was a forward who would quickly blend with the team, help to close the gap left by Larsson, whose departure was eventually accepted as a certainty, with only the fondest believing he might change his mind and offer his services for another term. Even after the cup final against Dunfermline and his last two competitive goals had secured the Double, many Celtic hearts willed that Larsson would fail to receive an offer that attracted him. The hope stretched on into the European Championship Finals where he had returned to international action but only until Sweden were eliminated – after he had scored three goals – and then declared his new club would be Barcelona.

It seems a crazy system that tolerates testimonial matches for players already multi-millionaires, where working-class people, most of them sacrificing to make ends meet, shell out to make rich footballers even richer. But there are supporters who would be offended if they were denied the chance to thank a player who above all others has given more than value for their money, and who has transformed a club – in Larsson's case unarguably so with his goal rate but also with his loyalty and devotion to the cause of returning Celtic to pole position in Scotland. In seven seasons he made 315 appearances and scored 242 goals; a phenomenal scoring rate that is unlikely to be surpassed at this level of the Scottish game – or anywhere else. His signing from Holland hardly caused a ripple outside Celtic Park, and very little inside on his arrival, so for him to go on and achieve what he has suggests some sort of dramatic if not divine intervention.

O'Neill would have to face life without Larsson in the full knowledge that the one year the Swede was missing, ruled out by a leg break, was the season Celtic were poor enough without his goal scoring to warrant the end of the then management team of Kenny Dalglish and John Barnes. Therefore, the 2004/05 season would be the first he would have to prepare for without the significant presence of Larsson. For O'Neill, Celtic and Larsson the decisive matches were the ones against Rangers which in 2003/04 were easy enough, though as always when the two meet you could never be certain of the outcome, however well one is playing, or however badly the other. It was as if Celtic destroyed Rangers' resolve in that first October meeting, made them realise they were a team prepared to concede the initiative. No? It is certainly the impression Rangers gave from the body language of a number of players – and it was an impression that increased throughout the season as Celtic's vibrant, powerful, positive approach – so much a tribute to O'Neill's style – had returned them to top spot and was to keep them there. They gorged on the domestic opposition put before them with such relish it took until the last week of April for them to be beaten, ironically by an undistinguished Aberdeen side in what was their 33rd match of the season. The opportunity to finish the season unbeaten had gone, punctured by a goal from David Zdrilic in the 90th minute after Larsson had given Celtic the lead in the sixteenth. The game was tepid, plain dull, what you would expect from the Celtic team anointed Champions at Kilmarnock only three days earlier. The 51,000 crowd wanted to see them, thank them, congratulate them. They didn't expect anything less than victory; defeat was to be Aberdeen's fate. Instead, the crowd suffered not only the first championship loss of the season, but also bore witness to Celtic's first home defeat in 32 months and 77 matches in all competitions, home and in Europe.

The temptation to say it was too easy should be avoided, although outsiders, particularly in England, have and had then little regard for the competitiveness of the Scottish game. They see it as very much a two-horse race, not even that in those seasons when one of the Old Firm is in decline or recovering from major squad surgery. In saying that, they forget to mention the domination of the Premiership by Manchester United, for so long in a position of supremacy which they shared from time to time with Arsenal. It would be wrong to suggest that the SPL required the same level of intensity in winning as the Premiership does, but on the occasions when Celtic have dipped their toes into the bigger and murkier waters south of the border they have looked anything but inferior either tactically or in fitness terms. There is an obvious gulf in overall quality, a gulf that can only be bridged with the availability of lots of 'dough', much more than is currently available to Celtic. They must make regular appearances in the Champions League and improve their reputation in European competition in order to attract bigger names plus the finding, development and most importantly the holding on to of home-based talent.

Celtic managed to improve their European street cred with the marvellous run that took them so gloriously on the road to Seville, albeit to eventual defeat from Porto. But the next step was the one the Portuguese have since taken after their victory in Spain – and that is winning the Champions League a year later. The relationship between O'Neill and the then Porto manager José Mourinho is justifiably strained after the play acting, the illegality of events in Seville. But the magnitude of Mourinho's achievement can only be applauded. Celtic's European recovery rate was impressive, but was exposed again by the shortcomings of O'Neill's squad when not even power and desire and fitness are enough for survival. That is not to discredit them. Defeat against Anderlecht was surprising; defeat against Bayern in Munich was not. A 2–0 home victory against Lyon – both goals being set up rather than scored by Larsson was a treat for Paradise – was not enough and a 3–2 defeat in the return leg was the fatal blow that stopped them qualifying for the final sixteen.

Celtic had reason to criticise the refereeing of Switzerland's Urs Meier before he cast his shadow over the England national side some months later in disallowing what would have been a Sol Campbell winner on 90 minutes and a place

in the quarter-finals of the European Championships. It was
Meier again playing his whistle to a tune different from the
one we know after Celtic had twice come from behind in
the Stade Gerland. With just five minutes remaining, Meier
decided Bobo Balde had deliberately handled the ball when
he rose to meet it alongside Giovane Elber. It was ball to
hand most objective people would agree, but no matter,
Meier saw it as illegal and Olympique Lyonnais converted
the penalty to finish as winners. So, it was Celtic's fate yet
again to seek amends from the UEFA Cup. Their main rivals
were to be two Spanish clubs of different status on the
international scene; Barcelona, renowned as one of the
world's great clubs, and Villarreal, who were comparative
nonentities. It was to be expected the Catalan club would
produce the greatest test. The meeting created two momen-
tous occasions, though the first was scarred by the terrorist
attack in Madrid earlier in the day of the match which left
so many dead. Should the match have been postponed?
Celtic would have agreed to that sensible decision immediately, but UEFA ordered it to go ahead amid accusations of
the governing bodies' insensitivity. Celtic dealt with their
performance superbly in the tragic circumstances, winning
the first 1–0 at Celtic Park and drawing the return in
Barcelona 0–0 to the chagrin of the Spaniards. Alan
Thompson, surely the best player not to be included in Sven
Goran Eriksson's England squad for the finals of Euro 2004,
scored an exceptional winner in Glasgow after goalkeeper
Rab Douglas had been shown the red card by German
referee Wolfgang Stark. Douglas had been involved in a
tunnel scuffle with Barcelona's Thiago Motta and both were
dismissed by the official who also showed the red to Javier
Saviola for a nasty tackle on Thompson. The Englishman
gained his revenge shortly afterwards with his winner.
David Marshall, Douglas's cool, youthful and talented
understudy replaced his Number One and played more
competently than perhaps was expected of him on such a
night. And it was his dazzling form in the return that as

much as anything ensured Celtic would progress justifiably full of confidence towards their next Spanish opponents.

Villarreal were to be eye-openers and not unexpected ones for those experts on the Spanish game. Celtic looked at times to be overwhelmed by them in Scotland. They conceded an early goal to Josico, but recovered with a Larsson strike to travel south to Spain with hope. It did not last long in El Madrigal, just six minutes, until Balde had opened the door with reckless defending and ushered Villarreal's Brazilian Sonny Anderson through. It was a gift the Spanish were relieved to receive and they made certain there would be no Celtic recovery, slim as it was, when Roger scored. Celtic's Euro adventure was over, not without honour, but prematurely.

When 60,117 Scotsmen, women and their children, many with strong Irish connections, decide to throw a party, it's bound to be some party, so you can imagine the appearance and atmosphere at Celtic Park the night they said goodbye to Henrik Larsson. The match against Sevilla was the loss leader – Celtic won 1–0 if anybody cared – a match to be endured in order for them to give the man the send-off they felt he deserved. Wim Jansen was present as the manager who had the incredible foresight to buy Larsson for a song. If they ever get round to erecting a statue to Larsson and his achievements, they are duty bound to place one of Jansen beside it.

The season was over, but there were still doubts about O'Neill's future, not helped by stories claiming that he was ready to take a break from the game. Strachan had done it, Gary McAllister, too, had walked away from Coventry City to look after his wife who was ill. The news on O'Neill was that his wife Geraldine was unwell, hence a perfectly natural decision on his part to spend time with her and the rest of his family without interruption. Celtic went so far as to ask the media to pull in the horns, basically give the man a break. That was honoured, with O'Neill back in harness by the end of June in time to start preparations for the new season, not the least of which was the task of finding the new Henrik Larsson, or more probably the system of play that could cover for his loss.

The success of the 2003/04 season, though, was there in the statistics at the top of the Premiership table:

1. Celtic 98 points
2. Rangers 81 pts

It's called a drubbing.

6. THE EARLY YEARS

Martin O'Neill was talking like a lawyer almost before he could walk. His mother Greta would take him to his dad's barber shop and find him a chair where he would be able to have conversations with the customers. It will come as no surprise to those who know him that Martin, the third son of the O'Neills born on 1 March 1952, could conduct meaningful discussions with adults when others of the same age were struggling to say hello. A wonderful scene is summoned up in the mind's eye, of this tot with his great mop of black hair sitting in the waiting room, elbows resting on the arms of the chair, his finger wagging at customers who were listening intently to such a precocious youngster.

Another tall story from the land of tall stories? Could be, but it was clear from a very early age that Martin was a smart young fellow, a high-flier academically, although at that time no one could have realised that football would be his chosen path to success. The two factors that have never changed in the life of O'Neill are his ultra-hyperactive behaviour and the ability to talk anyone he comes across to a standstill. He talks incessantly at all levels of emotion and degrees of passion, but does so with the eloquence of the barrister he could have been. This ability to project arguments, to convince others to do what he wants of them, has been one of his great assets as a football manager.

O'Neill was destined to be a survivor. When you fall out of a two-storeys-high window as a toddler and sustain nothing worse than a broken elbow bone, your family, and particularly someone as deeply religious as Greta, is entitled to believe you have been blessed in a special way. Greta and Leo surely felt that about Martin, the sixth of their nine children. It could have ended so differently, so tragically, and at such an early age. To their relief, and to the benefit of the country he played for with such distinction, the teams he has infused with his commitment and the clubs he has transformed with his insight as a manager, his life has since moved along at a pace he alone determined.

The O'Neills were an exceptionally talented working-class Catholic family. Martin and his siblings – Agatha, Gerry, Leo, Mary, Breedge, Eoin, Shane and Roisin – were inspired by the political and sporting interests of their father along with their mother's drive and ambition, academically and in choice of career, for her children. They weren't exactly awash with money – home was a terraced three-bedroom council house, and austere post-war Britain was short on luxuries anyway – but they found the wherewithal not to want for the essentials and had enough about them to have other interests, some of which – greyhounds and gambling – did not meet with the approval of the more prudish townsfolk. O'Neill grew up to be a punter, either laying bets or taking them, and it is an interest that has grown with him, earned him the nickname 'The Squire' and made the *Racing Post* essential reading.

In those days in the 1950s Martin was able to fulfil his liking for all things sporting – it was soon to become one of his obsessions – without ignoring his school studies. It was simply accepted among the O'Neill boys that sport was for you, an essential part of life, particularly because of their father's love of Gaelic football. It was a healthy, inexpensive way for young men to develop values about themselves and others.

Success followed Martin at school and on the playing field, and he was clever enough at his studies and talented enough on the pitch to be able to make a choice about his future. When the Forest offer came in from the East Midlands, Greta made it clear she wanted him to finish reading law at Queen's University, Belfast. There was a family gathering to discuss Martin's long-term future involving as many of his big family as could make it to the new home in Belfast. He had already made his first appearance for Northern Ireland, but his mother continued to argue in favour of his completing his studies before heading for England and a career in football. Martin said nothing, possibly for the last time in his life, until he was asked what he wanted to do. His answer was positive: it was to be football. Queen's University and the law would go on hold, never to be resumed, although the legal system and those caught up in it remain a lifetime's passion.

If it was a gamble it wasn't much of one, so talented was he as a Gaelic and association footballer. The nationalism in his family introduced him to the Gaelic game, but he knew the money and the glory would come from his mastery of the round ball. Leo, his older brother, told of the family photo of Martin's first steps as a toddler, of how he'd had a ball at his feet. 'He just seemed to have an attraction for it. We were always playing one sport or another. We would imagine great sporting events, but you know how boys are at that age.'

A story concerning Ferenc Puskas is used as another example of the adolescent O'Neill's persistence in search of sporting excellence. Leo had read that the great Hungarian was able to keep a tennis ball in the air two hundred times, a feat of endurance as well as considerable skill. It was inevitable that Puskas, at his peak as a player from the mid-1950s into the 1960s, would make an impact on a mind thirsting for knowledge. He was the 'Galloping

Major' – a reference to his style of play and his army rank – with the brilliant and innovative Hungarian national side. When the USSR invaded their country in the late 1950s that side was broken up, the players scattered over the rest of Europe. Puskas joined Real Madrid to become one of the reasons, alongside Alfredo Di Stefano, Francisco Gento and other players of stunning quality, why they emerged as the original masters of the European game. Puskas was a heroic figure in a game more read about than watched, in an era when television hadn't yet taken control. Real were the team for the young O'Neill to follow, to fantasise about, especially after their 7–3 victory over Eintracht Frankfurt in the 1960 European Cup final held at Glasgow's Hampden Park stadium. Puskas, who scored four goals that day, was among the best, playing for the best. That gives an idea for those unaware of Puskas's pedigree in the great game of exactly what the O'Neills were taking on when they decided to emulate what was only a 'fun record' to the Hungarian. Leo was the first to try, and he reached 20 taps before dropping the ball. Martin then made it to 25. Over the next few days the contest continued; Leo managed 50, then Martin reached 100. In less than two weeks he had burst through the 200 target. The story tells you a lot about the man in the making – the doggedness, the commitment, a conviction that anything is possible if you're prepared to work hard enough.

Still, being Catholics, the O'Neill boys leaned more towards Gaelic football. Dad Leo was a founder of Kilrea's Gaelic Athletic Association, the GAA. The association, formed for those who wanted to play the Irish game, was then, and is now, heavily associated with republican politics and civil rights. Martin's natural talent was recognised by his own family and was developed particularly by his brothers Leo, who played, and Gerry, who managed in the Gaelic code at the highest level. His younger brother Eoin was also an outstanding Gaelic footballer, and Shane, who came after him, was a talented footballer, selected by

England Schoolboys and on Wolves' books. Leo and Gerry were the ones who kept pushing Martin, not under orders to do so as a result of any pre-planning, but simply because they were there, bigger, stronger and more knowledgeable. He learned from them, instinctively and well.

O'Neill's sporting abilities and powers of concentration were total, it seems, at a ridiculously early age. Leo told of how he would lose at golf even though Martin hadn't played the game before because of the concentration he could apply to his putting. He was always focused, always had a target – something to aim at and surpass.

O'Neill has been credited with having a number of heroes and supporting a number of teams in his youth, but it would be fair to say that he was simply mad on sport and those who played it, and being a Catholic in Ulster, Celtic were a passion. It was his dad's team, and Kilrea had strong connections with the Glasgow club. A few shareholders lived in the area which meant regular visits from famous Celtic names who would gather in Leo's shop to chat and argue about football. O'Neill also followed Sunderland, through the form of their Irish defender Charlie Hurley, by listening to their matches on radio when they were available.

He played all the sports: Gaelic football, association football, cricket and tennis, depending on the time of year. There was a grass playing area in front of the cluster of council houses where O'Neill was raised, and he and his friends used it to develop their competitiveness. That edge, that will to win, must have been an instinct natural to him, but it had to be brought out, then honed. He never played simply for fun. Yes, they were able to enjoy their sport, but whether it be a Gaelic ball or the other sort, the older brothers were taught and they in turn taught Martin that winning was important, that there had to be some end result to their efforts. It sounds a bit too competitive, but that is to imagine it worse than it was. In truth, life was pleasant for Martin O'Neill during an era before the civil rights marches had begun to ignite the conflict that affected even outposts such as Kilrea.

His father found the cash to buy the boots and the sports gear they needed, and his sporting interests influenced every member of the family. They would have long debriefings to ascertain the rights and wrongs, the good and bad points of the Gaelic football match they had just been involved in. Their approach was professional, their commitment one hundred per cent, and clearly O'Neill took these experiences into adulthood and into his own professional career.

Kilrea is a tidy, unremarkable town 40 miles from Belfast and slightly less than that from Derry. It hasn't changed dramatically since the late 1960s when the O'Neills moved east to the big city. Its only high-rise is the church steeple, and it has everything a small rural town requires: a Bank of Ireland branch; J. Rainey the bookmaker's; a soft furnishings 'Emporium'; and the Mercers Arms, named after the English company who had an interest in the area. The main street is busy enough these days with its Cost-Cutter store and a New Golden House Chinese restaurant, but this is High Tea country (served between 5 p.m. and 7 p.m.), which means you can eat a heart-stopper breakfast twice a day. The O'Neills' house in Woodland Park, owned by the local council, is on the periphery of town, part of a small cluster of cream-painted semis with smart gardens – worlds away from the images of council estates associated with the likes of Belfast, Glasgow, Liverpool or any other major city. The area would have been as neat and tidy then as it is now. It is a town conscious of sectarianism but not obviously divided by it, certainly not in 2002: drive in from Belfast and through one of the country's linen villages and there is a union flag; drive out down Coleraine Street past an old-style red telephone box and a tricolour flutters above you – pockets of resistance, or more correctly neighbourhoods, who want to express their identity by flying their flag of choice. You must know where you stand, even in less desperate times. Catholics and Protestants share the town, which suffered far less than many but still suffered.

These were the influences that rooted themselves deeply in the O'Neill psyche. The political set-up in Northern Ireland in the 1960s when O'Neill was a teenager meant that Catholics in the province would have felt like second-class citizens because of the old Unionist-controlled gerry-mandering administration at Stormont. An expert on Northern Ireland politics and local to the area said, 'Nationalists would have grown up in those days feeling they were not adequately considered in important matters like education. Certainly things were very much Unionist-orientated. Unless you were Catholic, and we are talking thirty or so years back, you wouldn't have been very involved with the GAA. The assumption is the children from that sort of background will support the nationalist cause. The aim of an Irish nationalist is a united Ireland. It is an idealistic outlook now because what you find in the Republic is they aren't particularly interested in unification. Northern Ireland has become such a festering sore they are quite happy with the way things are. The younger people tend to look more to Europe these days. Dublin has a strong European outlook now.'

Despite difficult times, it is hard to imagine the O'Neills being anything other than strident about their lives, whatever the circumstances. Dad Leo set up the GAA in Kilrea, guaranteeing that Martin grew up in a strong, tightly knit nationalist environment with education and sport as part of it. To help understand O'Neill today you have to understand that side of his life.

He was named after a saint, Martin de Porres. That is a normal enough occurrence in Ireland, but the choice was unusual. St Martin de Porres is hardly known outside South America and the USA, though he is the first black American saint. So why did Greta decide to name her third son after him? It can only be because of Leo's trade. Martin de Porres is the patron saint of barbers, having worked with a surgeon barber as a youth in Peru. And this next piece of historical information is hardly the sort a republican would wish to hear: the name O'Neill can be traced in a direct line to one of the most famous kings of Ireland, Niall Glundubh, who fell fighting against the Danes in 919 and whose grandson was the first person to bear the surname O'Neill.

The O'Neills, under the guidance of Greta, made education their priority, and it paid off: all the children were highly successful at school, college and university. Martin's schooling began at St Columba's Primary in Kilrea where his principal was Lawrence Callan. The former headteacher – he retired in 1980 – was a neighbour of the family and still lives in the street where Martin grew up. He had no recollection of him being the motivated person he was to become. 'There was nothing outstanding about him, but he was a bright enough fellow. The boys were often in my garden chasing a ball. There always seemed to be a ball around no matter where Martin and his brothers were.' These were good, happy, comfortable years for O'Neill, close to his family; he was eventually moved out of St Columba's to Rasharkin Primary, where his older sister Agatha taught. It was, as expected, his first experience of loneliness, however, an unhappy time, but he passed his eleven-plus and went on to win a scholarship to one of the most famous colleges in Ireland, St Columb's Christian Brothers in Derry, where he attended as a boarder.

You sense that St Columb's was a surreal happening for O'Neill; a mix of good days and not so good, of stomach-churning worry and intense satisfaction. He worked hard at his studies and became more and more engrossed in sport, as most do in order to throw off whatever shackles they are bound by, but he missed his family and the surroundings of his Kilrea home. Miserable or not, that didn't mean he was going to be beaten by the system. He was there for a purpose: to learn and to excel at his studies, and to play Gaelic football. O'Neill was a superb player, a natural, one of the best in the country. He was going to follow in the footsteps of his brothers Leo and Gerry, who played in the All-Ireland Gaelic finals in Dublin, but for Martin it would be association football.

The standard of teaching at St Columb's was of the highest order, and it has produced a number of famous old boys apart from O'Neill. It is, for instance, the only school in the world that has produced two Nobel Prize winners, in John Hume, the distinguished politician, and Seamus Heaney, one of Ireland's modern men of literature. Brian Friel (literature) and Phil Coulter (music) are two more exceptional talents that flourished at St Columb's. O'Neill is revered there as a successful former pupil, and indeed returned in November 2002 to be honoured by his alma mater.

At the end of the 1960s O'Neill's father decided to find work in Belfast, and it was then that he uprooted the family, or at least those of them still at home. For Martin it wasn't a problem: he had a place at St Malachy's College in Belfast and had bid goodbye to St Columb's (where Gerry and Leo were also taught) and the boarding with which he had never been comfortable but which instilled in him the individual-ism, single-mindedness – call it what you will – that has sustained him, driven him forward, made him what he is today. There were times in the early years when being away from home during the school terms made him feel like a stranger in his own town when he returned for the holidays. He was a working-class boy moulded by the educational methods used so successfully by the English middle and upper classes. His studies in Belfast ended with three A levels – an A in Ancient History and Bs in English Literature and Latin – all the qualifications necessary to read law at Queen's. This ambition, about to be partly fulfilled, had derived from his mother's interest in the James Hanratty case (in 1961 he'd been accused of murdering Michael Gregsten in a layby on the A6), his trial and the perceived injustice of his execution.

O'Neill's development as a student, however, had been expected. It was the way he made progress as a footballer, first with the Gaelic ball and then with the larger ball he was to master so completely, which opened up exciting possibilities to him. He had pestered the local priest in charge of the Gaelic football side at St Columb's to give him a chance, and when he'd finally relented and played him, O'Neill had showed just how much natural talent he possessed and also how much he had benefited from those training sessions with his brothers. He was selected for the Schoolboy Minors Gaelic team that won the County Derry Championship at St Columb's, but at St Malachy's he upped the standard to an extremely high level. It was his first experience of pressure sport – of a mild kind, it has to be said, but still an arena in which you carry the expectations of others as much as your own.

Politics and petty-mindedness are close companions in Irish sport, and not exclusively in the north. Three decades ago, in the winter of 1971, the sports-mad O'Neill found himself at the centre of a wrangle that was big news then but appears ludicrous looking back from the beginning of the twenty-first century. The situation was this. O'Neill had developed into a Gaelic football player of rare ability, but there was a problem: he had also signed to play association football for Irish League side Distillery. The Gaelic Athletic Association had long since decreed you could not take part in both. The Distillery manager at the time, the late Jimmy McAlinden, had been alerted to O'Neill's promise by the glowing reports he had received about this young player who had moved from the Gaelic game into association football with the Belfast-based Rosario Youth Club. O'Neill was considered a Gaelic footballer, so it would have to be his decision if he was going to make the switch because of the spiritual hold the game had on its players – something 'soccer' clubs would be loath to force the issue on. A number of other Irish clubs had been monitoring O'Neill's progress, but it was McAlinden he committed to.

McAlinden thought so much of O'Neill's promise as a footballer that he forecast he would be snapped up by an

English club within a year. He was correct, but first someone had to find a way around Rule 27 of the Gaelic Athletic Association, which stated unequivocally that those who participate in their sport shall not take part in foreign sports or promote rugby, 'soccer', hockey or cricket – British sports, basically. Not only could they not play, according to the rule they were also banned from watching these sports. The GAA's rule had been instituted not so much as an anti-foreigners measure as to prevent non-Irishmen, i.e. anyone associated with the British garrisons in Ireland at the turn of the last century, from joining. O'Neill's success, both for St Malachy's and with Distillery in the Irish Cup, meant he was on a collision course with GAA officialdom.

If the rule was taken at full value, then neither his father nor his brothers could watch Martin play football. But the rule was not strictly adhered to across Ireland, and not everybody took it seriously. One of the legendary figures in Gaelic football at that time, Mick O'Connell, was seen watching 'soccer' at Cork. The very next day he announced his retirement from the game – panic over, though there were many who took that as another O'Connellism. For O'Connell, no lover of rules or those who make them, the game was all that mattered. Not even winning medals or trophies appealed to him. After captaining Kerry to an all-Ireland title, he went home with the ball, which was presented to the winning team's skipper, and left the Sam Maguire Cup under a bench in the Croke Park dressing room.

O'Neill had an arrangement with Distillery that allowed him to miss an Irish Cup semi-final against Glenavon in favour of playing for St Malachy's College in the Ulster Colleges GAA semi-final against St Mary's. McAlinden was relaxed about his young star's absence, saying, 'The college must come first. There will be no pressure brought to bear on him while he is at St Malachy's.' It was the GAA that was unhappy. They banned the Gaelic match from going ahead at Casement Park, Belfast, and switched it instead to Omagh, which was outside Antrim – a bizarre compromise. The outrageous ruling has long since been abandoned thanks to the power of the people and good common sense.

O'Neill was by now establishing himself as Distillery's only real asset, and that was confirmed when he scored twice – his second a goal Puskas would have been happy to claim – in the 3–0 Irish Cup final victory over Derry City. It was April 1971, he was nineteen years old, it was his first season, he had been with Distillery only four months and now top clubs from Celtic to Arsenal were recognising his potential. In the *Belfast Telegraph*, Malcolm Brodie reported O'Neill's first major triumph under the headline MARTIN IS CUP HERO. 'Distillery's name will be inscribed tonight on the Irish Cup,' he wrote, 'with this win over Derry City at Windsor Park Belfast before a crowd of only six thousand – but alongside it should be that of teenage inside-forward Martin O'Neill ... this 18-year-old [*sic*] St Malachy's schoolboy who with two goals [was] the basis for Distillery's first Cup Final success since 1956.' Brodie described O'Neill's first goal: 'After three minutes came a sensation. It followed what looked an innocent enough McCarrol free kick. Watson hit the ball over his head to Savage, who swept it to O'Neill, and the St Malachy's schoolboy did the rest. He gently but decisively placed the ball into the corner of the net near an upright.' O'Neill's football career had only just begun, and in this one match it went into overdrive with a second goal of even more outstanding quality two minutes before half-time. As Brodie put it: 'O'Neill beat three men with a mazy run, actually changed feet and hit the ball hard into the net. A goal that was breathtaking and spectacular. A goal that destroyed Derry City ... [it] will long be remembered by the fans who did turn up for the game. It was superbly executed, and another example of the potential which this ex-Gaelic footballer possesses. No wonder almost a dozen cross-channel clubs have made enquiries about him.'

O'Neill, by now a former Gaelic footballer, was short on breath but not on words as he described these goals in the self-mocking way that was to be his trademark. 'I thought I had taken too much time over the first and was relieved when it went into the corner.' Of the second, rated at the time one of the best goals witnessed at Windsor Park, he said, 'After getting through at least three tackles I thought I had muffed the final shot. That was a horrible moment, but I am looking forward to seeing it all again on television tonight.'

After such a display, it was only a question of time before O'Neill would answer the call from a top English League side. So many showed interest, so many had him watched in the weeks and months following that cup final – Everton, Manchester United, Arsenal, the list went on. All the major clubs had scouts patrolling Ireland for promising players in the days when players such as O'Neill could be scooped up. O'Neill had only missed being caught earlier by English clubs because of his studies and involvement in Gaelic football. Now he was being talked about as the catch of the season, particularly after he scored for Distillery against Barcelona in the European Cup Winners Cup.

It says everything about O'Neill's confidence in himself that he not only played well against the Spaniards – then, as today, a top-class team – but scored a goal the fans still remember as special for the club and for the player. Barcelona won, as expected, 3–1 at Windsor Park in the first leg of the tie on Wednesday, 15 September 1971, but the Distillery goal? Dawson Simpson, who is compiling a history of the club, was at the match, and he still marvels at the strike, which he described thus: 'The 77th minute saw 19-year-old Martin O'Neill produce a moment of sheer magic. He tried a one-two with Martin Donnelly, but the return pass was played behind him. Somehow O'Neill managed to stretch back, drag it forward and strike it in one swift, stunning movement, and it rocketed off the base of the post with the keeper staring in disbelief. It was a real masterpiece.'

By this time, O'Neill had already started his studies at Queen's but had primed himself to move the moment a suitable club made Distillery an offer they could not refuse. Distillery were so financially stretched that O'Neill would be their lifesaver. O'Neill knew his move to English football would have to be made soon or he could miss out, perhaps for good, though such a scenario seemed unlikely when in the autumn of 1971 Terry Neill named him in his Northern Ireland squad – a decision that, along with O'Neill's performance against Barcelona, sharpened English clubs' appetite for his services, if that were possible. But O'Neill's fears of being left on the shelf were real enough to him, as he stated at the time: 'It is now or never for me. I am nineteen and if the break does not come soon it could take another two years to establish myself in England. I have talked this over with Jimmy McAlinden and fully under-stand the position of the club.' He could hardly contain his excitement at the thought of playing in England, as he explained: 'It would be great being part of the big time. That is what I really want. Playing against Barcelona this week was such a tremendous experience.'

O'Neill signed for Nottingham Forest in October 1971 in a £25,000 transfer. He and McAlinden flew to Birmingham and were then driven to Nottingham to seal the deal. The fee looks minuscule today, when multi-million-pound trans-fers are common, but it was described by Distillery presi-dent Clancy McDermott as 'a good thing for Martin O'Neill, and for Distillery'. About the transfer of a player who had already scored ten goals, including the strike against Barca, that season, McAlinden added, 'I'm delighted for the boy's sake – I think he's a wonderful footballer. I've always said that since he came into our team. He'll make the grade all right, both in the English game and as an Irish international.'

Today, Distillery have what can only be described as a no-nonsense attitude towards O'Neill. In their official website he is given a short paragraph under the 1970s team as a 'reserve'. The description reads: 'Martin O'Neill was an inside-forward with a reputation for scoring wonder goals. He scored two goals in the 1970/71 Irish Cup final and later played for Nottingham Forest, Norwich and Manchester City, as well as becoming a Northern Ireland international.' From the moment he arrived in England, this scorer of 'wonder goals' never looked back.

7. CLOUGH – FRIEND OR FOE?

Brian Clough did not like Martin O'Neill. Clough might have said differently, and his opinion on the Irishman clearly changed over the years, mellowing to the point of being on friendly terms, but the relationship when they were manager and player was distinctly fraught. The man credited with the making of O'Neill actually came close to forcing him out of football. If he had, the chances are he would have simply blamed the player for destroying his own career.

There are few who escaped the sarcasm, the continuous mocking tones that emanated from the mouth of the old tyrant at Nottingham Forest. The Irishman was not one of them. It is difficult to accept that a man like Clough, steeped in socialism, a man so devoted to family life and high principles and who had such regard for the welfare of struggling groups like the miners in the years of the Thatcher pit closures, should have had such scant regard for the sensitivities of those who came into daily contact with him, including players who were sweating blood for Forest. Maybe it was O'Neill's exceptional intelligence, or his enquiring mind; perhaps it was his perceived arrogance, his freely given opinions on any subject, or that cocky questioning attitude of his. Something rankled with Clough, and it was bad enough for O'Neill to consider turning his back on football and returning to his law studies at Queen's University, Belfast.

In May 1978, acceptance of differences on both sides looked impossible. In those days it would be fairer to describe their relationship as based on grudging respect rather than brotherly love. O'Neill has always had a reputation for being super-confident and mentally tough, not the sort to be cowed by another man's reputation or intimidating behaviour, whether or not he was his boss. He coped with Clough's idiosyncratic behaviour most of the time, but as a player he simply could not understand the man's curmudgeonly attitude towards him. Not all horses respond positively to the whip, though it could be argued that Clough's methods worked, and worked superbly. O'Neill certainly improved as a player in double-quick time and we can only assume the improvements were a result of his ability to assimilate Clough's off-centre, off-the-cuff teachings. O'Neill had been looking up at the mountain top; Clough pushed him towards the summit.

Forest had been transformed from a struggling, depressed team into a promotion side who went on to win the First Division championship in 1978 and then successive European Cups – glorious achievements for any club, never mind a provincial one. The scene of Clough's greatest triumph, that first European Cup victory in Munich against Malmö in 1979, was drenched for O'Neill in bitterness, if not sheer hatred, when Clough refused to select either O'Neill or Archie Gemmill for the match. His decision was based on their lack of fitness, or out of fear of either of them breaking down during such a crucial match, but it was a decision that to this day neither accepts or accepted. They may have much to thank Clough for, but O'Neill and Gemmill will forever curse him for that one. There is no doubt, none whatsoever, that when Clough told O'Neill that he and Gemmill were out and Frank Clark would play, the hurt was so real, the wound so deep, that the scars remain. There are those who believe it to be a defining moment in O'Neill's career, but exactly how defining remains for the moment a matter between him and his family, his close circle of friends and his god.

The decision was typical Clough. There was a difficult choice to be made before the match and it was his job to make it for the good of the team and without consideration of the feelings of individual players. All three had approached the final carrying injuries, and two of them, O'Neill and Gemmill, were confident, not just of being fit but of playing. The only one not sure was Clark. The player given the nod explained, 'It was difficult, for everyone. On the morning of the match three players were competing for one place in the team, not just for any old match but for the final of the greatest club competition in the world. Martin had played in all of the previous matches and we knew Trevor Francis would play for the first time after Brian had signed him, and that he would play wide on the right – Martin's position. If Archie played, Ian Bowyer would play left-back; if Martin played, he would be in the inside position and Ian Bowyer would again play left-back; and if I came in it would be at left-back with Ian in midfield. Brian asked us if we were fit and we all said yes. I was fit, but certainly not one hundred per cent, but both Martin and Archie were adamant about their fitness. "Right," said Brian, pointing at me. "You play, Frank." I was delighted, but the two of them were devastated – I mean out of it, bitter. I asked Brian afterwards why he had selected me, and he said, "I was less likely to disbelieve you." '

Did Martin say anything?

'Nothing that could be repeated. I can understand his and Archie's disappointment. In football terms it is a horrendous experience. They didn't know that a year later Forest would be there again. But that night in Munich you just couldn't be that optimistic. It may be different if you are a major club like Juventus or the Milan clubs, Bayern Munich even

– they are regularly competing in the final, but not Nottingham Forest.

'We've seen plenty of each other since, Martin and me, and he always reminds me about that day. It's over, no grudges; there isn't a simmering argument. The only time we have argued is over the role of a director of football at clubs and him telling me about nationalism in Ireland – he's a republican.'

O'Neill's chances diminished because of the nature of his injury – a hamstring. Clough always argued that a hamstring needed two weeks beyond when the player said he was fit. Basically, his decision said, 'I can't trust you, Martin, or you, Archie, but I can trust you, Frank.' It was Clough's instinct, and only the team and winning the final mattered.

Gemmill's recollections of that morning meeting with Clough are just as vivid. 'I wasn't worried about Martin's feelings. I was only concerned about myself. Martin would have felt the same as me. I had played in every match up to getting injured in the first leg of the semi-final, when I ruptured my groin. I was told if I improved my fitness I was playing. I even played in a match prior to Munich, though only for half an hour. As far as I was concerned I was fine. And again, if you speak to Martin, he will say the same about himself. It was a dreadful experience, dreadful. It doesn't go away, but it is a lot less traumatic as a memory as the years go by. People would say, "Well, Archie, there's always next year." Forest did make it to the next final, and Martin did get to play, but by then I was long gone. In the summer after the Munich final Peter Taylor called me into the office and said, "Archie, you are finished here." Just like that.'

So there are scars, but they didn't stop Gemmill visiting Clough at his home outside Derby at least once every two weeks in recent years. He lived only five minutes away from his former boss, whose own departure from the City Ground was a sad tale involving relegation, worrying illness and a love of drink. O'Neill was smart enough on this occasion to 'kick the cat' and leave it at that, whereas Gemmill argued with Clough and Taylor, overstepped the mark in their opinion, and was sent to Birmingham City. Strangely, Gemmill hasn't talked to O'Neill about their non-selection, but he knew he'd taken it 'very badly, as you would expect'.

The European Cup brought the best out of Clough's teams, yet neither final was without controversy and embarrassment. Trevor Francis won the first of them in his debut European tie, heading a John Robertson cross at the far post – where O'Neill would almost certainly have been lurking had he played. There were no formal celebrations, Clough didn't believe in them. His ideal plan was to win, collect the cup, find the coach, arrive home, put the cup on top of the telly and watch *Match of the Day* with a relaxing drink or two surrounded by the wife and family he adored. But in Germany the players, including O'Neill, went out for a meal. That left Clark, whose wife was at home having just given birth to a daughter, to spend the evening with Gemmill, who was understandably miserable, Chris Woods, the reserve-team keeper, and former Stoke City boss Tony Waddington, who was enjoying this one as if it had been his own cup victory.

The final against Kevin Keegan's Hamburg in Madrid in 1980 was another commendation for the Clough style, with O'Neill in place this time waiting for the cross that never came from Robertson but celebrating when the Scot hit the winner. Robertson was unhappy with Clough's strict instruction to control Hamburg's giant defender Manny Kaltz. In his opinion it restricted his attacking possibilities. He moaned and moaned as the game progressed. When Kaltz was caught stranded far inside the Forest half, Clough jumped to the touchline screaming, 'Lay it off!' At that, Roberston collected a long throw from Peter Shilton, controlled the ball, ran on and scored the only goal of the game. It was the moment Clough had been waiting for, though the 'celebrations' were spoiled by his insistence that the players should party on their own despite the presence of their wives in Madrid. O'Neill was one of four players – Robertson, Kenny Burns and Larry Lloyd were the others – who ignored the boss's decision and ate with their wives instead. Clough was so furious he told them he was withdrawing their medals on the grounds of unacceptable defiance of his specific instructions. Madness, or a touch of genius? You can't argue with the manager of Europe's club champions. The punishment was quickly rescinded, the wounds healed, but again the scars remained.

Throughout his playing career, O'Neill was acknowledged for his workrate rather than the inspired football of a George Best. Some would say he was unremarkable, though that is not how the player saw himself – in fact, just the opposite. Clough would have called him selfish; O'Neill felt he wasn't given the opportunities to express his ability fully. But slowly Clough made him believe in his role, and he was eventually recognised as one of the first players to flourish in what could best be described as the modern wing-back position. Clough, like it or not, was the irritant that produced the pearl.

The Forest boss could be as gentle as a summer breeze to those he liked, for whatever reason. His judgement on individuals and their value to him was gauged on their commitment, but not always. There was no logic in his often bizarre attachments to his players. Clough was in so many ways a traditionalist: he believed in good manners, and discipline, and all the qualities that 'made Britain great'. Most of his players understood the guidelines from past experience and tended to do what they were told; it was so much easier than a confrontation they had no chance of winning anyway. He expected obedience, though he didn't always receive it, even from those he trusted implicitly.

You would have thought Clough would have been attracted by O'Neill's personality. Here was a young man with a strong voice in the dressing room who would argue for what he believed was right and who was not scared of questioning, at times challenging, what was said by the boss – surely the attributes of a leader. Was he just too much of a mirror image of Brian Clough and therefore had to be put in his place? Clough's response to O'Neill was zilch; worse than that, it often seemed he went out of his way to humiliate a player with a reputation for giving nothing less than one hundred per cent. He referred to O'Neill as 'the idiot on the right side' – a coarse, over-the-top description. It preyed on O'Neill's mind. Here was someone who from childhood had generally been sustained by the respect of others for his ability, his endurance, his droll quick wit, his well-ordered mind, the forcefulness of his argument and the eloquence of speech that would have made him a formidable advocate. But it was John Robertson the manager doted on. While the tubby Scot with the magical feet and the outward appearance of a slob received the praise – who would have denied him that anyway, considering what he was doing for Forest? – O'Neill had to live with the aggro. It was delivered without mercy, and presumably designed to make him subservient to his manager's demands.

O'Neill's value as a player increased under the Clough regime, but if Forest now had a better player on their books he could hardly have been described as happy in his work. Clough's refusal to acknowledge his effort ate away at O'Neill, fuelled by a sense of injustice. His own high intellect couldn't unravel the mystery, as he saw it, of why Clough dismissed him in quite the way he did. On one foreign trip, the Irishman cornered an acquaintance he knew was a friend of Clough and quizzed him about the situation. His questions were those of a man depressed enough to unburden himself at a chance meeting.

'You're close to him – what does he say about me?'
'Nothing, he doesn't mention you.'
'Does he slag me off?'
'No,' came the reply.
'I can't get through to him, he hates me.'
'He doesn't, you're wrong about that.'

'He calls me an idiot. I can get nothing from him.'

'Well, he has said nothing to me about you. He may say that inside the club, I don't know, but not to outsiders.'

The fact that by this time O'Neill had already helped Forest win a European Cup will prove to many the point that a manager can make a player grovel and still extract the maximum of effort from him. But Clough stunted O'Neill, of that there is not a shred of doubt. He slapped him down because O'Neill always wanted to chip in, to talk, to tell him what he thought. It came naturally for him to have his say, something he had learned during his elite schooling in Northern Ireland, but unfortunately it was the one characteristic Clough could not abide, certainly not from his players or staff. Billy Bingham, then the manager of Northern Ireland, was one of those who recognised the problem O'Neill had in coming to terms with his treatment under Clough. Bingham was concerned enough to talk it over with him, though he could do very little but confirm his own confidence in O'Neill's ability by making him captain of his country – the first Catholic to be made skipper in Ulster's troubled modern history.

O'Neill wasn't exactly easy for Clough to understand, and at least the arguments were about football matters, not about unruly behaviour or drinking too much. If only he had learned that the best policy with Clough was to say nothing and do exactly what he was told, all would have been well. O'Neill was certainly media friendly in those days, a fact that will surprise modern-day reporters who have to deal with him on a regular basis, now almost exclusively in press conference conditions. He would have been wary of what he said because of Clough. The Forest boss didn't stop his players talking to the press, but if O'Neill had said in print what he truly thought about Clough, he wouldn't have survived.

O'Neill has always shown a capacity for defending himself and his actions, though he was content enough under his first two managers at Forest, Matt Gillies, who signed him from Distillery, and the heroic Dave Mackay; less so with manager number three, Allan Brown, the former Luton player. O'Neill was considered confident without the brashness you associate with those who know nothing but think they know everything. His self-belief was based on an excellent schooling at two of Ulster's most prominent Catholic colleges and a natural aptitude for sport. Tolerance of others was not part of the deal; Brown and O'Neill constantly argued, usually about his place in the team. O'Neill believed he should play in every match, and for the full 90 minutes. As Frank Clark pointed out, his younger team-mate certainly never lacked an opinion on a variety of subjects, including himself. 'Martin was good, but not as good as he thought he was,' Clark added. 'It was only when you were playing in the same team you saw his qualities. He was very hard-working, but he wasn't a player you would remember scoring a spectacular goal, though he did score regularly.'

It has been a theme of O'Neill's career that if he has something to say he won't hesitate to do so. He will even respond to criticism in newspaper articles. A lot of players row with newspapermen, but very few take the time to write about their discontent. O'Neill is the exception. He was furious when in January 1974 the late Harry Richards, then sports editor of the *Nottingham Evening Post*, criticised him in print. What had angered him so much was Richards' inference that he should be grateful for being on Forest's books, not moaning about not being in the team. O'Neill wrote him a letter that was published and caused a bit of a stir in Nottingham for its audacity, when in fact it was written to counterbalance what he considered an injustice. The letter read:

Dear Mr Richards,
Since I received a 'letter' from you, albeit through the *Evening Post*, I thought it proper that you should have a reply, so I shall not disappoint you. You claimed I

made a 'song and dance' about a seemingly trifling affair, yet you found the matter sufficiently interesting to devote a column to it. What were you trying to tell me, Mr Richards? It is certainly your prerogative to criticise from the footballing aspect – although I wonder how many games you have seen this season – but I got the distinct impression from the tone of your article that my position in life prior to being with Nottingham Forest was in question. I am grateful to the club for giving me a chance, but I was 'plucked' from law studies at Queen's University, Belfast, not from the queue at the Labour Exchange. To use your own words, Mr Richards, it's a 'cold, cruel world'.

Yours sincerely, Martin O'Neill

O'Neill was 22 years old at the time, and his words again confirmed his single-minded approach to football. Until then it had seemed that most of O'Neill's letters were written to Allan Brown, asking for a transfer. There were club fines, including one for speaking to the press after being substituted. Brown tried to explain that the fine was no criticism of his play 'because he was doing well', confirming that the Irishman had been fined simply 'for speaking to the press without permission'.

Clark's views on O'Neill are particularly pertinent. When Clark joined Forest he signed as a defender greatly admired and respected by Clough. He was the old, experienced head among the young bucks desperate to achieve great things. When Clough took over from Brown in January 1975, both O'Neill and Robertson were on the transfer list at their own request. O'Neill had been out of the team, but Clough recalled him for his first game in charge, an FA Cup third-round replay at Tottenham, for the start of what was to become a gloriously successful period for both, and for everyone involved with the club.

O'Neill's preferred position was centre midfield, so the future began to look dismal when Clough and Peter Taylor signed John McGovern and John O'Hare from Leeds United. Adapt and survive was the message for O'Neill, and he did, not always to either his or Clough's satisfaction, but as time progressed he established a role for himself on the right side of midfield in front of defender Viv Anderson. Anderson became the first black player to be capped by England, and his development as an international full-back can partly be explained by his reliance on O'Neill to work that wing, to cover for him at all times. Still, O'Neill wasn't entirely happy with the way he was being played. When he put his point across to Clough there ensued what diplomats call a full and frank exchange of views. When he asked, 'Why does everything go down the left?' the answer was, 'Because John Robertson is there.' 'Look,' Clough would say, 'you stay on the right. If we get the ball to Robbo, he'll cross and you'll score.' What more did the man need?

With most Clough teams the emphasis was always on the other side of the field. They all tended to be left-sided: Alan Hinton at Derby, with the Gemmills and people inside, and of course Robertson, the most wonderfully talented crosser of a ball of his generation. It was just tough on O'Neill; there was no way the Clough/Taylor management team was going to upset Robertson to accommodate the less talented Irishman. It would have been much more helpful all round had Clough stopped talking up Robertson – something he didn't need to do, unless it was designed to belittle others, make them more aggressive. One of his favourite quotes, certain to inflame O'Neill, was, 'When you can cross the ball like John Robertson, you can start to call yourself a player.' Few had ever crossed it with Robbo's lethal delivery and it is hard to imagine a player coming along who could do it better than the fag-smoking Scot. O'Neill's head must have throbbed with the number of times Clough told him how much better a player Robbo was. He would often leave it at that, but would occasionally add that most of O'Neill's goals – he scored 8 goals in 38 matches when Forest became champions in 1978 – were directly down to

Robertson. He was absolutely one hundred per cent correct, and nobody was arguing; they just became fed up listening to the Clough mantra on Robbo. The tension increased, but not between O'Neill and the scruffy Robertson who were the closest of friends, family friends. It was O'Neill who turned to Robertson as his partner when they sold insurance, and then as his right-hand man when he managed at Leicester and Celtic.

Clark remembers these arguments vividly, but insists 'there was a mutual respect there. No matter what happened or what was said, Brian respected people who were prepared to work. He just wanted them to do it his way. What Martin did was give the team balance. We had Robbo on the left and Martin's industry and a willingness to work on the right. You were never going to get many goals from Robbo, though some of them were vital like the one that won the team their second European title, but he could always supply them. When you think extraordinary, you think John Robertson.'

Despite Clough's constantly comparing the workmanlike O'Neill with the star turn Robertson, Archie Gemmill, brilliant player that he was, the man whose goal for Scotland was voted the greatest of the 1978 World Cup finals in Argentina, has a high regard for O'Neill's talent. 'He was very under-rated. If you are a midfield player and if you can get into double figures every season then today you would be worth a fortune. Well, Martin did that year after year after year. They say he wasn't a star, that he wasn't the one you looked at, but if you talked to Martin I don't think he sees it that way. He thought, and quite rightly so, he was as good as if not better than a John Robertson or a Kenny Burns or a Larry Lloyd. He did his bit. Nobody has put in a better shift down the left wing. He could hold his place in any company; he wouldn't be demeaned by anybody. He was easy to get on with, that was never a problem. Martin has a great sense of humour but would still have his say with the boss.'

It was undoubtedly a coup for Forest to sign a player the Irish believed had enough ability to achieve great things. There were other clubs in the hunt but Matt Gillies was the one it suited O'Neill to sign for from Northern Ireland, where he was seen as a prodigious talent. But until the arrival of Clough and Taylor, Forest was a relatively mundane set-up broken only by the sights and sounds of confrontations between O'Neill and Allan Brown, but the rows became more heated under the new regime. Clough, chance-taker that he was, could dig up O'Neill with ease. It would be wrong to say Clough was suspicious of O'Neill, but he was wary of him. The Irishman was bright and forever reminding Cloughie of the fact. He would talk about resuming his legal studies whenever things weren't going well for him. 'Oh,' he would say, 'I might as well get off to university. In fact, I'm thinking of it right now.' In the end, Cloughie would tell him, 'Martin, I've got your flight ticket, you are going to Belfast, you are going to university tomorrow,' just to shut him up. He regarded O'Neill as a smartarse.

The relationship with Clough did mellow a bit as O'Neill began to perform on the field, and his rating rose when he started to score a few goals and establish himself as a valued member of the team, but the Forest boss liked to keep most players at arm's length and particularly he liked to keep O'Neill at a distance for selfish reasons. Academically, he had more than met his match in O'Neill, and he knew it. You could say, and close observers did, that O'Neill made Clough feel just a touch vulnerable – something else he didn't appreciate. O'Neill's legal interests suggest he would have been a barrack-room lawyer in the dressing room, and certainly he was never slow to express an opinion and other players did tend to look up to him. He was the sharpest knife in the drawer, but Clough couldn't tolerate an agitator in his dressing room, oh no. When he banged his fist on the dressing-room table, that was it.

Clough felt he had to batter O'Neill into shape. O'Neill argues that he wasn't battered into anything, he simply conformed sufficiently not to get under the skin of his manager, but Clough was always teaching him a lesson, or at least trying to. In one Charity Shield match against Ipswich when O'Neill had scored two goals he was promptly pulled off. He was furious. 'Boss,' he remonstrated, 'I'm on a hat-trick.' Clough replied, 'Yeah, I know you are. The trouble is, if I'd left you on I would have had to throw another ball on: one for you to keep to yourself and one for everybody else.'

O'Neill had no problems with the rest of the team. They liked his quick wit, his eloquence, his university style if you like, which was rare in British football, and still is. All the players were close to one another. He was serious about his football and he must have been bewildered at times by some of Clough's rather eccentric forms of match preparation. He would take them into red-light districts in Germany or Holland and not train at all before certain European Cup ties. You couldn't second-guess him. There was that extraordinary occasion when they travelled to Glasgow by coach for a European tie against Celtic with Clough instructing the driver to divert to David Hay's pub. They sat around and had a few beers before checking into their Glasgow hotel. Clough thought the lads would appreciate that, that it would relax them, that if there was too much tension among them this would take away the edge. You can imagine Cloughie thinking it through. 'Hang on a minute,' he would have mused, 'I think I've heard – oh yes, I think that David Hay has got a pub, hasn't he, somewhere? We'll find that.' They eventually checked in and earned the result that sent them through.

Nottingham Forest was in so many ways both the best of times and the worst of times for O'Neill. His folks Leo and Greta were immensely proud of all their children and had moved again from Belfast to the East Midlands. The family bought into a bookmaker's in Nottingham and were able to watch his success as part of one of the most extraordinary teams England has produced. O'Neill was there from the start, riding the curve from relative obscurity to unimaginable success. It started with promotion and a League Cup win, then a First Division championship for the first time in the club's history, two European Cups, another League Cup win, a League Cup defeat and a World Club Championship. In total he played 348 matches for Nottingham Forest, made 23 substitute appearances and scored 62 goals. He scored his only hat-trick for Forest in a 6–0 home win against Chelsea in March 1979, and twice in a 3–1 win over Arsenal on 21 February 1981 when he was also named Man of the Match. It was his final appearance for the club.

8. NORTHERN IRELAND – THE GLORY YEARS

M artin O'Neill was never happier than when he was playing for his country. There was something about international football, the cerebral freedom it offered perhaps, that made him a comfortable participant. He certainly enjoyed the respect accorded to him from within the squad, from the managers he played for: Terry Neill, Dave Clemence, the great romantic Danny Blanchflower and Billy Bingham. He appreciated the camaraderie of his teammates, all of whom, Catholics and Protestants, mixed well. And he revelled in the goodwill and support of the majority of his fellow Irishmen, which his instinct told him was out there despite the divided nature of the province.

It was Bingham who appointed him his captain, for the World Cup qualifier against Israel in Tel Aviv on 26 March 1980, at a time when the IRA v. Loyalist terror campaign was a violent and terrible reality. It was a brave decision to make the offer, equally brave of O'Neill to accept, even if at first he was suspicious he was being used to garner the Catholic vote. He was certainly the first Catholic to skipper Northern Ireland during these Troubles, and that meant hate mail of the most vile kind for both him and Bingham.

Bingham explained his decision to appoint a 'Taig', as Irish Catholics are traditionally referred to by the Prods in Ulster: 'Martin was my captain because he was the best man for the job. In my years as manager of Northern Ireland every decision taken was on the merit of the individual, his suitability as a player, or in Martin's case his suitability as a captain. The mail we received was abusive, dreadful stuff. I mean, poor people were still being shot and blown up at the time. We expected the abuse, but it didn't stop us, and the majority of my countrymen, I suspect, agreed the decision was the correct one. Martin asked me why I had chosen him. I told him it was simple: he was the best man for the job. It was as straightforward as that. He thought it was a political decision – he comes from a very political family – which considering the times was a reasonable enough thought, but it was not the right one. Of course I knew he was a Catholic, but his religion had no bearing on my choice. My decision was based purely on him being the best candidate. And Martin was a superb captain.'

O'Neill did indeed flourish in the role and went on to make a substantial contribution to Northern Ireland's emergence as a small football nation which gained the respect of much mightier ones in the 1980s. In 1983 he received the MBE for his services to football, but not before a family conference had considered the implications of his accepting such an award from Her Majesty the Queen. They knew there would be many in the nationalist faction unhappy about it, but the decision was made that he would accept what, after all, was an honour for his achievements at Nottingham Forest and Northern Ireland as the representative of his teams.

O'Neill was an articulate spokesman for the team and an exceptional player during what was to become the most successful period in the country's footballing history. His professional relationship with Bingham was therefore a significant factor in uniting the country during a run of remarkable results that climaxed with an unexpected but inspired victory over hosts Spain during the 1982 World Cup finals. It was an extraordinary 1–0 win, the goal, scored by O'Neill's long-time friend Gerry Armstrong, coming in the 47th minute, just before the Irish were reduced to ten men. The victory propelled Northern Ireland into the quarter-finals of the World Cup for the first time since 1958.

It was a win Bingham and O'Neill had considered possible when they talked privately in the build-up to the match. They were adamant it could be done, and O'Neill told the rest of the players how they could go about winning, as Armstrong confirmed. The match in Valencia is the most vivid of memories for the former Tottenham striker. Armstrong, who played part of his football career in Spain, explained just how perceptive O'Neill's view of future events could be. 'Martin's thinking was organised, not off the top of his head. He was always one step further on than the pack. That day, seven or eight of us were lying by the pool after training. We had gone on a light session, come back and were allowed usually about an hour by the pool before we had to get out of the sun. We were having a swim and a chat, and the game obviously came up in the conversation. There was a lot of pressure because we had to win after drawing our first two ties against Yugoslavia [1–1] and Honduras [0–0], and, to be truthful, nobody outside the camp gave us a chance.' Such little hope was there for Northern Ireland's survival that one London-based book-maker – run by a Belfast man, by the way – was offering odds on their group opponents Yugoslavia, whom he had taken for granted would qualify.

As well as Armstrong, the group round the pool included Sammy McIlroy, Jimmy Nicholl, David McCreery, Pat Jennings and O'Neill himself. Armstrong, who now commentates for television on European matches using his knowledge of the Spanish scene, recalled: 'We all had a little bit of a say, then Martin said, "Look, it's as simple as this. We are not good enough to beat them two or three nil, so forget about it. Look at the way they played the other night. They played like a team under a bit of pressure." He added, "What we've got to do is keep them under pressure for the first 25 minutes of the game, not allow them too many chances, let the crowd turn against them when they aren't having any joy with us, and you know what we're like, we'll create three or four chances on the counter-attack and we'll stick one of them in. That's how we'll beat them – one nil, and through to the quarter-finals." ' The accuracy of O'Neill's forecast would have delighted Mystic Meg or any of the tabloid stargazers, but, as Armstrong pointed out, 'He forgot to mention that we'd have one player sent off and we'd have to play with ten men for the last half-hour, but that's another story. It is an example of the sort of thing he would come out with. He always said it like he meant it.'

O'Neill had made public his faith in Bingham's squad before that poolside talk-in. It was the first hint that he and his boss had spotted a way through to the second phase, despite Northern Ireland having a miserable spring warm-up schedule with comprehensive, almost humiliating defeats by England and France. They had conceded eight goals in these two friendlies, four at Wembley and the same again in Paris, but that hadn't affected O'Neill's confidence, at least not publicly. On the way to Spain and without a hint of pessimism he made a point of declaring that they shouldn't be written off as no-hopers. 'They think we haven't a prayer,' he said. 'That's their opinion, not mine. I've been playing international football long enough to realise that the difference between doing well and not doing well depends on what happens on the night. You can make three chances and score twice, and if the opposition makes five chances but only scores once, you've won ... with a bit of pride, spirit and luck we'll get through. We will be playing the way we know how. If we do qualify it will be phenomenal. I honestly feel that we have the spirit to do something special in Spain.' O'Neill was playing his captain's role to perfection by dismissing the preamble, relaying Bingham's planning, and concentrating all his and the team's thoughts on the event itself.

It is reckoned that some 5,000 Ulster people travelled from where they were holidaying for the crucial match against Spain. Some had taken six hours to arrive by car, and they weren't disappointed. They stood in the Luis Casanova stadium for a good half an hour after the match, singing and applauding the players, who had remained on the pitch and were applauding them in turn. The Irish FA held a champagne reception when the team arrived back after one in the morning. There was no damage reported by local police; the fans had behaved impeccably. One member of Bingham's squad had a black eye, delivered, so it was said, by a team-mate in what was the only confrontation of the early-morning shindig, but nobody gave a damn. They had drawn against Yugoslavia and Honduras and had now beaten one of the favourites on their own patch, very much against the odds. The celebrations were special even for the Irish. Rob King, a journalist and former colleague who sadly died far too young, summed up the party atmosphere in the team hotel when he put together this crisp little piece for the Press Association: 'No one could find the fiddle, but Northern Ireland still managed to jig their way through the night. The biggest, rowdiest party Valencia's top hotel can have ever endured marked the Irish team's qualification to the second phase of the competition. For the whole squad it was an intensely emotional occasion summed up by full-back Jimmy Nicholl, who said: "You can forget your FA Cup finals, your League titles. There was twice as much happiness and euphoria in our dressing room after that game than I have seen before." As the champagne flooded the hotel, no one was thinking about Austria and France, the next-round opponents. Not much thought was given either to Spain, whose brutal tactics supported by a partisan referee from Paraguay left most of the players with a painful memento of their greatest performance. The ecstasy of the moment was everything, as families, friends and an army of extras crowded round.'

For Pat Jennings, at 37 and with 95 caps already, it was an experience he thought he would never taste. 'I have never been so proud of a bunch of lads in all my life. They were magnificent,' he said. And, as always, humour was to the fore. Centre-half John McClelland, who in a roundabout way kept the flag flying for the departed Scots – he played for Glasgow Rangers – had a dig at a Spanish journalist who had falsely accused the Irish of living it up in the nightclubs of Valencia. 'If that's what you get for supposedly haunting the discos, then we might have to give it a go for real,' he quipped. For the youngster of the party, seventeen-year-old striker Norman Whiteside, the whole thing was almost too much. 'I have just spoken to my mother back in Belfast and they are dancing in the streets outside my house.' Indeed, the full impact of that result back home was immense, and it was celebrated with unbridled enthusiasm throughout Northern Ireland. The craic, as they say, was something else. Those are the best of victories, the ones only the committed regard as possible.

It was Gerry Armstrong's goal that had sent Northern Ireland into a tizz and Spain into acute shock, a victory achieved in spite of a homer of a referee in Señor Hector Ortiz from Paraguay, who was officiating in a match in Europe for the first time and who dismissed Mal Donaghy for no more than a push on an opponent. Never mind, the straight cash benefits alone as a result of the win were considerable: the Irish FA was to receive £90,000 for qualifying and was expected to make a quarter of a million profit from the tournament. Not a lot by today's standards, but so much more than they had anticipated, and worth millions today. Bingham was ecstatic, as was his right, and over two decades later that feeling of joy has been diluted not a drop. 'I thought and said then it was the greatest night and the best performance ever by an Irish side, and although we had some quite outstanding results after that, this was special for many, many people. When I spoke to my mother she told me how they had celebrated back home in Northern Ireland. It was extraordinary, and to this day I feel proud at what was achieved.'

Top observers from the media were unequivocal in their view that O'Neill, the quiet man, had been at his best in such a situation, as leader, captain and forecaster, but it was Malcolm Brodie of the *Belfast Telegraph* who reported most memorably to the nation:

It is almost dawn. Seven hours have passed since Northern Ireland last night defeated Spain to top Group Five of the World Cup and qualify for the second phase. Yet in the stillness of the room, with the Mediterranean only a few yards away, the heart still pounds, the pulse races, the game is relived in the mind like a constant video-action replay. Everyone can remember what they were doing and where they were when President Kennedy was assassinated. In years to come they will say the same thing about the night Northern Ireland not only achieved soccer history, but produced one of the greatest ever performances of a British team in any World Cup. To do so with ten men for the last half hour of a match played in a temperature of 34°C is bordering on the miraculous. As manager Billy Bingham put it, they killed the Spanish bull in its own ring . . . Nothing compares with this in my book after watching every post-war Northern Ireland match.

. . . As I write this I am drained by the tension of it all, filled with pride at how a small country such as Northern Ireland with its limited supply of talent can reach such dizzy heights, finding itself almost unbelievably among the elite of the game and indeed with a chance, perhaps, of making the semi-finals. It is unreal, but it happened there on that pitch which the Spanish have called home for the last eighteen months.

Those final ten minutes were agonising. It seemed as if the electric scoreboard timer was not moving. Then it was all over and those ten heroes, the subs on the bench, and full-back Mal Donaghy, who had been ordered off in the 61st minute, were swamped with congratulations. Bingham, not the most emotional of men, but with tears in his eyes, his voice quivering, could only comment, 'What can I say?' High up in the stand the chants of Northern Ireland fans, some of whom had travelled six hours just for the privilege to be there, were hoarse after their 90-minute chorus of encouragement. They waved their Ulster flags, they danced, they grasped Spaniards in their arms, they shook hands. Dutifully the players, some unable to draw breath, their legs gone, perspiring bodies limp, went across to say a big thank you to them. Almost half an hour after the finish they remained there, before reaching the sanctuary of the air-conditioned dressing room, the delight of champagne, the luxury of the shower. Glasgow Rangers defender John McClelland was the last to leave, wearing Quini's jersey. 'I've never exchanged one of my shirts before in any match, but I thought, why not in this one? Why not get a Spaniard's shirt to remind me of the night? It is something I really treasure and I will have a special case in my souvenir cabinet.'

. . . The Spaniards body checked, crunch tackled, niggled constantly . . . yet the Irish gave as good as they got, including seventeen-year-old Norman Whiteside whose first-half performance was something to behold – the flush of youth, the brain of maturity, the strength of a budding Atlas. He shielded the ball brilliantly, was never knocked off it, never overawed by the passion of the fans chanting España, España as the confetti fell on us like snowflakes. Nobody has had a better World Cup series than Watford striker Gerry Armstrong, who hit the winning goal in the 47th minute, his second out here and the tenth for his country. The moment he struck that ball from twelve yards, a right-foot shot, will be imprinted for all time in the mind.

. . . No Irish team has ever produced a display such as this. That is not a statement made in the euphoria of going through, but can be backed up by assessment of the records. The back division had the Spaniards neutralised, with Pat Jennings bringing off world-class saves, including one which necessitated him diving at the feet of Lopez Ufarte in the first half to prevent a certain goal which could have been decisive at that point. 'It was the lads in front of me who must get the praise. Nothing I can say would be sufficient tribute to them,' commented Pat in his usual modest, almost shy manner. And he was ever so right. Jimmy Nicholl, Chris Nicholl, John McClelland and Donaghy all hit a peak, especially Chris Nicholl, rock-like in the centre of the defence, and McClelland, whose pace in recovery has been so invaluable. David McCreery was again a revelation, Sammy McIlroy too until he was injured, while Martin O'Neill played a captain's role, inspiring by example and effort.

. . . Thirty-six minutes came up on the scoreboard, 41 minutes, 43 and finally 45, but still there was no whistle. Suddenly, there was the blast, and on to the board flashed that never-to-be-forgotten result: España 0 Irlanda Del Norte 1. 'Remember Sweden 1958' has been the catchphrase in Ulster football for 24 years; now, 'Remember España '82' replaces it. Jennings, Nicholl, McClelland, Donaghy, Nelson, O'Neill, McIlroy, McCreery, Cassidy, Armstrong, Hamilton and Whiteside. They are among the immortal names now in the 102-year-old history of the Irish FA – and justifiably so.

The team went on to draw 2–2 with Austria in the second-phase Group D, a highly creditable follow-up for the

Bingham/O'Neill partnership. The France of Michel Platini was next in line at Madrid's Calderon stadium, and it was on the way to this match that Armstrong, nicknamed Don Quick Quote by the rest of the squad, claimed O'Neill put the frighteners on him with his peppy pre-match talk. 'We're on the way to the stadium, we're like ten minutes from it, and Martin is bubbly and positive as always. He was never negative, and he says, "Ah, this is great! How are you feeling, big man?" I say, "Looking forward to it." Then he adds, "Just think, we're ninety minutes away from the semi-final of the World Cup." I say, "What?" He says, "Well, if we beat France today, we'll be in the semis." Fuck! I hadn't thought of that. You wouldn't think that was possible, but in the aftermath of the Spain match I was not worrying about what lay ahead for us. He scared the shit out of me, but that's the way he was. We all lived for today, and that included Martin, but he also had his eye on tomorrow.'

The French were in spectacular form, and they won 4–1. It was all over, but still it had been a triumphant run, thanks in the main to Bingham's immaculate planning and a superbly balanced squad with a true leader in its ranks. Even now, 25 years on, it is an occasion that grips our attention.

O'Neill has never been shy to come forward, has always been the first to ask questions. He is the product of a warm family; he has won medals and lived a life somewhere between the heaven of winning and the hell of having to accept being the invisible man, as he saw it, in Clough's team at Forest. But the captaincy of a giant-killing World Cup side raised his profile and gave him the opportunity to impress radio and TV people as well as the general public. Things might have been different, however, had Bingham's planning not been so sound (some may say simplistic). O'Neill was vital to him as an attacker but a worry when asked to 'rotate' and defend. Bingham, though, knew the problem could be solved. 'Part of Martin's problem, and he'd hate me to say this, was he was good going forward but not particularly good defensively. I had a midfield slot for him: there was Sammy McIlroy and David McCreery and Tommy Cassidy. I was happy with Martin going forward because he could nick a goal now and again. He could be very creative, with tight control, but when we lost the ball he wasn't such a good defender. Occasionally I would put Gerry Armstrong on the right wing and say to him, "You're a right winger, but you're also a right-back." It was rotational. If Martin passed the centre-forward then the centre-forward would slot in for him. That is the system I used all the time. But I am talking about the negative side of Martin; the positive side was he was very good going forward, as he did for Forest.

'Now, when you have a squad you know them inside out, and when you talk to them you know if they are articulate, whether they are bright or not, if they are average. You sense that in people. Martin always had something to say, and that sort of person is smart. You don't always knock them, although sometimes they can be a nuisance – they're saying their point is better than yours. But it was obvious that Martin was a bright lad, and he was a Catholic. I had four or five Catholics in the team, it was balanced about fifty-fifty. I felt that if I made him captain the responsibility could make him a better player for me and the team. I didn't know for certain, though. I knew what the reaction would be from those people in the north of Ireland – by God, you get letters, don't you? Mind you, if I had taken heed of all the letters I received I wouldn't have had a team. "Why are you putting a Catholic in charge of the team?" You know all the ramifications of that. Then you would be asked, "Why aren't you picking a Catholic in such and such a position when he is better than the Prod?"

'I had been manager of Northern Ireland before, from 1967 to 1971, but I was too young. When I took over a second time it was because I was sick of the First Division as it then was. Your job is always on the line. I finished fourth with Everton and then got sacked the next year. That's the way it was. So, you have to understand why I went into that and how Martin O'Neill is linked to that because it was essential for me to have a settled team, to get them playing the system that suited them. We had to have power, strength and everybody working for the team. I knew Gerry Armstrong would run for ever on the right so I made him the right winger because we had other strikers. I was trying to make a little pattern so that we were always covered. That's when I made Martin captain. You know, I didn't say anything about the Catholic or Protestant thing – nothing like that. It worked because he worked his little socks off. He had the responsibility he needed. He felt, if I can say this, important. I don't mean it the wrong way. He felt important to the team; he wasn't playing his own game, he was playing the team game. So he settled in there and he didn't look back, and his game improved tremendously with me. I can't speak for Cloughie, but that's how I solved the problem.'

One of the main problems O'Neill had to cope with was his morale being shattered by Brian Clough's hostile attitude towards him. Again, it was Bingham who recognised what had to be done if Northern Ireland were to benefit from the player's considerable ability. 'Martin was trying to establish himself as a player of substance at Forest, but with Cloughie, chopping him here and there all the time, knocking him back so tremendously, it was difficult. I had talks with him just to build up his morale. Nothing destroys morale more as a player than being constantly in and out of a team. They were playing him on the right wing, they were playing him in the sort of semi-inside-right old WM formation, and he wasn't all that happy.'

O'Neill's personal coping mechanism could be described either as overly aggressive or merely enquiring, but it was the sort of attitude Bingham wanted from his captain, despite occasionally not being able to shut him up. 'He would run away saying things. I wanted that from him.

He would say to me, "How have we got this far, Bill?" And my reply was, "Because we're organised, we play as a team, we cover up our weaknesses, we use our strengths. We do all the things a good coach does." I am not on an ego trip when I say that, it was just up to me to spot the weaknesses. We never had an argument, though we had discussions about the team needs. He knew what I wanted, he knew the system I was using, and he'll tell you to this day it was the best possible for the team. You don't just select a system as some coaches do, saying, "It's 4–3–3 or 4–2–4." '

Rumours circulated in Spain in 1982 that all was far from well between Bingham and O'Neill, though they were denied by both men. The stories gathered fresh legs when the skipper was substituted in the match against Honduras and left the pitch looking sullen, dispirited. Bingham put the substitution down to injury, and when asked if any animosity existed said, 'No. Why should there be?' Bingham insisted he was satisfied with O'Neill's captaincy – still a highly contentious issue in some quarters because of O'Neill's Catholic upbringing – but added, pointedly, 'not his present form'. O'Neill was equally scathing of the rumours when he said, 'Unless you break a leg you wouldn't want to be taken off in a match such as this. I had been feeling good, feeling satisfied with my game.' And he could never be accused of having a romantic or inflated view about the importance of his role as captain when he posed the question, 'Does captaincy mean that much?' then answered it by saying, 'I see us having eleven captains in a match. Naming one man doesn't matter a heap.' Only those who excel can indulge in that degree of self-deprecation.

Perhaps Bingham's greatest effect on O'Neill in terms of his future career as a manager was the way in which he used psychology as a weapon before matches. Bingham related one such story, of how he followed the West German star Karl-Heinz Rummenigge on to Windsor Park before a European Championship qualifier in November 1982, a match Northern Ireland won 1–0. 'There he was,' said

Bingham, 'this Rummenigge, with his lovely suede shoes and his lovely suit, his hair slicked back, squelching on to Windsor Park. His shoes went slosh, slosh, the water was coming over his heel, and I followed him all the way out. His face was a picture of misery, and I came back into the dressing room with the rest of the players and said, "They don't want to know. Put them down on their arses in the wet. They see this as the worst place they could possibly come to." ' A lesson in motivation and morale-boosting that was stored in the footballing brain of Martin O'Neill.

From the outset, the young O'Neill was a player so richly talented it was only a matter of time before he was selected for Northern Ireland. He had been singled out for his academic and sporting potential. He mastered most things he tried, including Gaelic football, but it was the Brits' game 'soccer' that won his concentration and devotion, his signing for Distillery confirming that the greatest influence when it came to choosing a path to follow was his childhood hero Puskas.

George Best remains the greatest Irish footballer ever and the glamorous star of the period, and in 1971 he was at his peak and still regularly available for his country – when Manchester United decided he was fit. It was Best's withdrawal, along with that of Danny Hegan, from the squad selected by player-manager Terry Neill for a European Championship tie against the Soviet Union on 13 October 1971 that opened the door for the young man from Kilrea. It would be good to be able to say that O'Neill was attending lectures at Queen's University when he was intercepted and told the news; the truth was that he was found in the students union playing pinball football and then had to rush off, collect his gear and join Neill and the rest of the squad. O'Neill's immediate reaction was, 'I just can't take it in. I was terribly disappointed at not playing well at the weekend when I knew Manchester City were watching me, but this more than makes up for it.' It was

Martin O'Neill in a rare still moment reflecting perhaps on some advice or more likely a calculated insult shouted at him from the bench by his Nottingham Forest boss Brian Clough (© *Popperfoto*).

Above This time it is a right foot shot from 'yer man' as he prepares to direct a blaster at the Coventry goal. Right or left, he was equally adept. (© *Popperfoto*).

Left At last he has a grip on the European Cup with the help of team-mate Gary Mills as the celebrations begin after Forest's 1-0 victory against Hamburg in the Madrid final of 1980. Dropped for the previous year's final against Malmo in Munich, his face says it all – yes, it was worth the wait. (© *Popperfoto*).

Above Now hear this! For once he is saying nothing as he takes on board pre-match instructions with his Northern Ireland mates Jimmy Nicholl, Sammy Nelson and Sammy McIlroy. (© *Popperfoto*).

Right O'Neill revelled in the understanding and respect he received with Northern Ireland. He led the country as manager Billy Bingham's captain during a brilliantly successful World Cup campaign in the Spain finals of 1982. (© *Popperfoto*).

Right One canary always in flight. His three spells at Norwich, two as a player and one as manager, were short and not always sweet. (© *Popperfoto*).

Below On the bench as Wycombe boss and in typical pose saying something like, 'Look lads, I don't mind you taking my picture but in case you haven't noticed my team's playing in a game out there.' (© *Popperfoto*).

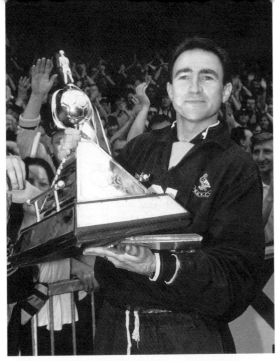

Left This is what he wanted – the GM Vauxhall Conference trophy. The month May, the year 1993. It meant as champions Wycombe Wanderers had achieved Football League status and O'Neill was to become a young manager in demand. (© *Popperfoto*).

Below The leaping Irishman celebrates Leicester's League Cup final victory against Middlesbrough in 1997 – a year after he had steered the club into the Premier League. (© *Popperfoto*).

Right O'Neill salutes Steve Claridge whose goal won Leicester the League Cup in their replay against Bryan Robson's Middlesbrough at Hillsborough – the first of three LC finals for Leicester during the O'Neill reign.
(© *Sporting Pictures*).

Below A faint smile on the face of the Irish tiger as he directs 'traffic' from the touchline while Leicester manager in January 1998.
(© *Popperfoto*).

Above Fulfilment of a dream as he raises the Celtic club scarf on the day he was appointed manager of the great Glasgow club with its strong Irish connection, on 1 June 2000. (© *Popperfoto*).

Below Rangers' Dutch manager Dick Advocaat didn't know it at the time, certainly not in the wake of this 2–0 defeat from Celtic, but Martin O'Neill's arrival in Glasgow would lead to his own departure. (© *Popperfoto*).

Right Hail! The fabulous Treble is secure as O'Neill carries the Scottish Cup at Hampden as the Celtic hordes celebrate the May 2001 final victory against Hibernian.
(© *Popperfoto*).

Left This is what it is all about – the Scottish Premier League trophy. For Martin O'Neill the ultimate domestic triumph, with three titles now under his belt.
(© *Popperfoto*).

also probably the last time O'Neill didn't come up with something original when questioned by the media.

He was awarded his first international cap as a nineteen-year-old a few days later when Neill used him as a substitute – the first of his 64 caps. If the astuteness of Billy Bingham produced a Northern Ireland team of substance and in O'Neill a captain respected by all, it was Terry Neill, the manager of Hull and soon to be manager of Arsenal and Tottenham, who was in a position to select the player and test claims that O'Neill was the most talented footballer Ulster had produced since it gave the world Best. When those who have worked with O'Neill try to explain his personality, they invariably use the word 'bright'. Not brainy or intellectual or aloof, but 'bright'. His first international manager is no exception. 'Very bright,' said Neill. 'He had skill on the ball and a lot of confidence. A lack of confidence certainly wasn't one of his problems. He was confident from the start when he came on against the Soviets, then he had a couple of other matches in 1972, and by that time he was at Forest. He had taken the step up and just became an automatic choice. There was more to Martin, a subtlety and a confidence and a composure that I don't always think Brian Clough fully appreciated. I wanted to sign him for Hull, but there were First Division clubs in for him and we had no chance when Nottingham Forest made their offer. That's how good he was. At Distillery he was very much the shining light who had that little bit extra.'

Despite his school and college success, way in advance of your average footballer, O'Neill had the capacity for fitting in. He was quite a bit above the rest in learning terms, but in this company he would be judged solely on his football expertise and his ability to work well within the team. Neill added, 'There wasn't much room, none at all in fact, in that Northern Ireland squad or any since, so far as I am aware, for objectionable behaviour. We all mucked in. He had his views and opinions, which he never hesitated to express.

He was like the absent-minded professor, happy-go-lucky, always bouncy. His room was like a tip, untidy, and from what I hear, nothing has changed. He would question everything and come up with what he thought was the solution, though he wasn't aggressive with it. All the squads I've been involved in have had inquisitive individuals, so there were regular lively exchanges, but again, I can't remember Martin or anyone else causing friction in the camp. He could be as daft as a brush when he was in with the group, but like all footballers of that era we could all act up. He never rammed his education down people's throats or had an air of superiority. If he had, it wouldn't have lasted long before he was slapped down. For ninety per cent of the time we were the underdogs, so that produced a closeness among the players. We depended on one another to survive. We stuck together, and Martin was very much part of that.'

It was O'Neill's extraordinary competitiveness that set him apart as much as a fistful of A levels. Neill added, 'He was more competitive than the average player, and driven. I use the word "driven" in the nicest sense. There was a determination there. For a guy who could be laid-back and happy-go-lucky off the field, he made it quite clear he wanted to get results. You don't have to be po-faced to be determined. Maybe the way he grafted at Forest had the effect of deflecting certain people from the ability he had, and in my opinion his ability was immense.'

Neill, like Bingham, dismissed sectarianism as a possible source of concern inside the Northern Ireland squad in his days as player-manager, and since. 'There was a wonderful man, Peter Doherty, who was the role model for all Northern Ireland managers. He was a Catholic, and Danny Blanchflower's right-hand man. Danny was Protestant, but between them they were a great driving force. Billy Bingham was Protestant, and in my time George Best, a Protestant from east Belfast, and Pat Jennings, a Catholic from Newry, shared a room together. They were big pals, so with these examples there was never any big deal about what you were among the players or the management.' But politics affected the team in other ways, in particular when Neill was in charge and the Troubles had just begun. Foreign teams weren't prepared to play in Belfast or anywhere else in Ulster for the justifiable fear of being caught up in a bomb attack. Over a period of two years, Neill's teams, including the young O'Neill, played matches against the likes of Spain, Cyprus and Bulgaria wherever they could through Neill's contacts at Hull, at Sheffield Wednesday, at Fulham – any club who would take them on.

Former Leicester City defender John O'Neill, now back in his home town of Derry where he has a wine and spirits business, offered some further insights into his namesake's philosophy – what made him tick during the years when they played together for the national side. The two O'Neills had gone to the same school, but as Martin was older they never met until Big John was called into the international squad in Blanchflower's days in charge. 'Danny Blanchflower turfed Martin out of his room, which he shared with Chris Nicholl, because he thought I could learn from a more experienced defender,' John recalled. 'Billy Bingham completely changed things when he took over from Danny. For example, with Danny, if you wanted to stay in your room and watch television a while longer you would go down for your meal when you were ready. Sometimes players were sitting apart in threes or fours. Under Billy, we all ate together at the same table and at the same time.

'The fact that he made Martin captain was a masterstroke. And Martin did great for him. At the time, perhaps we thought that Chris Nicholl would have been favourite, the ideal skipper. I had, and have, a lot of respect for Martin. He turned out to be a brilliant captain. He got on well with Billy, who was difficult to get close to. Martin always got you going. He was a great motivator, and has obviously taken that into management. He always encouraged you. It was his sheer enthusiasm. Mind you, if he didn't think you were giving one hundred per cent he had a way of letting you know. Martin never suffered fools lightly. Perhaps he was never going to be the greatest coach in the world, but, together with Chris Nicholl, he looked as though he possessed the right temperament for management, although at that time he didn't seem to look very far ahead. But he was always a man who studied form. When we lost a qualifying game for the 1982 World Cup finals against Portugal, he was at the back of the bus working out how many points we needed and so on while the rest of us just wanted to get a drink and forget about it for a few hours.

'I remember once we went on a tour of Australia and, to be honest, it was not very well organised from their end. We went to a function and Martin had to speak. Others might have been more diplomatic, but Martin, while saying we were glad to be there, told them the ways in which the tour wasn't good enough. He was never afraid to speak his mind.'

Martin O'Neill's love of a gamble also plays a major part in the Derry man's memories. 'Chris Nicholl was a deep thinker, but when he saw Martin coming he would rush over knowing he'd get odds on anything. Steve Davis could be five frames up in the snooker but Martin would always give you the odds on him getting beaten. He was having a bet all the time. It kept everyone going and it was great fun. Then I always thought Martin was more of a bookie than a punter, but he was a gambler, and took a great interest in it. I think he just enjoyed it – I don't know whether he spent much money on it. I remember after playing a game in Portugal we went for a drink in a casino that was next door. We walked in, and there he was playing the tables. And I mean the tables. He must have been playing ten at a time. There were chips everywhere. God, he loved it. He worked out the odds on everything.

'I'd class him as a friend, but he is the type of person it is difficult to know that well. He has a private life. And that's his life. A great family man. And he is a hero over here. He is mobbed wherever he goes. I remember when he joined up for internationals he used to bring stacks of letters from fans and he used to sit down during our stay together and personally answer every one. He had, rightly so, a great reputation with the fans. The 1982 team had a reunion recently and he must have spent three hours signing autographs. He is a nice guy, and was a fair player. He was a man after my own heart in the fact that he did little in training, but, God, did he love playing.

'When I went to Leicester, the late Jimmy Bloomfield, a lovely man, was the manager, and I heard they'd been disappointed about not signing Martin. They'd spoken to their scout in Northern Ireland at the time and asked why he hadn't recommended him, because of his outstanding form at Forest. The man said that for long periods Martin hadn't been in the game he'd watched, and then he would suddenly pop up and score the winner. The chap couldn't make up his mind about him.'

John O'Neill is another witness for the defence in the argument that sectarianism was divorced from sport in Northern Ireland. In recent times the abuse of Celtic's Neil Lennon has bewildered those who know how both sides work in Ulster. If it is the start of a new trend then it is a deeply disturbing one to all who have been and are involved with football in the north. It is there, simmering, among those with extreme views, of that there's no doubt; but sometimes you can be concerned without foundation. John told an amusing fear-without-reason anecdote involving Martin O'Neill when he had returned to Belfast for a match and was invited to open a new sports shop in the Shankill. 'Martin told me, so I can only assume it was true. We were staying at the Culloden Hotel. Billy Bingham, Martin, John McClelland, who was captain of Glasgow Rangers at the time, and a couple of players were asked along to the opening. Martin was standing there signing autographs and the place was full of Rangers supporters. Then he saw this big burly guy burst through the crowd. He was wearing UVF badges and tattoos and making a beeline for him. He was afraid the fellow was going to fill him in, so he sidled up to John thinking he would be safe standing next to the Rangers skipper. The guy still kept coming, and he was worried about what might happen. Then the fellow shoved an autograph book at him, asked him to sign, and whispered into Martin's ear, pointing towards John Mac, "Who's your man?" Threat over. No threat at all, in fact.'

Of the future, John O'Neill added, 'Martin's had marvellous success in management and you wonder how far he can go now at Celtic. But those of us who know him understand what he is about, how determined he is about the things he wants and where he wants to go.'

Ian Stewart, another ex-Northern Ireland player and now a coach for the IFA, has no doubts either. 'I would put him alongside Sir Alex Ferguson and Arsène Wenger,' declared the ex-Queens Park Rangers winger. 'And I'll tell you what, he could manage England and make a greater success of it than anyone. I can also see him managing a big European club like Barcelona. Terry Venables was the best coach I worked under. He was always thinking about the game. Martin is the same. He was also a very clever player who could see things happening during a game and change it, which was a great asset for our side. And was he a talker. He could talk a leg off a stool. Mind you, he couldn't talk as much as Gerry Armstrong.'

Armstrong is as close to O'Neill as anybody outside the Kilrea family group, with the exception of John Robertson, Steve Walford, his assistant and coach at Celtic, and his friend from the Distillery days Alan McCarrol. The friendship between O'Neill and Armstrong is based on trust. They keep in touch, they talk a lot, they share secrets; both spent a long time trying to find managerial posts and maybe felt their Irishness was against them. They know each other's families, and O'Neill uses Armstrong's vast knowledge of European football as and when required. Gerry has strong opinions on O'Neill and was happy to share them. 'I've only seen him upset two or three times in the ten years I played international football with him. One of them was just after he'd come back from winning the European Cup with Nottingham Forest, and the coach Tommy Cavanagh had a pop at him in training. I think basically it was a bit of sour grapes because, you know, Tommy was at Manchester United at the time. He was saying, "Just because you won the European Cup you shouldn't think you don't have to train now," that sort of stuff. It wasn't the case, because that wouldn't be Martin. Maybe Tommy was having a bit of fun.

'There was talk at one time, rumour really, that another player was critical of the way Martin trained, but international football is different. I don't think training was so important with the national team. All of that had to be done at your club. I knew Martin never trained hard with Nottingham Forest because he used to tell me stories about when he came in and Cloughie would say on the Monday morning, "Right, I don't want to see you until Thursday so you can clear off." He'd kick them out for three days and let them do what they wanted. Martin is clever enough that he will take a lot of the philosophies of Brian Clough and he will look at them and say, "That's one I agree with and I will go along with it." But there are others he wouldn't agree with, so he will take the best from Clough and the best from Billy Bingham and the best of Danny Blanch-flower – the best from all the managers he has worked under – and then he'll use them.

'Martin was the first choice to be Northern Ireland captain, and there was no trouble about that. How could there be qualms? He had just won two European Cup medals with Nottingham Forest, and everyone was one hundred per cent in agreement with him being captain so far as I know. I thought he showed then he had the qualities to be a manager. They say he wasn't interested enough in being a boss, but I know differently. Billy Bingham took over a side that had suffered mixed fortunes under Danny. He was clever by coming in and organising us, playing to our strengths, and his changes meant we were in excellent shape from 1981 right through to 1985. We never lost a game at Windsor Park for five years when Billy Bingham was manager and Martin the skipper. The strength was the back four – solid, as good as it gets.

'There were no stars, and Billy just kept on tinkering. I had been playing up front with Billy Hamilton through most of the qualifiers, and then about four months before the finals in Spain he looked at the situation and saw Norman Whiteside coming through. We had no naturally left-footed players, not one. Mal wasn't, Sammy McIlroy wasn't; then you had David McCreery who was the engine and Martin who was the brains, a good passer of the ball and very astute. He then decided to use me as a right-sided midfield player, to give us more power and pace in the middle of the park, and he stuck Big Norman up front with Billy Hamilton because Norman was naturally left-footed, though only seventeen. Not many would have taken that gamble. It was a stroke of genius.

'Everyone you talk to about that era for Northern Ireland will tell you how much it meant in bringing the country together. If only it could have stayed like that – not just the understanding, but the progress of the team. It affected all of us. It was a delight to be part of it all, and Martin was especially proud at being captain. To be honest, what talks he had with Billy would remain private between them. Both had strong opinions, and I don't doubt that Martin had his say. You have special times in your life, and professionally it was a great one for all of us. It was clever, well thought out. You felt changes were made for the good of the team, not for show, for the sake of making them.

'We had enough about us as a team to put any opposition under pressure. We beat West Germany in Belfast [in November 1982] and then went over and beat them 1–0 in Hamburg. No team had done that before. We played fantastic stuff. I was talking to Billy afterwards and it was a very significant night because he bought everyone a drink and he didn't always do that. It was my fiftieth cap, and Big Pat bought me a bottle of champagne. We were having a bit of a do and Billy was feeling so good about the way the team had played. "What a great performance," he said. "We took so much stick for the first 25 minutes, but once we had taken it everything went into gear. Do you know, Gerry, we had six Catholics and only five Prods. Not a bad wee game." There was no favouritism, although there will be people who'll always think there was. After matches in Belfast we used to have a party. The bar would reopen about midnight and we'd have musicians. It would go on until five, six in the morning. That was after *every* match, though Billy used to be in bed most nights by eleven. There would be sing-songs, and the families would be there, Martin's and mine.'

Bingham insisted on the highest professional standards from each of his players, and they were personified by O'Neill's attitude, but alongside the celebrations there was also a relaxed atmosphere around the camp, a friendliness that is missing from the modern game. Before that Hamburg match, Clive White, then football correspondent for *The Times*, sat next to O'Neill on the team coach on the way to the stadium. White, who has covered many great football occasions, recalled, 'It is remarkable when you look back and remember just how welcoming they were. There we were, Martin and myself, chatting away before he went out to face one of the world's great teams. Extraordinary. But then that whole era with Northern Ireland was just that, extraordinary. It was a wonderful experience for everyone involved.'

Armstrong also noted the chaotic side to the relaxed but focused O'Neill. 'If ever you went into his room when he was a player, oh, it looked like a tip. There were *Racing Posts* strewn all over the place, there were letters; he was in the middle of writing letters all the time. But he knew where everything was. He was disorganised in an organised way. He is manic, but he has always been like that. In fact, he is at his best when he is doing fifty things a day, when most people would struggle to try to do five. He seems always able to be on top of it.

'Martin'll always phone you back, but rarely when he should. After that Celtic match against Valencia when they were beaten he phoned me and said, "Listen, pal, what are you doing tomorrow? Keep your mobile on. I've got to go now, but I'll phone you." That was in November [2001]. I knew he wouldn't phone. Anyway, I heard nothing from him, and then it was Christmas Eve and I was going to a party with my wife about four o'clock one afternoon when my phone rang and he said, "How are you doing, mate? What are you up to? Sure, I told you I'd phone." That's him to a T. He always gets back to you, but never the next day.

'I wasn't surprised when Martin went to Celtic. He is a quality manager. It was a great decision. What did surprise me was success coming so quickly for him. I would have thought he needed a year or two to sort things out, so he has done a hell of a job. Mind you, when you think of where Scottish and Northern Irish football is in comparison to some countries who have gone forward not backward, well, you just cringe. Celtic and Rangers must produce their own players. It's a big job, but there must be a positive attempt at trying to do that. It's a vital job for somebody to undertake, and you can be certain Martin has been working on it. If I was to have a bet, I'd say he'll sign a new contract at Celtic.'

The Troubles could have been one reason for the decline in the production of top-quality players from Ulster, and again it was predicted by O'Neill as long ago as 1979 to an English journalist. Even that far back he saw how the curtain would eventually fall when the peak was reached and then passed. 'You only have to look at the length of time since the last player emerged at the very top level. The few that are coming across are going to the Third and

Fourth Divisions, and this is reflected in the international squad. I was watching a programme on television that was saying how politics seem to have come to a standstill in Northern Ireland, and you can draw the same parallel with football. That, too, seems to have ground to a halt. There is more interest in living than in playing football – and who can blame them? It is a very distressing situation, and quite clearly it is going to get worse with even fewer players coming through. The managers and scouts have been going south anyway. They feel it is safer – it's as basic as that. No one wants to find themselves in an embarrassing situation in a bar or an hotel just because they have an English accent.'

Whatever the reason, it has been impossible to replicate these glory years for Northern Ireland. That team of Bingham's qualified for the 1986 finals in Mexico too, a marvellous achievement, along with England and Scotland. O'Neill didn't make these finals because of an injury that was to finish his playing career, but he battled until virtually the last minute in an increasingly hopeless attempt to make the trip as a player. His age and all the years of satisfying the demands of international and club football had caught up with him. One week before Billy Bingham was due to name his squad for Mexico, O'Neill, then 34 and with 64 caps, announced he would not be available after aggravating a knee injury in a match against Swindon reserves. His playing career, which had been relatively undistinguished since 1981 with Norwich City, Manchester City and Notts County, was as good as over, and when it did finish there was to be no quick move into management.

9. GRANTHAM – THE FIRST STEP

Martin O'Neill was undecided – not an unusual state of mind for the Irishman. Was he to continue trying to find a way back into football as a manager, or should he forget about that side of his life and focus his considerable energy on selling insurance as a former high-profile footballer? O'Neill had been for sure trying relentlessly to find a job with a club and had so far failed. He revealed his frustration long afterwards when he remarked, 'The number of clubs, including Fourth Division ones, who didn't give me an interview shows how soon you're forgotten.' It was a depressing scenario. Here he was, a former captain of Northern Ireland, an expert survivor of the winning methods of Brian Clough, a championship winner in England and twice in Europe, yet embarrassingly often he never even received a reply from lower League clubs to his letters kindly requesting an interview. Didn't they know? At the very worst he could have sold them a policy.

O'Neill knew that if he continued to fail at making the breakthrough into management then the chances of ever doing so would quickly recede and finally disappear altogether. The longer he was sidelined, the harder it would be. Insurance, on the other hand, was in boom-time with seemingly limitless opportunities for making money. O'Neill was perfect for the role, too: charm itself when required, highly educated and ambitious with a name well known enough to open the right doors. Find an ambitious non-League club, and maybe he could do both.

Sammy Nelson, a team-mate in the Northern Ireland squad, had introduced him to the insurance business when O'Neill had been forced to quit playing. Former Arsenal defender Nelson has never really been tempted by football management, is still involved in insurance and lives in some style at one of the best addresses in Brighton. But O'Neill just could not make that kind of break; his addiction was football. There are arguments about his motives; was he really interested in the game, or was management simply a means to an end? If the latter, then some end.

To O'Neill's great credit, he was prepared to start at the bottom and learn the hard way. If he had taken in the good teachings of Clough, Bingham et al since the early days, maybe, just maybe, with the essential lucky breaks such as being in the right place at exactly the most opportune moment, he could make a success of it. There was no limit to his ambition, and unlike for some the job was never going to outstrip his ability. But he needed the chance to prove himself within the game; he needed an impressive CV beyond the one he had earned as a player. Several ex-Forest players had found a toe-hold in the Midlands non-League scene, and that is where O'Neill's first offer came from.

They say the two best things to come out of Grantham are Margaret Thatcher and the A1. There may only be one, depending on your political stance. The man who took O'Neill on, took the gamble at a time when the club was in danger of extinction, was Tony Balfe, newly installed in 1987 as chairman. Grantham were struggling for survival in the then Beazer Homes League, Midlands Division, two mighty steps away from the Conference. The club was operating at a loss, with debts of around £40,000 on gates of 150. They had decided to advertise the job but had then heard that O'Neill, who had been doing some writing for the *Sunday Times*, was on the market, and a meeting was arranged with Balfe and a co-director at a pub-cum-B&B on the A52. It was exactly what O'Neill had been looking for. The association was to last two seasons, and ended in an unfortunate argument over the money being made available to bring in new players. But at the beginning all was optimism as the lives of both Balfe and O'Neill entered a new and exciting phase.

When Balfe took over the club it was within 24 hours of folding, weighed down by financial problems. 'I came in very quickly with a few other people to form a board,' Balfe recalled. 'There were a lot of creditors, many of them local businesses who had their own cash flow to consider and were chasing the club. So a new board was formed pretty quickly, and then in a short space of time the existing manager and I had a parting of the ways because I felt that if we were going to clean the club up and clear the club out we needed to do something. I wasn't terribly happy with the preparation for the new season, so I took the radical step with the board and sacked the manager six to eight weeks before it started, which when you look back you think was a bit of a heavy decision. But there were problems in the club, like all clubs, politics and so on, and I wanted a clean sheet.

'We met Martin at the Haven on the A52 between Grantham and Nottingham. This other director and myself sat outside waiting for him, and actually watched him walk by. It was one of those wonderful situations where you could sit quite openly because we knew what he looked like but he didn't know us. There was a lot of trepidation on my part because I was new at the job, and as a younger man I'd watched Martin and the rest of them play at Forest. They were our idols in one sense. To be there, ready to discuss a job with someone you'd looked up to, was quite unnerving. But as Martin would always say about this sort of situation, "They're only people."'

'We thrashed a few things out. He wanted to come and join us from the off, but he needed to know how ambitious we were. We informed him we were a new board, that the club did have some problems but that already at that stage there was the potential of a new ground because the old London Road ground was due to be developed for what is now a Safeway supermarket. If we could save the club, stabilise it and give it some impetus, we felt Martin would be the sort of person, because of his local attraction, who could help drive the club forward.

'You could tell that Martin was very keen to get in at the ground floor. I think Martin, by his own admission, had stopped playing and like a lot of pros had sat back and waited for the phone to ring, thinking, "Where is everybody?" Privately, over many conversations, he articulated that attitude. Then along came Grantham, and one of the things I think attracted Martin was that, as with all his moves to come in the future, there was a challenge there. The club was struggling financially, had had a mediocre season the previous year and consequently gates had gone down to 150 – pretty low even by Grantham's standards. Without telling any obvious falsehoods we gave him a good picture of the new board and what we were planning to do. He could see the place had the potential for Vauxhall Conference football. That was his aim, he told us. He was very enthusiastic and ready to get cracking.'

Balfe's opinion of O'Neill was confirmed during that first meeting. As so many had found before him, O'Neill was different from your average footballer. 'Martin's not an open book,' Balfe added, 'he's one of those people that takes it all in but doesn't warm to you immediately. You have to work with him; he's not an easy person to get to know. And of course he doesn't suffer fools, so it was a question of building trust initially. He explained what his ambitions were: he wanted to get into football management, he did see this as an opportunity, but his main concern was knowing there was going to be an opportunity for him to make his mark. His attitude was that five years was the time he'd set himself to get the club into the Vauxhall Conference. His message was a confident "I can deliver – can you?" '

Balfe also discovered – and he wasn't the first to do this either – that O'Neill was not always the stridently confident character he appeared to be. Clough had done a pretty thorough job of knocking the self-belief out of him with his put-downs, and even for someone of O'Neill's privileged academic background and prodigious sporting talent it must have had an effect whether or not he recognised it or admitted to it. 'He didn't always have the greatest confidence in his own ability,' Balfe confirmed. 'As with all focused people, he would chase himself harder than anyone else. Like a Roy Keane. There was this inner turmoil. Driven people want to prove it to themselves on a daily basis. I think anybody who's successful in what they do fears failure. When I see him on TV now, I see the same things. It doesn't matter if he's won the treble at Celtic one year, and the title the next. Not doing well in Europe is going to be a real sticking point with him.

'I probably got closer to Martin on and off the field at Grantham than a lot of people. Just when you think you've got him, though, he does something. He's contrary. He's in the Clough mould. I've never worked out how much of that is Martin and how much of it's deliberate.'

O'Neill had no qualms about taking on a job he had been advised from the first interview would be dominated by severe cash restrictions, even by non-League standards. 'First of all, he made no demands financially, as such,' declared Balfe. 'He was interested in what the budget was, and we had to make it clear the club was in a bit of a state. Martin's first salary as a football manager was miserly, £60 a week. The budget we gave him was probably too high in retrospect, £600 or £800 a week. We said, "Show us what you can do and we'll discuss things again for next season."

'In the early stage of his management, Martin was fairly easy to deal with on that side because I think it was the carrot of the job that motivated him more than what he could earn out of it. He wasn't well off; by his own admission he'd had a few aborted business attempts, a string of bookmaker's offices or shops, and had taken some losses. We provided him with a little car as he didn't have his own wheels. I think it would probably have been one from Grantham Motor Company, the Ford company – it might have been an Escort. It was part of a sponsorship deal. That got him back and forth from training twice a week on Monday and Thursday, with matches on Saturday and Tuesday.'

O'Neill was not the only former top-flight personality to turn up at London Road. First to arrive, before even O'Neill, was his old Forest pal John Robertson, followed by his soul mate from his playing days at Norwich, Mick McGuire. Balfe was the first chairman to benefit from the presence of football's version of The Odd Couple: O'Neill, the hyperactive, shy intellectual, and Robertson, the laid-back, gregarious bon viveur. 'Robbo acted as a foil,' said Balfe. 'He was a bit more one of the boys at Grantham than Martin, almost Martin's man in the engine room. Martin trusts Robbo's judgement, which is a great compliment to Robbo. They are very good friends, but they're the most unlikely ones because Martin is the opposite end of the scale, in football and in life. One appeared to have no ambition at all, the other was totally fired by it. Also, of course, Martin used to hear Robbo getting all that praise at Forest, and you'd have forgiven him for thinking, "How can that slovenly slob be talked about like that?" He probably didn't think like that, but others did. They've had little spells on their own, but basically they've been together ever since Grantham.'

O'Neill took on the job on the understanding that he would be free to carry out a previous short-term engagement to coach in the USA. He arranged for Robertson to look after the pre-season training, so it was Robbo who prepared the Grantham players for the opening league match of the 1987/88 season at Merthyr Tydfil in August. 'Martin was due back the day of that first match,' said Balfe. 'As I recall, we sent a director to pick him up from the airport, and he did take charge of that first game, even though he hadn't done any pre-season. There was Martin, coming back from the States, hadn't seen his family for weeks, but instead of going home to West Bridgford and Geraldine and the girls he was happy to come to Wales straight away.

'We lost 3–0. Bob Latchford was centre-forward for Merthyr and was still a good player. They were to be our rivals that year for the championship. We had a poorish start to the season, probably because it took Martin a while to get things sorted. I felt the pressure a bit because I'd made the decision with the board to appoint Martin, but there were no real doubts as far as Martin was concerned because whatever the results he was always striving to get it right. I suppose out of the first ten games of the season we got only about eleven points. It didn't look very good, but there was a good, close-knit camaraderie about our club, as there is about any small-town football club.'

Poor start maybe, but by Christmas Grantham were top of the league. Although he would not admit it himself, Mick McGuire's arrival in September had something of the same inspiring effect on Grantham that O'Neill's own move to Carrow Road had on Norwich earlier in the decade. The cultured midfielder, newly retired from the game after ending his League career under Joe Royle at Oldham, had almost turned down the chance to play for his former lodger, but having taken up the offer he quickly saw in action the foremost quality that has defined O'Neill's managerial career: the ability to pick a player then manage him in such a way as to extract the absolute maximum from him.

'I'd retired in June 1987 and done a month non-contract at Blackpool with Sam Ellis,' McGuire recalled, 'and I didn't fancy it because they were hoofing the ball and I'm not a hoofer, I need a touch. Martin rang me and said, "Micky, come and play for me." I was 35 and I didn't want to go. I didn't want to play semi-pro and I'd always said I wasn't going to play again. He said, "Come and play on a Saturday and I'll put a few quid in your back pocket." I drove down there and still didn't want to play to start with, but he and Robbo got me going. I played four seasons there.

'He was fantastic to work for because I saw a side of him which still applies today. It's about managing people. What I saw in him was something I hadn't seen in any other manager, not even my best friend Joe Royle whom I really enjoyed working for. Martin could keep that distance as a manager. There was always that slight fear factor with Martin. It wasn't that he scared you into playing, but he had that distance, even with me. There was a feeling I had to do it for him; I felt it even as I was driving down there. He was expecting things from me. He never said, "Micky, you've got to do it for me." His knack was to find the right characters. He'd do anything to encourage me. He'd say, "Micky, come and trap it," and every time I did, I'd hear from the dugout, "Brilliant, Micky!" It got to the point that even I needed it, despite having played First and Second Division football for seventeen years, having captained sides in both divisions and having played in the cup final in America for Tampa, a total of 500 games. There was all that, yet I still looked forward to him shouting over to me. I'd only have to knock it three yards and he'd shout unbelievable praise at me.

'I know why he brought me in: I was a good character, I was strong-willed and he knew I'd come and bust a gut for him and be a good role model for his younger players. Without being unkind, I've never seen so many players of limited ability improve at that level. Like Gary Crosby. Within twenty games he'd been sold on. He had uncanny ability, and enthusiasm to die for.

'Martin had an innate knowledge of what made people tick. You can't always treat every player the same. It needs a special astuteness to get the best out of each individual. If you look at his later career, there were players every manager had trouble with until Martin got hold of them – without naming any names.' Stan Collymore, John Hartson and Chris Sutton spring to mind. 'He knows players, picks strong characters like Cloughie did and treats them firmly. Look at Kenny Burns and how many red cards he got at Forest. Under any other manager these days ... well, it would have been a holocaust. Martin had Cloughie's strength.'

McGuire is not convinced by the argument that O'Neill's positive and considerate approach to his players was a reaction to the abuse he suffered under Clough at Forest. 'I think it was more a case that he realised that playing football is not just about ability. It's about maximising what you've got, getting the best out of that individual. If it suited he was not afraid to distance himself from somebody and slaughter them. You need intelligence for that, a bit of foresight, and most of all an ability to be able to suss people out. That's why some people want to follow, some want to lead and others want to direct. The only people who can direct, I believe, are those who have that ability to get the best out of every individual – slaughtering one, distancing yourself from another, patting somebody on the back four times a week, whatever it takes. That's the ability he's got. I don't think it's about being downtrodden at Forest; he was by no means the only one who got that treatment from Clough. He told me about what Cloughie used to say, things like, "Fucking give it to Robbo and let him get on with it! O'Neill, fucking run up and down that other flank like your life depends on it because you haven't got his fucking ability!" Or words to that effect. That stood him in good stead, but stressing that wouldn't do the man justice.

'What he achieved at Grantham on limited resources was amazing. I played under some great managers, like John Bond, Norman Hunter and Noel Cantwell, but when it came to man management, no one was in the same street as

Martin.' But at the same time, McGuire is always keen to point out that there was and is more to O'Neill's success than sound man management. 'He's not a master tactician, as anybody else will tell you, but no one should belittle him and say he can't read a game and know when to change it. People think the hardest thing is to set out your team, but more important is to be able to see what is going wrong and knowing how to change it. Don't let anyone tell you that Martin can't do that. He knows his style. He plays a very simple, basic way: you need pace and you need strength in all areas, and you must be one hundred per cent committed when they have the ball. Anyone who doesn't want to play ball will be moved on, but if you do, he will protect and support you to the death. He believes in playing, but playing in the right areas, so if you need to hoof it out of defence, that's what you do. He could assess and find quality and potential in a player and get it out. He wasn't Houdini. I know players he's had that haven't done it. You can't get it right all the time, but, God, what he's got, very few have in this game.'

O'Neill's methods soon began to bed down. The players got the message, and those who didn't react positively were told to look elsewhere. Balfe recalled, 'Slowly but surely, his influence started to show itself in the dressing room. He was a great one for team spirit. Travelling back on the coaches, we didn't have a lot of money but we'd pull in and he'd buy the players fish and chips. He'd have a few beers at the club after games, sing songs on the coach if we won. He wore his heart on his sleeve. He was just like he's been at Leicester and Celtic. He'd be dancing up and down the touchline, he'd be over the dugout. He'd even argue with the crowd, because in a small crowd you can hear a lot of what is said. He would turn around and start an argument if someone had shouted something he didn't agree with. He was just enthusiasm personified.

'People did not cross him twice. There were one or two players who slowly but surely were weeded out. When they came out of the dressing room, his players were going to give 110 per cent. Nothing less was going to be acceptable as far as Martin was concerned. He was ruthless. He could leave people out on a whim. Sometimes you wondered what he was doing – "Why the bloody hell has he left him out this week?" – but there would always be a reason for it. One of Martin's strengths was getting the best out of people. He could make an average player a good player by making him believe in himself, by drumming in the need to do the simple things well.'

Quality former pros can find it difficult to work with those less talented than themselves – those who can are one step ahead of the herd – but O'Neill proved with at least one player at Grantham, Chris Curtis, that he had the patience to teach him how to improve, how to become a valuable member of his team. Balfe explained, 'Chris hadn't played at Grantham's level before. He came in and was the weak link, but by the time Martin had finished with him he was a solid member of the team. He used to get some stick, but if you responded to Martin's cajoling and you could take a rocket and didn't want wet nursing, you'd do for Martin.'

But as well as making the most of limited ability, O'Neill knew a true gem when he saw one. It was O'Neill, as already mentioned by Mick McGuire, who spotted the potential on a wet and miserable night in Gary Crosby, a young non-League footballer playing in a county match that, as luck would have it, had been scheduled for London Road. O'Neill was confident that Crosby would be good enough to play First Division football, given the proper grooming and encouragement, but Grantham's pursuit of him led to an accusation of tapping.

'I went to watch,' Balfe recalled, 'and Martin came across from Nottingham to see what talent there was among players he hadn't had a chance to see playing for other sides in the county. Crosby was on the wing on the far side in the first half. He went by people as if they weren't there, and London Road was like a bog. Gary was going past people at will and putting the ball in the net every now and then. Martin immediately wanted to know who he was, and we found out that he wasn't on contract with Lincoln United. We got hold of him, and were reported by Lincoln to the Lincolnshire FA for tapping him up.'

Mention the words 'he was tapped' or 'I'm sure he was tapped' in the company of any group of people associated with the running of a football club and they will shuffle their feet and look at the ground. For those who do not know, tapping is the illegal method used by the unscrupulous to snatch a player or a manager from another club. It is illegal in the sense that the clubs themselves have agreed it is something so underhand that those caught tapping, if not quite cast from the land, are disciplined, slapped over the wrist and ordered to pay a fine. It is one of those rules that draw big headlines when a club is found guilty, but to most it is ludicrously unworkable. When a club wants to sign a player the process should be conducted club to club, either through the managers, the chief executives or the chairmen. Some do, some don't. Those who prefer to know whether the manager or the player they have targeted would be happy to join them contact them without the permission of their clubs, and if the vibes are right they might try to entice them away. There can be complications; a contract, for instance, can be a difficult hurdle, but not an insurmountable one.

Lincoln's complaint to the FA certainly didn't stop the deal being completed in Grantham's favour. 'We went over to see Gary at his house just outside Lincoln,' Balfe continued. 'His parents were big Nottingham Forest fans. We were treated like royalty. We persuaded Gary to sign a contract. He was worried about doing that because there was talk of scouts watching him, but I needed him on a contract because I would have been shot as chairman if he'd left soon afterwards.

'Martin's ability to charm the birds out of the trees was crucial in persuading Gary to sign. At the same time, Martin alerted Forest to the fact that he had signed a little gem and they should come and have a look at him. We were playing Banbury when someone came from Forest to watch Gary. He didn't have a particularly good game, but they took him and a player called John Humphreys, who was a good one and our club captain, to play in a reserve-team game so that Cloughie could run his eye over Crosby. Cloughie being like Martin, or rather the other way round, it wasn't sufficient for someone to tell him a player was good, he had to see for himself. He took one look at Crosby and said, "We'll take him." Gary was only with us for about two months.

'Looking back, they got him for a song. If I was doing the deal again, I would want more than £15,000. But we were cash-strapped. As for Martin placing Gary with his old club, a few people made noises about it. There was always rumour and counter-rumour about arrangements. As club chairman, everyone comes to you with tittle-tattle.'

Crosby was not to reach the City Ground without a flea in the ear from Alex Ferguson, who at the time was building a competitive side at Old Trafford and was also very much interested in the young player; during Crosby's short stay at London Road, one of the local United scouts had pestered Balfe to let him take Gary up to the Theatre of Dreams. By doing a deal with Forest, O'Neill unwittingly crossed swords with the man he would later be hotly tipped to replace.

'I trusted Martin and was led by him in this because he knew the people at Forest,' said Balfe. 'I had made Gary a promise in front of his parents that if he signed the contract and Forest came in for him, I wouldn't stand in his way. Of course, I got a battering for that at boardroom level. Gary was a bloody good player. He had the trick of going past people and he had pace. One of the things you'll always find with Martin is that pace is the big thing.

'I went over and picked Gary up myself. I drove him to the ground, and Martin came over from West Bridgford. Then we all had a meeting with Ronnie Fenton [Clough's assistant]. Brian Clough didn't attend, but we agreed terms. Gary wanted to go to Nottingham Forest, even though he'd had Manchester United on his back, as had I. In fact, Ferguson actually rang him. There's me, driving Gary Crosby to Nottingham Forest, and he says, "Oh yeah, Alex Ferguson rang me last night." Alex Ferguson wasn't yet the big man he is now, but I still wondered at the conversation. "What did he want?" Gary says, "He just rang me up and said who he was and that all he wanted to say was that I'd just made the biggest mistake of my life, and put the phone down on me." Gary's a lovely lad, and all he added was: "It wasn't very nice, that, was it?" ' In a word, no. Crosby signed for Forest.

'Gary, of course, was moved very quickly into Forest's first team. I'd got a deal that was going to provide us with £15,000 and so much more if he made so many appearances, plus 50 per cent of any further transfer, but a few years later when Gary had knee problems he went, you guessed it, on a free. I could have screamed. He'd played in League Cup and FA Cup finals for Forest. His transfer value would have been at least £100,000.'

By the end of the 1987/88 season O'Neill's team at Grantham was a now-familiar blend of existing players made better, new young talent and old friends – steady, experienced journeymen. O'Neill used his friendships with former team-mates and his name to persuade some big names to play for him, and Robbo continued to attract 'names' when he had a spell as manager for a while. Kenny Burns and Ian Bowyer, who were in the same great Forest team as O'Neill and Robertson; fellow European Cup winner Alan Kennedy, formerly of Liverpool; Terry Curran; future Forest manager Paul Hart – all would pass through London Road in the space of four years.

The success O'Neill was bringing was enough to have a dramatic effect on attendances, too, as his first season drew to a dramatic climax. 'When we played Merthyr Tydfil at London Road we had 1,200 people here. My first game as chairman the previous year had been Merthyr, and there were only 150 there. The chase went right down to the wire. Merthyr had already won the league; we had to win, Moor Green had to lose heavily. We went over to Bilston and gave them a footballing lesson, winning 3–0. It was a very exciting time, there was this impetus building up with so much happening, but unfortunately we missed out on promotion by one point.'

That disappointment was offset by the thought of what could happen the following season, 1988/89, O'Neill's second at London Road. Balfe was certainly up for it, more convinced than ever that the appointment of O'Neill was a masterstroke. 'We were feeling very confident and we were one of the favourites for promotion. But we had a slightly indifferent season in many ways and finished fifth. Martin rang the changes a bit, brought in a few players, but there were situations cropping up. We lost Glenn Beech, who went to Boston United. I remember Martin ringing me; he could ring you up at any time of the night. He really wore it on his sleeve. He was so determined. He rang me very late at night, it must have been quarter to twelve, to tell me Glenn had signed for Boston United. He went ape. He ranted and raved against Beech for what he'd done. He felt deeply hurt because I think Beech had given his word he wouldn't do that. He was a very important player for the team, left-sided with a hammer in his foot, could score goals from anywhere. He was a cracker. There were a few other things that went against us through the season. We lost our way a little bit and didn't carry on the momentum from the previous year. We had our ups and downs.'

It was during one of the downs that Balfe got an insight into just how much failure hurt O'Neill. 'There was one match, for instance, at Sutton Coldfield where we got a right thumping. I think it was one of the last times John [Robertson] played; he realised he couldn't do it at that level any more. I seem to recall it was 5–1. It was a terrible performance. Martin was tearing his hair out on the touchline. I remember going into the boardroom afterwards. They were a good board, and the whisky was flowing. Time must have crept on. Suddenly there was a knock on the door and it was the assistant trainer, Nigel Marshall. He said, "Excuse me, Mr Chairman, Martin's asked me to tell you we're ready to go." I looked across and said, "Excuse me, Nigel, you tell Martin the coach goes when I say and when I'm ready. OK?" "Is that what you want me to say?" Nigel replied. "That's what I've told you to say. Thank you." When he shut the door, there was cheering in the boardroom. I hadn't done it for that. I was bloody furious. I'd had to sit and watch that crap and I'd probably paid the wages or half the wages that week. It was a poor performance, and Martin had obviously sent Nigel. I could see where Martin was coming from afterwards, but I was drowning my sorrows.

'Eventually, we left. We got on the coach, and it was like . . . well, Martin never looked at me once. I sat opposite him and he never uttered a word. In the end I went across and sat next to him and started talking to him, and he gradually loosened up. He was obviously deeply hurt by the performance, that was the most important thing that came out of it. He wanted out of there. It was an indication of how much he took it to heart. He'd never done it before and he never did it again. Only Geraldine can say what he's like to live with.'

Perhaps so, but two years was enough to give Balfe more than a glimpse of some of his manager's idiosyncrasies. One of them, presumably inherited from his mother as a result of her interest in the James Hanratty case, was his long-held interest in murders and the criminal mind; more than once on away trips he asked the coach driver to divert in order to travel past a location that featured in the infamous careers of the likes of the Yorkshire Ripper. Another was a curious reluctance to spend money. 'Martin hates spending money,' said Balfe. 'He gets very embarrassed. I think it's because if he spent a lot of money, there would be more pressure. He spent £500 when he was at Grantham on a player, a quick, greased-lightning striker. The guy had run us ragged when we played Gloucester, we'd found out he was unhappy there, Martin decided on the way home that he wanted to buy him, and Gloucester said we could have him. We went over to Spalding to watch him again. Martin worried all the way over, but we bought him for £500. In his first game there were 700 or 800 watching and he didn't give good value. Martin never forgot that. He'd be withering if you asked him about it.' This discomfort with money, or the worry of wasting it, was to resurface later in his career, particularly at Leicester.

O'Neill was not to follow through his five-year plan for Grantham Town. Club officials including Balfe had become certain before the end of the 1988/89 season that their man, having failed to build on his promising first season, had been approached by another local non-League side, Shepshed Charterhouse, who were trying to establish for themselves a new future and were looking for a manager. An approach was bad enough; then they realised that O'Neill was so impressed with the Shepshed offer that he was ready to accept – that is, if he couldn't agree a new deal with Grantham. It was a considerable blow for Balfe, who regretted the way things finished.

'We were moving towards the end of the season when these rumours started,' Balfe recalled. 'After the semi at London Road of the floodlit Evans Holdshaw Cup competition, a dour game that we won, I'd arranged with Martin to sit down and sort out the third season's budget. We were sitting there having a drink, celebrating the fact that we were in the final. Slowly, people began to drift away, but a director, the secretary Pat Nixon, and a couple of others stayed around for the discussion. Without realising it at the time, it was the last meeting I was to have with Martin at the club.

'I knew what I could afford for the following season, and I felt that the last season had been a bit disappointing given the fact that the budget had been slightly higher than the previous year. Martin was on more money, too, I think about £180 a week [others say a lot less, not much more than the £60 he started on]. He was in a very deep mood, very guarded. You could tell he was very distrustful of what I was offering him, or how it was coming across. He could go into these little phases. It was all writing things behind his hand, that sort of business. A little bit at arm's length.

'The discussion went backwards and forwards. Eventually, I think I said £800 and that's it, the weekly budget, and he was quite pleased with that. Then he said, "Well, what about mine?" I said, "You can have as much of it as you want, but it's £800." Maybe it was the way I put it over to him, maybe he perceived it as clever-arse. Whatever, he was not very happy. "What are you saying?" he said. I replied, "You can have what you want. If you want £200 for yourself, you've got £600 left." "I can't build a team on that," he remonstrated. "That's what we've had this year. If we need new players, I need more money." But I hadn't got any more money.

'We knew at some stage in that third year we were going to have to leave London Road and move to Spalding. It wasn't going to be a normal season where we could rely on home games. We'd already arranged to share Spalding's ground, pay them a rent and keep the gate, but we weren't going to get that many people travelling 25 miles down the road for so-called "home" games, so I had to be fairly tight. I was adamant I wasn't going to bust this budget.

'It was close to about midnight by now. I forget how it ended, but we reached some kind of impasse and Martin left the boardroom. He didn't storm out, he just called it a day and went, saying he would be in touch. That left me and the secretary wondering what the hell to do. The Evans Holdshaw Cup final was coming up that week. I wasn't going to be there because I was due to go on holiday that weekend, and I didn't want to come back with things up in the air. I was fully expecting Martin to say he was off. So I told the secretary to advertise the job in the *Nottingham Evening Post* the next day. It probably wasn't the right way to handle it. I wouldn't do it that way again, but we all get to a point where we say enough's enough. I personally felt that Martin was pushing me to a point where he had a reason to leave. He, I subsequently found out, felt that I had more money than I was prepared to give him.

'He was furious to find out that I'd advertised his job. He did turn up for the final at Mansfield, but he was not a happy man, and told me so on the phone when I got back from holiday. He was never abusive to me, nor I to him, but he told me he'd been deeply wounded by my actions. I told him that we felt he had one foot in the Shepshed camp. It was the parting of the ways for us. Martin was still not happy, but he went to Shepshed.

'Tommy Docherty once got stuck into me at a dinner, saying I didn't know what I was doing, getting rid of Martin O'Neill. "I couldn't afford him," I said. "You couldn't afford not to have him," Tommy replied. Basically, he was partly right. Our finances were wrong.'

Whatever the rights and wrongs of O'Neill's departure from the club, Balfe had had the privilege of being the first chairman to appoint O'Neill the manager, and to assess whether or not he was going to be a good coach or a motivator, whether or not he would be able to operate in the transfer market as a good buyer and seller, whether or not he would be able to balance the books, and whether or not he would be able to spot potential in players. But more intriguingly, he had also come to an understanding of the extent of Brian Clough's influence on the Irishman and the importance of John Robertson to his future. It was clear to Balfe, or at least it was his opinion, that Clough's approval was important to O'Neill.

'Oh, definitely. I don't think there's any doubt. I think Martin and Cloughie saw a bit of themselves in each other. I got that impression whenever Martin talked about Cloughie. Martin pulled Robbo's leg and vice versa because

Robbo was one of Cloughie's favourites. Cloughie used to say that whenever he was feeling rough he went and sat next to Robbo and immediately felt better. Martin always seemed to believe that no matter what he did, Cloughie would find fault with it. Martin's nickname at Forest was "The Squire". Even in those days, he acted a bit like a shop steward. Cloughie thought Martin was a bit of a smartarse and was a bit wary of him because he had a bit of a brain and the rest of them weren't the sharpest knives in the box. Martin used to be the mouthpiece for the players; that was the impression I got from talking to him. Both Martin and Robbo would talk about the old days, especially if we'd won and after a few beers.

'I only met Cloughie the once, when we were doing the deal for Gary Crosby. He looked me in the eye and asked, "What made you get into football then, Mr Chairman?" He said it in a way that made you think he was questioning your right to be involved in football. But he also told me, in no uncertain terms, and in front of Martin, "You've got a very good manager there. You look after him and he'll look after you. You've made a very good choice." I felt Martin was seeking the rubber stamp from Cloughie. Cloughie [was] very proud of him, regarding him almost as a son. I think Martin finally got the approval he needed.'

Even before the Grantham job had come up, O'Neill had already decided that his assistant would be Robertson, a man whose judgement in all matters football was far greater than his fashion sense. He was O'Neill's trusted confidant. Balfe observed, 'Martin and Robbo worked very well together. Robbo's influence on how far Martin has gone should not be underestimated. Martin always used to say with John that if he got a Football League club, Robbo was going with him. It was an agreement they had made many moons ago. I heard a rumour at the time he was going in for the Forest job when Frank Clark left. Someone told me that they would have had Martin, but they wouldn't take Robbo. I don't know if that's true.'

Having played under both men at Grantham and kept in contact with them, Mick McGuire has watched the O'Neill/ Robertson axis develop into a formidable partnership. 'Robbo is a cracker,' he said. 'He's got very good knowledge of a player. In my opinion, he's not a manager like Martin is, and never will be. I don't think he ever wanted to be, although he enjoyed his spell as manager at Grantham, but he was more forced into that. I think he's more comfortable doing what he's doing now.

'People don't know what Robbo is really like. He does *The Times* crossword. He used to do one every Saturday. At that time it was the *Telegraph* and no one else could get a single clue. I went into Leicester one day and he was there in the laundry room with Wally [Steve Walford], because it was warmer, doing the crossword. He's that sort of guy, a deep-thinking guy. I think he is a sounding board for Martin, but what Martin loves about him was his ability as a player. He always used to do himself down and say of Robbo, "That's a player, by the way." It helped that they had the same views on players, on how they should play. Robbo always had that playing side, instead of just hoofing it. Get it to feet and pass it.

'You don't go together that long if you're not good buddies, and they were good together socially. They're men's men, very into the racing. It's not a double act, though; it's not a Clough and Taylor. Robbo didn't always go where Martin went – to Norwich, for example. He couldn't bring him into the Wycombe or Leicester set-ups straight away either. But when Robbo opened his mouth, the players, especially at Wycombe and Grantham, listened, because of what he'd achieved.'

As for other driving forces, there was little sign of the strong religious upbringing or childhood passion for Celtic which emerged when O'Neill went to Glasgow. Balfe said, 'I introduced my father, a Dublin man, to Martin before he died. He knew I was a Catholic but we never talked about religion. As far as I know he never spoke about it to anyone at the club. Martin O'Neill came from West Bridgford, that was it. He did talk to me in the early stages about bringing his mum over from Ireland, but I probably learned more about Martin's upbringing when he went to Celtic. I didn't even know he had this passion for Celtic.

'Without any qualification for saying it, I would say that everybody's upbringing shapes their future. You get your confidence, your ability, your perspective on life and the standards you live by from your parents and grandparents. Martin's no different. If he was brought up in an age when bigotry was evident, then coming from a fairly large family and being in a mainly Protestant town, it will work in good and bad ways. It could create insecurity and make you a little bit suspicious of life. It's why people have to prove themselves.'

Balfe and O'Neill soon settled any bad blood over their parting of the ways, and remained friends. Although the Irishman's profile was to change dramatically over the years, his former chairman recognised some of his old traits, such as a (well-hidden) lack of self-confidence, a drive to succeed and a devotion to football that excluded all else. 'Years later, on more than one occasion I remember talking to Martin about the Norwich job when it came up and he was agonising over whether or not to apply. Martin is a very humble sort of guy. He doesn't always have the confidence in himself that others have in him, which I put down to the fact that Martin drives himself harder than he'll ever drive anyone else. He had to admit, "Tone, you're right, I've got to throw my hat in for these things."

'After he left Shepshed there was a bit of a hiatus, and I went back in for him. The day he said yes to Wycombe I was going down to a chairman's meeting in Oxfordshire, and we listened to the radio on the way back. The first voice I heard was Martin O'Neill's. We needed a new manager because the guy who had replaced him, Danny Anderson – well, it was more interesting watching paint dry, although to be fair he had done the job we'd hired him to do. But there was just no atmosphere. The buzz Martin had brought had gone, so when I got back I dug out the black book – Martin was still at West Bridgford – walked past the phone a couple of times and took some deep breaths, because I hadn't spoken to him for a long while. I shouldn't have worried as I got a very warm welcome. "Thanks so much, Tone. If you had rung me last week I would have jumped at it, but you'll never believe what happened. I met Alan Parry, the Wycombe director . . ." Alan had said to Martin on several occasions, "Get your name in for the Wycombe job," but again Martin wasn't confident enough to put his name forward. That particular day, Alan had asked him again and he'd agreed to go down for an interview.

'Then he said to me, "Talk to Robbo. Robbo's doing nothing." We had a laugh about that because Robbo's never doing anything. "Give Robbo a ring, he'll come and do it." With Robbo, what you see is what you get, while Martin weighs you up and sizes you up over a period of time. You have to prove yourself to Martin more than once to be accepted as someone he can trust. That's the impression I got early on. Clearly, our working relationship ended on a sour note. I suppose that was an indication that however much you got to know him, however close you thought you'd become, maybe there was another part of him you weren't privy to. But that's what makes him what he is. That's why players are always on edge with him, and that's why he gets the best out of them. Just like Cloughie. If he was so easy, you'd work him out very quickly, and then how would he motivate you?

'His motivational skills are amazing. His passion is infectious. He's got this get up and go, this great desire to succeed that is rare in people. But I can still see some little insecurities there when I see him on television. He knows that unless he gets some European silverware he can't be talked about like Jock Stein or Brian Clough. There is that little bit that makes him what he is, keeps him driving forward all the time, so that whatever he achieves he will always think he's got to do more.'

In this quest for success, O'Neill has earned himself something of a Nutty Professor reputation, founded on the sort of anecdote Balfe relates about the time he and Robbo, then manager of Grantham, were invited by O'Neill to be his guests when Wycombe played Kidderminster in the FA Trophy final at Wembley in 1991. There's comedy in the tale, but more than that it exemplifies O'Neill's total involvement in football matters to the exclusion of everything else.

'Wycombe were staying at Burnham Beeches hotel, where England stay, and the idea was that Robbo and I were going down on the Friday night and Martin was booking us into the hotel. We would then go down to Wembley with the team. I remember ringing Martin from my office on the Friday afternoon to check he'd made the booking, because he's not totally reliable when it comes to things like that. If it's not what he wants to be thinking about, it's not happening. Sure enough, he replied, "I haven't, but what time are you coming down?" I told him, but all the way to Burnham Robbo was saying, "He won't have booked us in. I can guarantee he won't have booked us in."

'We could see as we pulled in to park that the players were having their evening meal. We walked round to the front entrance, and Martin met us there. "Hi," he said, "put your stuff in here." It was a broom cupboard. "I told you," said Robbo. "Are you going in the bar?" Martin added. "Only I've got to get back to the meal." So there's me and Robbo, and no evening meal.

'Martin eventually comes in and calls us through, and we sit down at the dinner table. We're eating the scraps off the plate as we talk about football matters. Later on, we hear, "Psst, psst, get your stuff and come with me." Martin takes us to his suite, and by this time Robbo was a bit gone. Martin said, "Right, one of you is on the sofa and the other's in this bed with me." Before we knew where we were, Robbo was in the toilet, dispatching. So Martin said, "Robbo, you're on the sofa."'

'So Martin and I ended up sharing a king-size bed the night before Wycombe beat Kidderminster at Wembley. We had a long chat, until about two in the morning, about football. It was at that point he actually admitted to me he'd realised afterwards that my stance about the budget at Grantham was true, and that I wasn't just trying to fool him.

'The last time I spoke to Martin on the phone, in February 2000, he rang me from that hotel bedroom the night before Leicester's Worthington Cup final against Tranmere. He said that being in that room again had made him remember how we'd shared a bed all those years ago. But if I picked up the phone this afternoon, he'd talk to me as if we'd spoken last week, and if I wanted tickets, no problem. He was at my wedding when I remarried in 1992. I also went down to one of the Nottingham Forest European Cup-winning team reunion dinners. When there was a break in the proceedings, there was a huge queue at Martin's table for autographs. I met Robbo in the toilet, and he insisted on taking me over and disturbing everyone. "Look who's here," he said. Martin leaped up and asked, "Where are you, where are you sitting? I'll come over." He spent fifteen minutes chatting at my table, asking about my wife and the business and so on.

'I like to feel I have a good relationship with Martin and John, and they've kindly made remarks about the importance of our early relationship and the opportunity it gave them.'

In truth, O'Neill's time at Grantham was far from an unqualified success, but it was at London Road that he learned he had the most important attribute of all successful football managers: the ability to get the best out of players, to inspire them to great deeds. It is fitting, therefore, that the last word in this chapter should go to one of his charges in Lincolnshire.

Having been so reluctant in the beginning, Mick McGuire had soon found himself having a ball. As he says, he and

O'Neill connected as people partly because of a shared cynical outlook on life, but the way he speaks about his time at London Road suggests he rediscovered some of the simple pleasures of football there.

'It was brilliant. The pitch had a slope on it – I'd love to know what the angle was from top to bottom. It was a good craic. He put attendances on and made everybody around him believe in it. We had no resources, but it was very, very enjoyable. I didn't want to play beyond that first season; I only did it as a favour because of our friendship, and then I found myself at the age of nearly bloody forty chasing around and getting angry with people when I'd said I didn't need it any more. The lovely thing was, he never, ever called on me to go training. He just trusted me to put myself in the right condition to play. I didn't train with them once. I didn't even play some of the midweek games because of my work. The lads liked me because I did OK for them and treated them with respect, and, as I was with the PFA, they could ask me questions about contracts. He'd give me cash in my hand after every game, which was nice, but it was because I kept fit and because I did it for him. I wouldn't have thought I'd keep on doing it once Martin left, but I did because he'd left such a legacy. In fact, I stayed for another two years. If someone had told me I'd play that long semi-pro, I'd never have believed them.'

Outwardly confident but apparently plagued by inner doubts, in 1989 Martin O'Neill would not have believed anyone had they told him he would end up as the most coveted manager in Britain. Especially after what happened next at Shepshed.

10. SHEPSHED – THE WRONG POLICY

Shepshed Dynamo sounds like a club from one of those innocent but avidly read boys' comics of the 1950s and 1960s – not the main club, but the one Roy of the Rovers would score five against in some fictional cup final. It may be a bizarre combination, Shepshed and Dynamo, but it was the club Martin O'Neill managed after his somewhat acrimonious departure from Grantham. The club's strong feeling that he was being difficult over the Grantham players' budget, that in effect he was playing to be off, would not sit well with O'Neill who has never been known to give less than one hundred per cent. But he *was* tapped by Maurice Clayton, Shepshed's flamboyant executive chairman, as Grantham boss Tony Balfe suspected: 'We were aware he was being tapped up by clubs like Shepshed. They had a chairman with a big wide-brimmed hat, quite a wealthy guy, Maurice Clayton. Martin's views on Maurice would be interesting to hear. I know they didn't get on. Anyway, it was clear Maurice Clayton was ambitious and could tempt Martin with a bigger budget. I simply wasn't prepared to get into an auction.'

It is difficult to remember an occasion when the director of a football club has volunteered information about illegally snatching another's manager with a tempting job offer. If Balfe felt at the time that Shepshed Charterhouse, as they were called at the time before reverting to their original name Dynamo, had made a back-door approach for Martin O'Neill he couldn't prove it – until now, with Clayton freely revealing his involvement in appointing the Irishman without Grantham's permission. It is hardly the crime of the century, nor is it rare for directors to ensure that the man they have approached agrees to join them before they take part in official talks with his club. Managers, too, have used the same method in order to find out if a player is looking for a transfer rather than alerting others to their interest and possibly losing their man to a club with more money or a more glamorous name. What makes this case unusual is Clayton's frank admission to his dealings with O'Neill in the late 1980s, which at the very least will now satisfy the suspicions of his opposite number at Grantham, even if it has come fifteen years late.

Maurice Clayton had first met O'Neill some time earlier through the then Shepshed manager Ian Storey-Moore, a highly talented former club-mate of O'Neill's at Forest, on a day when O'Neill had just been for an interview for the Bradford job and received yet another rejection, though this time he had come tantalisingly close to an appointment, finishing in second place. 'He had quite surprised himself by getting to number two,' Clayton recalled. 'He was delighted to have got that far because I don't think he thought he'd be in the running. He said to me, "I can't believe it." But you would have thought, why not? Go and try for another job in the League. I don't know why he didn't.' But O'Neill's move to Grantham, as we know, went well for him, and he soon had a decent managerial record for all to see. Clayton said, 'I wasn't aware of any arguments over money at Grantham, but I tapped him up, that's the truth of the matter. He and I had dinner together. I made him an offer and he came over. We went down to see a game at Redditch and he was chatting away in the car. He was a very intelligent, very likeable person. He struck you as a great motivator. We were looking for a manager, so we made him an offer.'

It is unlikely O'Neill had wanted his position at Grantham to deteriorate as it had to the point where he had no option but to accept Clayton's offer to join Shepshed Dynamo. Was it in fact a game of bluff with his former club that went wrong? Did he misjudge his ability to cajole some extra cash for players out of Balfe? But accept Clayton's offer he did, though his stay at Shepshed, alongside John Robertson, was distinguished only by the shortness of time he remained as manager. The unofficial Shepshed website records his coming and going with a gentle touch of humour: '1989 – July – appointed Martin O'Neill as manager'; '1989 – October – sacked Martin O'Neill as manager. Wonder what became of him.'

Non-League clubs such as Grantham and Shepshed represent the grassroots strength of the English game. They keep the game alive in communities where it is neither convenient nor cheap to watch League football. They produce and nurture those players who are late developers, or who have in one way or another slipped through the professional net. For budding managers, too, they can be excellent testing grounds, though with few exceptions the modern-day retiring Premiership player would consider nothing less than the Nationwide First Division and £500,000 a year, and that as a last resort, as a suitable venue at which to learn the necessary skills of management.

O'Neill's stay at Shepshed was, at four months, far too short to make any significant inroads into team matters, but it was long enough for him to impress Maurice Clayton before the two parted company. Clayton had taken over in the 1970s when the club was called Shepshed Albion; at the time they were bottom of the second division of the Leicestershire Senior League. 'I was approached by someone from our company, Charterhouse, to help out,' Clayton said, 'and for the 1977/78 season we renamed the club

Shepshed Charterhouse. I wondered what I was getting myself into – it was very run-down. We put up a new clubhouse and began a recovery, but they really were strugglers to begin with. Originally I got together with a couple of people who really knew their local football, and we just avoided relegation in the 1976/77 season. But after that we won the second division, then the first division for three years in a row. We were then promoted to what was called the Midland League. We won that, too, and that was when Ian Storey-Moore joined us. Next was the Southern League, Midland Division. We were runners-up, and got promoted into the Premier Division. Then the geographical boundaries changed and we were moved from there to the Northern Premier League, a direct feeder for the Conference. We were ambitious, and this is when we decided to seek out enthusiastic young managers like Ian, first of all, and then Martin to sort out the team. There was a reasonably good budget by the standards of those years, and remember, Martin wasn't very well known at that time. His salary? I do remember what it was, but I don't think I should quote it.

'Martin's a very serious chap, deep-thinking, but very likeable with it, and quite humble. He's also very articulate and very, very vibrant. John Robertson once said to me, "You know, before a game, Martin will come into the dressing room a minute before the match and within that minute he'll really turn them on. It's a gift, a gift of motivation." John is quite a character, too. I remember one reserve game when he put himself on as a sub. He's a very heavy smoker, John, and not the fittest, but the magic was still there; he could turn on a sixpence, no one could take the ball off him. It was magic to see it. That's a gift, too.'

Clayton, who owns the Shepshed Dynamo ground, the Dovecote, and leases it to the club, has never used the word 'sacked' when describing O'Neill's departure, and has only stated the fact that the decision to part company was made because of the manager's external involvement in selling insurance. The reasons for O'Neill's leaving are of no great concern, but it does appear odd that a man who thrives on work, who we are told can do 'fifty things a day', should have stumbled when asked to do two. 'We did quite well under him,' Clayton owned, 'but in real terms he was only with us for a few months. He was very much involved in his business, and I think John might have been working with him at the time. It all got too much for him. It was a very successful business, with a lot of pressure, so he decided to take a break and to get out of football for a while. He couldn't handle the two responsibilities, really. If I remember rightly, he just felt he'd taken too much on. He came along to me and said, "This is all getting too much. I've got this job and I've got to do it; I can't do the football as well." I was disappointed. I can't remember if I knew he had the job when he joined; I probably didn't.

'But you have to remember we were training twice a week in the evening, and sometimes the travelling for games could be long distance. It's a real commitment to be a manager of a non-League football club. It's not a job you can do half-heartedly. You're either in it or you're not. For some people, football can act like an outlet as a pressure job, but Martin already had that, selling insurance: the expectation to succeed, being paid on commission. At the end of the day, people like Martin weren't highly paid as players. They left football and they all had to work. I was later told that when Martin joined Wycombe, he was the highest-paid non-League manager. I suppose I could have offered John the job in his place, but they were peas in a pod, those two. When he joined us, it was on condition that John came. John was the coach, Martin the inspiration.

'He's a great family man, Martin. At that time his daughters were probably about seven or eight. His wife, Geraldine, is a charming woman. He is very, very devoted to his family.'

So, O'Neill left that October, but he was to bump into Clayton again, after he had taken over at Leicester, this time at school. Clayton recalled, 'It was the end of term, his daughters had joined Oakham School, and he was there talking to the rapt attention of the boys. When I heard him, it was as if he'd never been away. It was probably six years since I'd seen him. I never expected him to go on and do what he has done. No. He was just known as a footballer. As a manager, I have to say, he was to me an unknown quantity.'

O'Neill's decision to quit Shepshed Dynamo, and the reasons given for it, confirmed the belief among people close enough to him to offer a worthwhile opinion that he had not settled in his own mind on what career path to follow between insurance and football management. But you don't have to apply greasepaint to sell insurance, and O'Neill had been slapping it on all through his professional life. Football would, almost inevitably, win the vote, but it would take time before he made his re-entry at Wycombe.

11. WYCOMBE – A DREAM COME TRUE

The notion that somehow the Irish are inordinately lucky doesn't look quite so daft when you consider the outrageous good fortune that accompanied Martin O'Neill's appointment as manager of Wycombe Wanderers. When you bump into an acquaintance in the toilets at Norwich City Football Club and he happens to be a director of a non-League club and he says they are, at that very moment, interviewing candidates for the job of manager, and you're out of work; when he says he'll put your name forward, only for you both to find out that the job has been offered to another manager, but then that other manager unexpectedly turns it down, all within a few hours, and it is offered to you instead – well, that's luck. There shouldn't ever be a bad time to relieve yourself, but come on, how often does so much spring from a simple pee?

The man O'Neill met that night was Alan Parry – television commentator, Liverpudlian, football nut and Wycombe director. It was a chance encounter that transformed O'Neill's career: it was both an opportunity to prove his credentials as a manager of the highest calibre and a springboard into, first, a hiccup at Norwich, but then a bigger, more lasting appointment at Leicester City and on to one of the greatest managerial jobs of all at Celtic. O'Neill had been searching for just such an opportunity and Wycombe had been looking for just such a young boss. The partnership was to the huge benefit of both.

O'Neill, like all ambitious romantics, retains the capacity to dream, and the moment he took over at Wycombe in February 1990 he began to dream of championships and cups and Wembley; most of all, he dreamed of the day he would lead the forward-looking little Buckinghamshire club into the Football League. All that was in fact achieved inside five years. It was remarkable, miraculous even, but proof that with the right man in charge, with good coaching and with outstanding man management; with an understanding chairman – and O'Neill had that in Ivor Beeks – and a board that backs you to the hilt, anything is possible in football, anything at all. By the time he left, lured into yet another personal misjudgement, Wycombe Wanderers, formerly of the Conference League, were happily and successfully ensconced in the Nationwide Second Division.

They carry the worries that all football clubs have to cope with in a deep recession, though less than most, but are now established as a Football League club, thanks to O'Neill and their own excellent long-term planning. You would have been able to name your own odds at such events unfolding, so unlikely was the outcome. His Wycombe bosses didn't believe it could happen so quickly; initially, they were sensibly looking for steady progress to go hand in hand with the move from their old ground at Loakes Park to a compact, modern stadium at Adams Park.

Even now, Parry looks back on it all with wonderment. As a commentator, he had interviewed O'Neill on a number of occasions and had enjoyed his company when they met at the Football Writers Association's Footballer of the Year dinner in London some years before. O'Neill was still with Nottingham Forest, and they'd kept in touch when his playing career took him on to Norwich, Manchester City and Notts County. 'I am not being unkind, but he was brighter than most of the players of his generation,' Parry observed. 'He had a lot to say for himself. Martin was lively to be with. I'd not say we were great mates, but I'd known him socially for a few years before he got the opportunity to come to Wycombe.

'I'd actually put him forward for a managerial vacancy at Wycombe some months earlier. He received an interview when he was managing Shepshed, and also working for an insurance company. I wasn't on the board then, and anyway he didn't get the job. At the time he hadn't sent in an application. When it came round again he never applied and we'd sort of lost touch, not spoken for a few months. I literally bumped into him. I'd gone to watch Liverpool play at Norwich, a cup-tie I think, and he was there for the BBC and I saw him in the loo. He started talking about Wycombe and I said that very day they were interviewing candidates for the job. He said he wished he had known, and I replied that I doubted the club would have appointed anybody on the night. I said I would ring the chairman on the way back to find out exactly what the position was. That's when I found out it had been offered to Kenny Swain, who used to be a player at the club in his very early days and was then assistant manager to Dario Gradi at Crewe. I told the chairman, "I've just bumped into Martin O'Neill," etc., and he said, "Oh well, we've appointed Kenny." But Kenny went back to Crewe, where they offered him more money and promoted him from coach to assistant manager. He changed his mind, rang back and said he wasn't going to take the job. Just like that. It was in Martin's favour that they hadn't been impressed by anyone else they'd interviewed, so the chairman asked me if I could make contact with Martin. And that's how it happened.'

It was something of a gamble to go with O'Neill, who had yet to make any real impact on the game as a manager. Grantham had given him a good start, but the manner of his leaving the club had left an area of doubt over his commitment and his temperament. And the short spell at Shepshed was a definite blip on the CV. Parry's faith in him was unbridled, however, and based on instinct; he didn't regard the new manager as anything other than a good bet to take the club forward.

Parry added, 'On the face of it, Martin had done well at Grantham. I wanted him badly, and I persuaded the chairman, Ivor Beeks, but there was one other director called Brian Lee, who, you may remember, used to run the National Sports Centre at Bisham Abbey and was a former manager and chairman of Wycombe. He goes back to the old-school days of Walter Winterbottom and 1950s coaching badges and all that, and I thought he wouldn't take to Martin because he is such a one-off. We were interviewing Martin, and I was thinking, is Brian Lee going to put a spanner in the works? But when Martin left Brian enthused about him so much, and I actually remember him saying he would be a breath of fresh air for this club. That clinched it. They didn't interview anyone else.

'He's very effervescent, Martin, very bubbly company, and I don't think he particularly tried to sell himself and he didn't come up with any "I'm going to do this for the club – take them into the First Division" stuff. It was my belief that Martin would be good because he had the background as a player, and you know what players are like. We had seen it with other people at Wycombe. If you haven't got that background as a player it is very hard for them to accept you. You might be a very good coach, and the club had previously had people who had their FA badges, as it was quite an old-fashioned amateur club for many years. But if you are trying to move on in a good semi-professional environment like the Conference, then you must have someone they will listen to and respect. I knew Martin would be respected in the dressing room, that he could turn on the charm to a degree in order to impress the directors, that he had the enthusiasm to get through to the supporters. I thought he would be good at the job, I just couldn't say how good. I never thought he'd be as good as he turned out to be.'

Alan Hutchinson, former club secretary and still working at Wycombe as media director, knows O'Neill as well as anyone outside the Irishman's family. Hutchinson was in on the decision process that clinched the Wycombe job for O'Neill, and said, 'One of the main reasons for our decision was that we had seen him for the same job before the appointment of our previous manager, Jim Kelman. Martin was then working for Save and Prosper, and the fact that he didn't get the job was quite extraordinary and to do with the fact, I suppose, that he didn't come across too well in the interview. He wasn't nervous, but overanxious. Too keen. I was to discover this was very unusual for Martin.

'His second interview was so different from the first. He was quite excellent. There was no doubt, he was by far the best person we'd seen. He made quite an impression. He was very honest in all matters. For instance, when I asked him about coaching, he said, "Oh well, we don't do too much of that, but I can guarantee the lads will be ready on the day." It was the way he came out with it. It was obvious that he knew what he was doing. A lot of Brian Clough had obviously rubbed off on him and he had picked up one or two things from Billy Bingham at Northern Ireland. That was linked to his own personality. It was charismatic. He was a motivator, and I had not met anyone like him. He got the job.'

O'Neill's annual salary was set at just under £25,000, with bonuses built into the contract.

Hutchinson added, 'He was so different in so many ways. With all other managers you would ring them to keep in touch and they would ring to find out what was going on at the club, but you couldn't get hold of Martin. Whenever as a result I said to the chairman, "I'm not sure about this fellow," like a magician he would appear. We had to work closely together, and I must admit neither of us was too sure of each other at first, but we became very good friends and we still keep in touch. You really have to get to know him. Martin is his own man, but once he feels he can trust you everything changes without you ever getting really, really close to him.'

O'Neill's single-mindedness was noted by Hutchinson before his first game, on 10 February 1990, when he arrived back from America and met up with the new Wycombe coach near the Severn Bridge. O'Neill mistrusted strangers, particularly ones who were allowed to travel with his team. Hutchinson explained, 'When he got on he asked, "Who are all these people?" So I told him it was the committee, and he said, "What, they travel with the team?" I explained it had always been that way, that this was non-League football. "Oh Jesus," he replied, "it's like travelling with Northern Ireland on away trips." That lasted about two weeks. It was one of the first things he changed. In future it was only to be the team and the people he wanted around him. I was glad to say he included me in that group all the time he was at the club.

'In that first game at Merthyr the players got their first taste of his matchday approach. He didn't tell them what he expected of them, he started off by telling them what he didn't expect. He said he would not tolerate any indiscipline in any shape or form on or off the pitch by any player. He didn't want to see people arguing on the pitch or having a go at the bench, and that if they kept these things in mind they would get on fine. They took it on board. One of the best things I heard him say, and I'm sure it was a Clough thing, was, "One of the most important things is this, and you cannot do without it." And suddenly he scooped up the ball and held it in the air.

'Martin was the first really big professional player we had as a manager. We'd had Sid Cann in the 1950s, who was a former Charlton and Southampton full-back. He was excellent, but he was a dour Devonian and a run-of-the-mill player. Here we had someone who had played at the highest level with Brian Clough in European Cup finals and had won 64 caps for Northern Ireland and been to the World Cup finals.

'When he joined we were still at our old ground, so for the first few months we were waiting to go to Adams Park. It was then I said to him we ought to fix up a game against Nottingham Forest for the opening match at the new stadium. He thought that was a good idea and told me to get on with it. It was all sorted out, then on the day of the game I spoke to Archie Gemmill on the phone and he told me, "The gaffer isn't coming." I told him that could not be, that we had posters and bills out all over the town saying that Brian Clough and Nottingham Forest were coming. "He doesn't feel like it," was all Gemmill said in reply.' It would have been a crisis had Clough not turned up, but when Hutchinson told O'Neill about the problem and asked O'Neill to ring Clough to try to persuade him to come to the match, Hutchinson was told, 'We have a problem because I don't get on with him too well.' True to form, after all this Clough did turn up.

Despite this tale of hesitancy, O'Neill was perfectly capable of taking tough decisions. He was, after all, being asked very politely to drag Wycombe, one of the great stalwarts of the amateur game, kicking and screaming if necessary into the twenty-first century. It was a task that demanded a ruthless approach to those he perceived to be standing in the way of both the club's and his chances of success, though that sounds far more draconian than the reality of it. Martin would stand for just about anything provided his or the club's good name was not damaged, provided his players were prepared willingly to donate some blood in the pursuit of results, and provided his arguments were listened to and obeyed unless there was a convincing counter-argument.

His players have talked about the 'O'Neill Regime' over the years, and yes it was tough at times, but it was toughest on the man himself. They sensed from the very first day that this hyperactive Irishman might just possess the key to better days than they had experienced. Wycombe were struggling in the wrong half of the Conference when he took over, yet within a year they had sprouted wings and were ready for take-off. Classic little stories have done the rounds of the boardrooms, retold like legends, of the methods O'Neill used with the most basic of materials to mould a club into one that believed only the sky was the limit. O'Neill was never going to accept any form of insubordination from the players, and Hutchinson highlighted how he dealt with even the best of his players when he judged they had overstepped the line.

'The longer you worked with him the more you realised he had certain principles, and you had to admire that. He was convinced he knew what we needed and where he wanted to go, and it was too bad if other people couldn't see it. We fell out once for a couple of weeks over something he'd said. We had a game against Cheltenham Town over the Christmas period, and he told the players, "Win this game and you can have the next day off. That's what I'm asking you to do." We had a lad playing for us at the time called Nicky Evans. He was a smashing player we'd bought from Barnet, when Barry Fry was manager, for £28,000, which was a lot of money. Martin didn't buy him, he inherited him, and he hadn't seen much of him as he'd been injured. As soon as he got back into the team, though, he started banging in the goals as if there was no tomorrow. Mark West, who was a local boy and had been at the club for a long time, partnered him up front, and they were terrific together. Cheltenham's main striker was Kim Casey, a very good player. We were two goals up with twenty minutes to go, then Casey hit two. Martin went absolutely loopy and told the players, "You're in for training tomorrow." At that, Evans said he wasn't coming in as he had made family arrangements. "What do you mean you're not coming in? I told you, you had to win or you're working." Evans just said, "Well, I won't be here." Martin said, "I'll tell you now, if you're not here it is the end of you at this football club." And he was our best player.'

Hutchinson told Martin he should think about the decision, but he was adamant: Evans had to go if he didn't turn up. There was a lot of discussion among club officials but O'Neill's dictat stood. 'I'm the manager,' he said, 'and he's going if he doesn't turn up.' Hutchinson added, 'Evans didn't turn up for training so Martin contacted Barry Fry, and in less than a week Evans was sold back to Barnet for the same money. Martin was absolutely right. He went out and bought Casey from Cheltenham, the lad that had scored these two goals against us, and he turned out to be a terrific player for us. What he did had a considerable effect on the other players. They knew if he would do that, take that sort of action against our best player, he would do it to anyone.'

Another of the stories involved their veteran Scottish midfield player Dave Carroll, who saw the signs and succumbed to the man's charm, but only after an early brush with O'Neill's authority. Carroll made the mistake of turning up late for O'Neill's first training session, then compounded that failure by again turning up late for the second training session of the week. The result? He was dropped from the team. Lesson learned.

O'Neill's primary task from the outset was to build a team and clear away those he thought might not be good enough and those who were talented enough but lacked the necessary ambition to make a worthwhile contribution. But the process of acquiring new players wasn't without its frustrations, as Glenn Roeder, who had got to know O'Neill when he played alongside him at Notts County, explained. 'When I was manager at Watford I wanted to sell a player called Roger Willis to Birmingham for £150,000. Their manager, Barry Fry, had had him when he was at Barnet. We had shaken hands over the phone, so to speak. The deal was done. A few minutes later the phone went again and it was Martin from Wycombe. He said he wanted to buy Willis and would I take £60,000 for him. I told him that was impossible, I'd already done the deal, and anyway they were paying £150,000. Yet he went on and on trying to convince me that I should let him go to Wycombe. I thought that call was the end of it, but an hour later there was a knock on my door and it was Martin. He'd driven over to Watford. He virtually came in on his hands and knees to beg me to change my mind. I couldn't, of course, but that was Martin. We had a cup of coffee, and eventually he left.'

There was a bit more behind the Roger Willis tale than Roeder stated, and the episode was to prove another tough managerial lesson for O'Neill. Former Wycombe secretary Alan Hutchinson takes up the story: 'Martin had seen Willis at Grimsby and recognised his talent, but had made the mistake of saying after a game that he was off up to sign him that Monday. Barry Fry, then manager of Barnet, heard about it and beat him to it. Martin was furious and rang Fry. He was told, "No offence. I like you, but this has just been a little learning curve. Tell nobody nothing." Barry had worked out that Martin was a good manager and an astute judge of a player who knew what he was doing, so he'd thought, "If the lad is good enough for O'Neill, he's good enough for me." '

Parry, who watched O'Neill progress from the inside, said, 'It took Martin two seasons to clear out the dead wood, bring in his own players and get his ideas across. There were one or two players who wouldn't listen and not take on what he wanted to do. There were dressing-room lawyers, and he got rid of them as quickly as possible and gradually brought in his type of player. He's volatile and dogged in his views. He could be a ranter and a raver but he doesn't go around shouting at people – except in the dressing room. I've been in there when he was at Wycombe many a time, even at half-time. This was one of his strengths. He had some players who would regard them- selves as the stars of the team and he would, if he felt he had to, belittle them with one sentence. It would reduce them to rubble. But equally, a player with a more modest, too modest, opinion of his worth, he would encourage.

'I'll give you two examples, because they are reasonably well-known players. At that time we had Keith Scott, a striker and a bloody good player who later went to Swindon and played in the Premiership. Now, he was a bighead in the nicest possible way. He couldn't work out why Real Madrid hadn't come in for him. Keith was full of himself, and he was the target for most of Martin's jokes. Steve Guppy was the opposite: he was incredibly talented, even then, but very unsure of himself and didn't really believe he was as good a player as people said. Martin would build him up and knock Scotty down. He used psychology as well as any manager I've known, and they never knew what was coming next with him. He is really quick-witted with a very good sense of humour and a very good line in caustic put-downs. He became impatient with people who didn't share his vision, if you like, and he had no time for pettiness. If a club official wanted to earwig him for ten minutes about some change in the regulations, he didn't have time for that. He's impatient and restless and difficult to pin down.'

O'Neill was merciless when it came to the sort of on-field indiscipline shown by centre-back Jason Cousins, who was sent off twice in successive matches, the second time for a foul that would have had him arrested on the street. O'Neill was having none of it. Whether it was the loss of his own player from the match, the thought that Cousins would be suspended for important matches or the realisation that one of his players could have crippled an opponent has never been revealed – even Cousins doesn't know – but retribution was swift. O'Neill dragged the player out of the shower, flung him into the corridor naked, took the captaincy from him and banned him from the club for one week – after returning his clothes. He doesn't hold grudges – it was O'Neill who brought his Scottish champions Celtic to Wycombe to play a testimonial for one of his old boys, the very same Jason Cousins – but he does have a long and sharp memory, as Parry knows. 'Loads of old players used to come back, and Martin would be holding court in the bar afterwards and would pick on a particular player and ask him to remember that day at Bolton when he'd missed that sitter. He would then go into details of where the ball was, everything. It was extraordinary, he had remembered the lot.'

O'Neill's main objective while rebuilding his team was promotion to the Football League, in common with every other non-League club in the country. It was an ambition rather than a demand, but an ambition shared. He knew he would be praised for winning what could be described as the minor battles – the FA Trophy, for instance – but he would surely allow himself satisfaction if he could realise the dream and lead his troops from non-League to League, from the Conference to participation in what is considered the greatest league system in the world.

In a short time Wycombe had discarded what was a slightly dusty image and replaced it with a new vibrancy, as Parry explained. 'They were running in a very old-fashioned style. It wasn't many years since the team used to be picked by committee, and the ground in the first year Martin was here was so very old-fashioned, with a sloping pitch. It was steeped in amateur history and needed to be pulled into modern times. The new ground at Adams Park and Martin's arrival were just perfect, and it all came together in 1993. The season before, Martin's second, we had been pipped for the title by Colchester, who had been relegated from the Football League. We had finished level on points but Colchester had taken it on goal difference. We were part-timers and matched them stride for stride. It could have slipped away from us then. You remember play-off teams who don't make it through and suffer terrible hangovers as a result. Everyone was a bit concerned that that could happen to us, but it was the opposite. Martin strengthened the team, and his enthusiasm carried everyone through what could have been a miserable summer. We bombed through the 1992/93 season; another trophy, and then promotion.'

Hutchinson remembers the emotions of that watershed moment. 'One thing Martin said when he took the job was that in two years he would get us into the Football League. In his second season we were joint top with Colchester on 94 points. It was ludicrous not to go up with that amount of points, and that almost finished Martin. "I'm out," he said to me. There were just the two of us in his office. I asked him what he was going to do and he admitted he didn't know. I told him, "What do you mean you don't know? That's rubbish. You have to stay and we will have a go at winning the championship next season." He said there was no guarantee, but I insisted, "You can't leave now when you have done so many good things." Everyone was disappointed. AP [Alan Parry] was in tears. It was terrible. Anyway, we all went out and got absolutely legless and on the Monday we were up and running again. Even then we nearly got elected when Maidstone went to the wall. The Conference were pushing the Football League to admit another club, which was us. It came very close, but they decided not to go down that route. We did have to stay in the Conference, but the next season we won everything. Martin had by then made a tremendous impact on the club. Because we were so successful the money was rolling in. The game wasn't like it is now. There was money in the club in every area. We had a highly successful manager of a team that never lost.'

The 4–1 FA Trophy win over Runcorn in 1993 was a real fillip. 'The FA Trophy means a lot to non-League people,' Parry explained, 'and we took 28,000 to Wembley, which was a record and still is, I'm told. Martin is so good on these occasions, talking to fans and getting everyone involved. On the touchline he kind of lives everything, and I think fans love that. You could see Ruud Gullit sitting back when 40,000 fans are cheering. I don't like managers like that. I think crowds respond to managers who are as involved as they are. I know it doesn't suit everyone, but because he was like a dervish they warmed to that.

'I remember nights at Wycombe when everyone else had gone home and it would just be his family and mine left in the boardroom. We'd order a Chinese takeaway and eat it on the boardroom table watching *Match of the Day*, drinking the bar dry, his two little girls, Aisling and Alana, falling asleep in the corner because they were really young then.'

O'Neill is a superb ad-lib speaker, and at the club dinner to celebrate the Trophy win he performed a spontaneous 45-minute routine after just a couple of glasses of Liebfraumilch. 'He had the room in stitches,' Parry recalled. 'He was absolutely brilliant. I remember, everyone was there – players, wives. He had the whole place spellbound he was so funny. He's Irish, and he has the gift of the gab; with a few glasses of wine he's off and running. He's not a big drinker, a couple of glasses of sweet white wine was his limit, but that's all it took. Loquacious, I think you would call it.'

Parry found O'Neill's deep interest in criminals and the law refreshingly different, even mystifying, though his visits to court cases and murder scenes were what you'd expect of someone who had read law at university and was fascinated by crime. 'Martin has a passion for it, it's his great hobby. His favourite case is the old A6 murder, and for years and years he insisted that Hanratty was innocent until they did some DNA tests that showed, so far as science could tell, that Hanratty was involved. He won't accept it.' Parry wouldn't be surprised if some time in the future O'Neill revealed that the only reason he took the job at Wycombe was the club's proximity to the Hanratty crime scene. He added, 'Within a week of coming down here he took his two daughters to the cornfield where they [lovers Michael Gregsten and Valerie Storie] were in the car, and he retraced the steps and drove all the way up the A6. He was so obsessed with it he even went to see the judge who'd presided over the case. Martin probably knows as much, if not more, about the Hanratty trial than anyone. He went to the Fred West trial, too, and visited many other murder scenes in the area. He can tell you all about them. Martin has a great eye for detail and would be a good Trivial Pursuit player because of his memory. It is easy to label him a great motivator because people see him jumping up and down and see the obvious passion when he's interviewed and things like that, but I think that is overlooking a lot of other qualities he has.'

Those who have studied O'Neill's style claim he is not just a tub-thumper, or someone who can go in at half-time and turn things around. It is agreed he is not what modern coaches would call a coach. There were many times when he wouldn't turn up at the training sessions at Wycombe, or only put in an appearance ten minutes from the end. But, again, those who have watched him operate at close range reckon him a superb judge of a player with a wonderful ability to spot what is going wrong and, just as important, a knack of being able to transmit what he had seen.

He proved this with his transformation of previous manager Jim Kelman's squad. He knew how he wanted them to play: in a style that could be described as simple, effective and good to watch – when it worked. Parry explained, 'Even at non-League level it's not practical to chuck a whole team out, so he had to modify what he wanted to do. But once he turned the squad around the results came. He loved wingers feeding a big centre-forward and a variety of strikers playing off the main man. He had powerful defenders, too. Like I say, it was simple enough, but so effective, and he was never afraid of making a change.

'I spoke to him just recently about Leicester and that play-off match against Crystal Palace when Stevie Claridge scored in the last minute as the game was about to go to a penalty shoot-out. His regular keeper had been absolutely brilliant. He'd stopped everything, yet Martin was about to substitute him for a massive Yugoslav who was on the touchline ready to come on. Martin felt that in the penalty shoot-out he would be a better bet because he was a big bloke, about six foot six inches, and he filled the goal. I thought, imagine if he'd taken off a goalkeeper who had been magnificent during the game and put another one on cold and they'd stuck six penalties past him. If you look at the video, he was literally on the touchline ready to come on. He has to be on before the end of the match to take part in the shoot-out. It was then that the ball was wellied upfield and Claridge let fly. That was it, they'd won the game. Just imagine, it could have all gone wrong in thirty seconds and people would have been saying, what the hell was Martin O'Neill doing changing a goalkeeper?

'There's another funny story about him that I was thinking about today which kind of sums him up. Until you have experienced it, you have no idea how disorganised he can be. When we played Preston North End in the play-off final [in 1994] it was the biggest game in the club's history. He came to the board and said, "I want to do this right. I want to stay at the Burnham Beeches hotel," which is where England stay. So off we went for three days of expense. Martin had his team meeting in the morning, read them the team and said there would be motorcycle outriders so we would have to be away promptly at one o'clock. He reiterated that instruction: "on the coach by one p.m." At ten to one all the players are on the coach, the motorcycle outriders are revving up, but where's the manager who's been warning them they mustn't be late? The physio is sent to the reception to ask if Mr O'Neill has checked out yet. "No. Shall I ring his room?" Ring, ring – nothing. So the physio, whose name is Dave Jones, nicknamed Jona, goes up, knocks on the door and hears water splashing. He shouts, "Martin, is that you?" "Yes, Jona, hang on a minute." Martin comes to the door, now just two hours from kick-off, with a towel wrapped round him. The physio goes in and has never seen a room like it. Newspapers everywhere, clothes in every corner; they had to run around like two madmen sticking it all into bags, and we ended up leaving fifteen minutes late because the manager couldn't get his head round what time it was. Typical of a man who used to keep his belongings in little plastic bags.'

Hutchinson can laugh now when he thinks of those plastic bags that were always carried on to, then off the team coach at away matches. 'Martin would take three black sacks with him that contained correspondence and all kinds of stuff. He said he would soon have the time to sort it all out, but he never did get round to it. A chap called John Reardon, who was assistant secretary, had the job of making sure they were taken on and off the bus and taken to his room. Week in, week out he would do that, and they would remain untouched. But on one occasion Martin actually opened one of these sacks and found a contract he had signed with Brian Clough. "If I'd known that was all he was paying me I'd have asked for a lot more money," Martin said. "He got me on the cheap."

'Not ever being able to get hold of Martin on his mobile phone was one thing I could never get the directors to understand. Our chairman, Ivor Beeks, is the best chairman you could ever get. He is brilliant, he is a very good man, but he could never get his head around the fact that Martin's mobile was always turned off. He used to say, "He never answers his phone. I can never get hold of him when I ring him at home." In the end I told Ivor I had been through the same thing when he first came. I realised it didn't matter a damn. He kept winning matches, and that was the most important thing. The fellow is a winner, and he is lucky. What more could you want? Having a manager like that was like opening Fort Knox. If we can't get hold of him on a Wednesday, don't worry about it. I had given up worrying. I knew that come Saturday we were likely to win.'

Beeks, and everyone else at Wycombe, soon realised that O'Neill was very much his own man, accomplishing things in his own way and in his own time. He was not going to be a manager easily bullied, in fact he was not going to be pushed at all into obeying what would even be considered reasonable behaviour, such as answering telephone calls. Hutchinson didn't see his non-conformity as a problem worth worrying about, so long as results were good. And he knew O'Neill's motivational techniques were second to none.

'We had a player called Terry Evans who had come from Brentford. A terrific fellow. He was captain of the team. He was six foot four and a real agricultural defender. Very, very strong, brilliant on the pitch and a great leader. On an away trip once, Martin told him, "Listen, Terry, I want you to get it through to the lads that I will not stand for losing away games. We don't have to win, but I don't expect to lose. Always get a point, and I'll tell you if we have a chance of three." He instilled a fear in them about losing away. You couldn't perhaps get away with it these days, but if they lost there would be no beer on the bus, they couldn't play cards and there would be no music. They might get some fish and chips, but more likely not. They went away afraid to lose. They knew that if they drew or won they'd get something extra. I thought that was brilliant. He set it up so all they had to think about was getting a result. He built a team and got it right in all departments. Even if we stayed at a hotel and lost, they would never stay at the same place again. We always had to find somewhere else. He was unpredictable.

'There was another strange motivational incident before our FA Trophy final against Kidderminster. He told the players to report to a particular room at twelve o'clock and he would announce the team. When he got there he said he had decided to wait until 12.30. At 12.30 he changed his mind again, and it wasn't until we were getting on the bus that he finally told them. It really wound everyone up because they were anxious to know if they were in the side. I never understood why he did it, but it worked because we won. We got to Wembley five times with Martin, if you include two *Evening Standard* five-a-sides.'

It may be justified to credit O'Neill fully for Wycombe's rise from non-League to Football League status, but it was the club's board of directors, chaired by Beeks, who planned the move to Adams Park and the beginning of the upward spiral. It was a partnership. The club needed a winning team, and a winning team needed first-class facilities, not necessarily up to Old Trafford standards but up-to-date facilities nonetheless, capable of offering safety and comfort for supporters and players.

'It was, of course, phenomenal getting into the Football League,' Hutchinson added, 'and the move to Adams Park was part of the plan. We must have looked at fourteen sites over twenty years, but the local council didn't want us moving into the town. They blocked it, and in the end we had to go to Parliament to win permission. The aim then was Conference football and then the Football League. I think at one stage we would have settled for the Conference because the ground only had a capacity of 6,000 when we built it. As soon as it was obvious that with O'Neill we would go further, the whole thing really took off.

'The big thing was not just getting into the Football League but into the Second Division in one season. I remember our play-off Wembley final with Preston in 1994 because our goalkeeper Paul Hyde had been ill all week with awful diarrhoea and sickness. But he said he would play and we went off to a hotel in St Albans. He played in the first half and was all right, but when he got back into the dressing room he was terrible. Two of the lads and Martin had to help him down the tunnel. Yet he actually played the entire second half not really knowing what was going on. It was amazing, because we were 2–1 down at half-time and went on to win 4–2. It was quite remarkable. The substitute goalkeeper was Chuck Moussaddik, a chap from Morocco who we'd got from Wimbledon. He was a great shot stopper, but when a cross came over he was nowhere. I don't think Martin was prepared to risk him. It was quite a gamble, though. People also forget that in that first season in Division Two only the top five clubs were involved in the promotion battle, and we came sixth. Under today's circumstances we would have had a chance of getting into the First in two seasons. And in those days we had the finance to do it.'

Money was certainly not scarce at the club, but there had to be a limit to what could be spent on improvements to both the team and the stadium, which would also have to be constantly updated. O'Neill felt he was going to be the loser in that process, that the stadium would drain his hoped-for resources. Hutchinson, for so long so close to O'Neill, was in fact surprised that he stayed in place as long as he did when there were other, bigger clubs interested in him. 'I think Martin knew that we would not have the money much longer because we were building this big stand on the far side of the ground which would increase the capacity to 10,000. I remember him saying to one of the directors, "Why not make it just 8,000, which would be £1.2 million instead of £2.2 million, give me the difference and I'll get you into the First Division." Had we gone that way we might have kept him.

'Come 1995, he obviously felt he had gone as far as he could go at Wycombe. He was far too good a manager for us. I really was amazed he stayed as long as he did. At least three clubs I know of came in for him: Leicester, Bristol Rovers, when they were in the Second and we were in the Third, and Norwich City. We knew we could not keep him much longer. I was organising interviews for him with all kinds of people and joked that he was "flagging up his career", but that was fair enough. Suddenly he had made Wycombe Wanderers very well known in football. It was just a shame about the stand. I've got to say we only ever filled the ground four or five times and that was during our great FA Cup run [in 2000/01, when they reached the semi-final]. Martin was not far wrong about the right capacity. It would have been different had we got into the First Division because of the big away following of visiting clubs.

'I took him to the door when he left. I'll never forget it. He was actually quite emotional. It was a hell of a wrench because he had got quite close to a few of us and he loved the area. We shook hands, and he told me, "Remember, Hutch, they only miss you when you're gone." And he turned away and got into his car. No matter where Martin goes he will be a success, and no one can say anything bad about him. That's unusual in football.'

Keith Ryan, who had been with O'Neill at the club since day one, was also present when O'Neill left that day. 'You could not have written the script for those five years,' said Ryan, who was a carpet-fitter and remained a part-time player, as did all the squad members, until they moved into the Football League. 'It was unbelievable. They were amazing times. He signed me from Berkhamsted in the summer before our first game at Adams Park. Our first game was the opener against Nottingham Forest, and it all took off from there. There was a real buzz about the place.

'I found he had a very infectious style. I didn't have anyone to compare him with because I was from non-League football and my previous managers were just mates, but he was really enthusiastic. He was driven by what he wanted to achieve in a very short space of time. Early on he earmarked people he thought weren't doing the club much good. I think he saw that. He didn't alienate anyone, but he felt some were holding other people back. Once he had sorted that out he got together the lads he thought could do something. Anyone that was going to stand in his way I think he was going to get rid of.

'He kept his distance from the players, but I think you have to when you are the manager. Much as you might know him, he would keep you at arm's length. I would like to class him as a friend, but I think it is difficult to become close with your boss. He wanted to know everything about me of course, and about all the players, so he knew my family. I was unfortunate enough to lose my mother . . . As soon as he heard he was straight on the phone and came down for the funeral. It was typical of the man. He did not have to do that. Because of things like that I would class him as a family friend. If you put out for him he will return the favour ten-fold. That's how I see him. A very honest and honourable man. He did not like cheats. One quality he has above a lot of other people is that he knows the character of people. He knows how to get the best out of them.'

O'Neill had an easy enough working relationship with all of his players, but even in the early days there was a boundary over which none of them would cross. Whenever they did, those were the moments when the forthright Clough attitude to management became more apparent. It was the kind of regime under which O'Neill had to live at Forest, and now he was utilising important parts of it at Wycombe, although no doubt he would argue it was a style that came naturally to him.

'You toe the line with Martin,' Ryan said. 'What he says goes. He would drag you into the club on a day you didn't want to be there, but he would reward you so highly when you won. There were plenty of days off. I think he will tell you that rest days are as important as training days. We would work very hard during the week, but close to matchdays we would really ease off. And if you were winning games under Martin O'Neill you would barely be training; you'd just keep your fitness up and be ready for Saturday. When you were in work you were on your mettle, focused. There were little incentives, too. If he won so many games on the trot or so many points over a spell he would perhaps arrange a trip to Spain. You would think he was definitely going to come, but on the morning you were leaving he'd say he had a few things to do at home. Still, when you were out there there was no knowing whether he might suddenly turn up. On the flip side, the penalties he imposed on the journey home from away games we had lost was psychology that worked. We knew the beer was under the coach, but we weren't going to get any.

'Martin O'Neill is a very intelligent man. He knows how to push people's buttons. His motivation skills were brilliant; you'd want to tear the dressing-room door off to get on to the pitch. He would make you feel like a great player even when you knew you weren't. I'd played in the lower leagues all my life, but there were days I went out playing for Martin when I thought I was the best player in the world. There were little things he would say to you individually, not necessarily before a game but in the days building up to it. If you performed for him he would really, really pat you on the back. Don't get me wrong: if you underachieved he would come down quite hard on you. You had to take the knocks until the time came when he would praise you. There were even times when we were in non-League when he would praise me too much. You'd be thinking, here's a bloke who has played in the World Cup finals and has European Cup medals . . . It really had an effect on me, and on the players around me. Without any doubt he got an extra ten per cent out of us.'

Ryan felt that O'Neill's man-management skills were extraordinary, as exemplified on the day when Wycombe lost their centre-half and skipper Glyn Creaser, who had been injured in an accident at work while driving a fork-lift truck. 'He was the heartbeat of the side, so it was a real body blow when the news filtered through that he would be out for the rest of the season,' he explained. 'Martin organised a meeting with the players and more or less just said, "Look, one of you here is going to rise from beneath and above everyone else. One of you is going to do that. I don't know which one, but there is someone in this dressing room that will tear up trees and be absolutely fantastic for us for the rest of the season." He was saying, "make it be you". There were maybe twenty people in that changing room and every one of us wanted to be that person. I sat there and thought it was going to be me. That meeting started with us in a desperate state, knowing we would be without our captain for the rest of the season, yet we left the dressing room so refreshed and so focused on what we had to do. It was unbelievable.

'He had a good sense of humour, too. We had a goalkeeper, Chuck Moussaddik, who was a bit of a poseur. He was posing in front of the mirror once when O'Neill walked past and spotted him. He said, "Here, Chuck, you look just like Joe Bugner." Chuck puffed out his chest and said that was a big compliment. Martin replied, "You both wear gloves for no apparent reason." One hit, that's all he needed. You could not take him on verbally because he was too sharp, too clever. Before a match, you would always put your programme down and look up when he came in. You were in awe of him. He was just a good man. He helped my career and instilled in me what I needed for professional football. He remains influential in my life, as he is in others'. They were brilliant times that can never be recaptured. All the lads got on well and he created that atmosphere. I don't know how he did it, but he did.

'When we reached the play-off final with Preston it was easier for us because we had been in FA Trophy finals, but he still took us away for four days. He took us to the theatre to see *Buddy*, which helped relax everyone instead of us sitting around and getting worked up. A couple of days before the match he told us that if we wanted a couple of drinks that was fine – do what you need to do to get ready for the game. A couple of lads were even up playing snooker until one or two in the morning on the eve of the match.'

By 1995, Ryan and the rest of the players knew there was no possibility of O'Neill remaining at Adams Park for very much longer, though they felt he would join Nottingham Forest and were surprised when he left for Norwich. It was an emotional time, and Ryan remembered that aspect of it when he said, 'I was one of three lads who were hanging around the ground when he was off to Norwich. He took us into his office and told us we might as well know from him that he was leaving. He thanked all of us for what we had done for him. "You have been brilliant," he said. I had just done my cruciate ligament and he told me that had I been fit I would probably have been going with him, which was nice.

'When I got that injury – a career-threatening one, especially in those days – I was upset, and I think he worried about me. He certainly came to see me at home. He told me I'd be fine, and said he had one piece of advice: there's a fellow who works out of Cambridge called David Dandy who's supposed to be the best knee surgeon in the country, so get the operation done by him. So I went to the physios and told them what I had been told. It caused a bit of friction between myself and them at the time. They argued that we had a club surgeon, and how was he going to get any recognition if he had no players to work with? Well, all I was worried about was getting my knee back in shape so I could play professional sport. I told them that if the gaffer suggested Mr Dandy, it was good enough for me. And he did the surgery. Just another little story about Martin caring.

'I don't think he was great having one-to-one talks with people. Perhaps he didn't need to because he was brilliant in collective situations. People say managers lack man-management skills, but he was good at it. He knew there were players that needed a rocket up their arse; he also knew that others needed a kiss and a cuddle. And he knew which was which. Mostly in football everyone gets tarred with the same brush, and that's not necessarily the right thing.

'I remember, too, one thing he used to say about Northern Ireland. If you were ever nervous about going out in front of 3,000 people, he'd say look where I stood as a Catholic captain of Northern Ireland. That was pressure, so don't complain if you get abuse shouted at you by two men and a dog.

'Every club seems to suffer after life with Martin O'Neill. Wycombe certainly did: we were nearly relegated for a couple of seasons after he left, and Leicester did go down after his departure. At the time you think the success is going to last for ever, but it doesn't.'

O'Neill was certainly a hard act to follow, and in Wycombe's case fate decreed that the man to be handed the chalice, poisoned or otherwise, was former Crystal Palace manager Alan Smith. Smith's experiences give an insight into just how complete the Irishman's control at the club had been. He was to suffer from and finally be beaten by the legacy. Smith thinks that only recently has a manager, in this case Lawrie Sanchez, been able to operate freely without being handicapped by the O'Neill legacy. Smith took on the job after being sacked by Palace and was a popular choice, but that did not make it any easier for him.

'In every aspect of the job,' he recalled, 'I was confronted with what had gone on before. On reflection, and it is on reflection, I don't feel anyone would have been able to cope at that time. Martin had a unique style of management. It was difficult for anyone to follow that.' Yet Smith had the impression there were people at the club who welcomed the chance finally to flex their muscles without having to bow to O'Neill. 'When I went to see the chairman, Ivor Beeks, who is a very nice guy, I got the feeling that he was pleased to be interviewing somebody and that he was making his own appointment. Martin had run the show from top to bottom. Perhaps that did irk some of the people on the board.

'I don't think it helped me that Martin still lived in the area and was very friendly with Alan Parry, who was his great ally. Parry was, of course, still on the board. It was not an overriding factor, but it was always there in the background. And sometimes the press would ring Martin for his opinion on what was happening at Wycombe. Everything I said or did got back to him. Not that I'm suggesting he deliberately interfered, it's just that Martin still seemed to have a hold on the club. That applied to the players as well. When I took over there wasn't a player there he hadn't brought to the club. And he had ensured they were well paid, too. I was surprised that a club like Wycombe was paying such high wages. That was obviously down to Martin. They had been indoctrinated into his extrovert ways. A new manager obviously has his own ideas, but I always felt I was battling against the aftermath of his reign.

'Martin had simply engulfed the place. As manager he had been unpredictable. He always kept the players on their toes. They never knew from day to day what they were going to do. And if they didn't do it his way they would soon know about it. I found that any time I tried to do anything different, just in general, there would be the same comments: "Well, Martin never did it like that", or, "We used to have Mondays off", or "Martin didn't make us train twice in a day". But don't get me wrong: Martin had done a phenomenal job at Wycombe. His success at other clubs proves his managerial talent, and I always found him straight and honest. But for me personally, and in the circumstances, it was one hell of an act to follow.'

It was one hell of an act, one that could not continue ad infinitum. As Smith implied, the relationship between O'Neill and Ivor Beeks became strained before the end, more out of frustration than anything – on O'Neill's part because he felt he had taken the club as far as he could, and on Beeks' owing to a feeling that he had lost control. 'I honestly think Martin had realised himself that he couldn't take the club any further,' Parry confirmed. 'We had achieved promotion and gone straight through Division Three, through the play-offs and the next season, and we were within three points of making the play-offs again in 1994/95, the season that turned out to be his last with us. They had just changed the structure in the League that season; before or since then, we would have been in the play-offs again. I think at that point he felt that was probably as far as the club could go.

'When Martin was with us, to my knowledge he turned down a number of jobs. I think he was beginning to feel –

and ironically this came out again long after he'd left Wycombe – that people might be getting the impression he was too cosy and he wanted to stay where he was liked, without taking on a challenge. All those things were going through his mind during that summer of 1995, along came Norwich to offer him the job, and that was it. It was good timing as much as anything.'

O'Neill's presence had created a marvellous winning atmosphere at Wycombe. He had taken the club to Wembley for the FA Trophy final in his first season, won the GM Vauxhall Conference League in 1993 to gain Football League status, plus another Trophy victory, and then taken them from the Nationwide Third Division to sixth place in the Second Division. Still it was asked of him, will he be able to do it with a bigger club? Could he, for instance, survive in the Premiership?

12. NORWICH – NEVER RETURN

Blink, and you could miss the part Norwich City played in the professional life of Martin O'Neill. But if his spells there as both player and manager were relatively short, that shouldn't detract from their importance either to him or the club.

The good folk of Norfolk will not appreciate the description, but second time round – that is, as manager – the six months Martin O'Neill worked under the chairmanship of Robert Chase suggest that Carrow Road was treated as not much more than a bolthole before taking up the reins at Leicester City. The facts, however, tell a different story; even the supposed rows over the lack of cash to buy players he believed were essential have been explained by Chase here for the first time. For all that the premature severing of his Norwich connection was unfortunate, the evidence points to O'Neill having considerable affection for the club and its supporters. It was at Norwich that he made lasting friendships, where he linked up with Steve Walford, Joe Royle and Mick McGuire, now deputy chief executive of the Professional Footballers Association. And despite O'Neill's abrupt and surprising departure at the end of 1995, he is still remembered with affection not just by the fans but, surprisingly, also by Chase, whose intransigence was supposed to have been the main reason for him quitting. There were certainly differences between the pair, but that is not unusual in football clubs, and Chase cites perfectly acceptable reasons for the split.

If Chase was at war with O'Neill, then it is hard to understand why he should have given Leicester a glowing account of the Irishman's ability – after he had resigned at Carrow Road. Stories about O'Neill and his Norfolk days come easily to Chase, and without any rancour. He laughs when he recalls some of them, none more so than the day when O'Neill, then a player, put in an unannounced and uninvited appearance during a Norwich board meeting chaired by the late Sir Arthur South. It was in 1983, when Chase was vice-president and O'Neill's playing career was beginning to draw to a close; he was on the transfer list, the fee for his services tabled by Notts County about to be deliberated by an independent tribunal. It was an extraordinary, perhaps unique intervention that saw O'Neill lecturing them on how best to deal with the tribunal, but again it typified the man. If he had a strong point of view, he expressed it; if it meant gatecrashing the corridors of power, then that too would be done. After O'Neill had finished, Sir Arthur turned to his colleagues to declare, 'If only he could still play football as well as he could talk.'

'At the board meeting we were discussing the fact that Martin was leaving,' Chase explained. 'Very roughly, Notts County were talking about a fee of £15,000 but we were asking around £100,000, and the matter was going to a tribunal. Suddenly there was a bang on the door – not a tap, a bang – and in walked Martin. He spoke extremely fluently. He gave the directors some advice on the way he thought affairs should be conducted, and on how he should be remunerated in respect of his move from Norwich. He commanded a great deal of respect.

'The amazing thing when trying to describe the man and his time with us as a player is that there were two aspects.

Firstly, as a footballer he was magnificent and he did Norwich a great favour by playing for us. Secondly, there are not many players that could barge into a board meeting and speak as well as he did. He had a message for us and he delivered it clearly. He certainly wasn't congratulating the board on the way it was conducting things, but he did not go behind anyone's back and waffle about it. He came straight to the meeting, commanded his audience and delivered it in a forceful manner. Martin left us on good terms, but the point really is that how many players would have the courage or the ability to address a group of men off the cuff – he had no notes – and tell them exactly what he thought? And I have to say he had a jolly good argument. He spoke very, very well and had a good hearing. The chairman thanked him for his intervention, and then Sir Arthur made that classic comment about Martin. I was on the board for ten years and it was the only interruption I witnessed. I often felt that that incident helped him get his MBE, for Sir Arthur carried a lot of influence and was able to make recommendations about such awards.'

The manner of O'Neill's first transfer to Norwich, in February 1981, illustrated how fractured his relationship with Brian Clough had become at Nottingham Forest. Norwich manager Ken Brown was convinced that under normal circumstances the deal would have fallen through. 'I seem to remember that he was officially on the transfer list and we agreed a fee,' recalled Brown, who was more recently one of England manager Sven Goran Eriksson's scouting staff. 'We were playing that week on the Friday night [20 February] against Birmingham, and he agreed to come along to watch the game and meet us. But on the Thursday night he rang to say that he had been selected for the Forest game against Arsenal at Highbury. Obviously he could not make it. Then, on the Saturday, Forest beat Arsenal 3–1 and he scored two goals. I thought that was it; they weren't going to sell him now. I was really down that weekend because I felt I had lost him. I resigned myself to it. But on Monday he telephoned me. "Aren't you interested in me any more?" he asked. I told him that in the circumstances I thought Cloughie would want to keep him. "Well, no one has said anything to me, so as far as I'm concerned I can go," he replied. And that was it. He came down, signed without any trouble and did marvellously well.'

John Deehan, who played with O'Neill during his second spell at the club in 1981/82, and who was later to manage Norwich, observed, 'Martin was a puzzle but a fantastic person, and he had great ability as a player. He was like a firework waiting to go off. Off the field, anything would ignite his imagination. He could talk on any subject that was brought up. He always had an opinion, and his timing was always perfect. He had a silver tongue. You could not take him on. He was so well educated. You had to be wary of him at the far side of the dressing room if you wanted to say anything. He was certainly an intriguing character, but to me he didn't stand out as someone who would take on the shackles of management. He was going to be a success whatever he did, but I thought he would probably be a writer. He had such a deep knowledge of words. He was always reading what you'd call the big papers, not the mickey-mouse ones.

'On the field, he was a player who was always available to take possession. He could create openings, and he was good in front of goal. He also had the capacity to turn losing situations into winning ones. He was an individual and a leader of men. Sparrows and swallows fly in flocks, but Martin was an eagle flying high above.'

Brown, too, had nothing but praise for his Irish footballer, though he found it strange that 'he was hopeless in training. You would not recognise him as the player who played on the Saturday. He was the same as Trevor Brooking at West Ham in that regard. Both of them were a waste of time in training. They just wanted to play. But Martin was a great influence in the dressing room. An hour before a match, he was full of it. Whether or not he was just working himself up, I don't know, but it worked. He did a great job for us. He was great with the fans and great with the club. It was a pleasure to have him in the team.'

'Speaking as a supporter', Chase, too, thought O'Neill was an entertaining footballer who also contributed so much effort. 'Only a player of his quality could have had such a long and successful career with Brian Clough at Forest. Clough was obviously a great influence on him and his approach to life.'

Mick McGuire's first impressions were similar to these. Of course, first impressions are important, but they aren't always the most accurate judgement; time can and often does allow you to see what the other man is about, particularly in a professional game riddled with jealousy, but there were no such problems between McGuire and O'Neill. They hit it off the moment they met up at Carrow Road, and in the more than two decades since then their friendship has flourished. Norwich were in deep trouble in that 1980/81 season, struggling – vainly, as it happened – to stay in the old First Division. O'Neill was brought in from Forest like the cavalry to help save the club from being scalped, and McGuire could not believe the confidence that oozed from him. 'My first reaction was that he was a man who totally believed in his own ability and wanted to pass that on to boost everyone else's confidence. He really galvanised us, and also made sure we went out as a team. He stirred everybody up and got the best out of me, too.

'Our initial friendship was partly formed by the fact that he was glowing in his praise of my abilities on the pitch. I'd had a time when I'd been out of the team because of a falling-out with the previous manager, John Bond. Ken Brown had taken over, and I had a bad start under him, in and out of the team. I had just started to play half decently when Martin arrived. I think his first game was against Brighton [on 28 February 1981]; we won 3–1 and I scored the first. Martin was exceptional that day. I'll never forget that game. I gave probably one of my best performances, but it got overshadowed simply by Martin's presence. He always tended to get the plaudits because he did turn us around, but to his credit he came up afterwards and told me how well I'd played, what a good player he thought I was.

'We also shared a cynical approach to life, and often the same opinion of players. I remember, years later, when David Ginola was getting a hard time after leaving Newcastle, I rang him and said, "Martin, please tell me what you think of Ginola." "Micky," he replied, "I think he's a fantastic player." At that point in time, I think only he and I thought so. A few months later he said on TV in front of Alan Hansen that he would have Ginola in his team any day. We often thought the same way.'

McGuire also found himself intrigued, as Tony Balfe, Alan Parry and others were, by O'Neill's interest in murder and murderers. 'He got me reading that bloody book by Paul Foot about the Hanratty case. I'm an expert on it now. He got me the book because he said Hanratty never did it. He has been to the Old Bailey with Pat Jennings in other cases, as members of the public. When we were going for promotion from the Second Division in the spring of 1982, we were playing Barnsley in an evening game. During lunch in Sheffield, he said to me, "Micky, come on, we're going." "Where?" I said. "We're going to the Ripper's house." "Are we bollocks. I'm going to put my feet up." But I'm sure he went anyway. It wasn't morbid, he just had this fascination for murder cases from his time studying law. When Martin opens his mouth, you listen, so I got quite into that.

'I think he joined Norwich because he wanted a challenge. I vaguely remember him saying he wanted the challenge of dragging us out of the mire. Certainly no one is stupid enough to think that if everything had been hunky dory, he'd have bothered coming. It probably wasn't exactly right for him at Forest any more, either, but I just think he relished the challenge of turning Norwich around.

'He lived with me for a while when he first joined. I'd say he and Joe Royle are two of my closest friends. We were the three senior players at Carrow Road at that time, and we were soon helping to give the club a fantastic chance of staying up. We beat Everton away one Saturday and Tottenham on the Monday. We then had to beat Leicester at home; Sunderland, also battling relegation, were playing at Liverpool. We were 2–0 down after five minutes, and Jim Melrose ended up with a hat-trick for them in a 3–2 win. Sunderland beat Liverpool. It was so disappointing. But Martin made the difference in that fight. Mark Barham was on the right, Dave Bennett on the left, with me and Martin in the centre. He was given free rein to do what he wanted.

'From what I remember, it was always going to be the case that he wanted to stay in the top flight. It was disappointing when he left, but not a shock, presumably because we knew when he arrived that he would leave if we got relegated.' McGuire was right. O'Neill did leave Norwich after they had been relegated, and it was all perfectly legitimate, as his former boss Ken Brown confirmed. 'Martin had a clause put in his contract stipulating that he could leave for the same fee if we were relegated. He nearly helped turn the corner for us, though. His debut brought our first win in seven games, yet when it looked as if we would get clear we lost our last two games and went down.

'I had taken over from John Bond, who had gone to Manchester City, and while I was on holiday in Ireland the club secretary rang me and said that Martin had gone to City and the deal had been agreed. City were paying half then and the other half the following year. I checked with the Football League and discovered they could do that, and I managed to get, I think, another £25,000.'

This was the purposeful O'Neill in action, no longer the man having to battle with Clough, up front and with a mind sharpened by his legal studies, knowing all about his rights and how they should apply. But the Manchester move was not a success. O'Neill played just thirteen League matches for them without scoring. There was a difference of opinion between him and Bond after one below-par performance when he was accused of not putting in enough effort. What Bond didn't know was that O'Neill had been punched so heavily in the chest by City's goalkeeper Joe Corrigan that it had affected him for the whole match. McGuire, privy to the information, remarked, 'He told me he was punched by Joe Corrigan, who had a habit of going around punching players and thinking it was funny. Martin said that afterwards he couldn't run during the game. He got slaughtered by the manager for not being able to run, but it was down to Corrigan.

'I don't think he had the same free role at Maine Road as he did when he was with us. At Norwich, the attitude was, if he wants it, give it to him, let him express himself. At City it was more regimented. Right from the beginning he didn't like it, and he didn't do particularly well.'

Manchester City didn't do particularly well either, and they were relegated at the end of the season; but by that time O'Neill was long gone – and back at Carrow Road. 'Martin jumped at the chance of coming back,' said Ken Brown, 'and, I seem to remember, for about half the price. It was great for us.' O'Neill's return in January 1982 once more galvanised the team, producing the incentive that earned Norwich immediate promotion back to the First Division. McGuire, for one, acknowledged the role his Irish midfield friend and colleague played in their success after what was a poor start to the 1981/82 League campaign. 'The first game we had after relegation was at Rotherham, and we lost 4–0. Everybody went, "Bloody hell, welcome to the real world." We had a very indifferent four or five months. That November I remember coming out in the press and telling people to leave off Brownie, to give him a chance. Mike England was being touted as a possible replacement for him.

'Martin was instrumental in the run we had from March during which we won ten out of the last twelve games to go from thirteenth into a promotion place. What started it off was a game at Bolton in which Martin scored with a shot that bounced about seventeen times before it went into the corner. That set up the run. It was no coincidence that it started just after he arrived back in the February. That was one of Ken Brown's masterstrokes, bringing Martin back.

'I was captain that season. We were probably the strongest players mentally in that team, and the game that really got us up, in retrospect, was about four from the end of the season: we went to Leicester and won 4–1. Coming back from Filbert Street we knew we were in pole position, but still, for the last game of the season we thought we had to win against Sheffield Wednesday. They scored first, we equalised, then we lost 2–1, but we still went up because Leicester lost. What was interesting, though, was that at 1–1 the ball was crossed and Wednesday's Gary Bannister headed it in from inside the six-yard box. One of their fans was actually in the six-yard box as well and dived as if he was going to head it. The funny thing was that nobody noticed until afterwards. We carried on for five minutes, lost the game, found out we were up, and then somebody said, "You've got to look at this." They put it on the TV and we couldn't believe it. The guy was wearing a scarf. If we'd lost and not gone up we'd have had to appeal against the result. But we'd had such a good run, it didn't matter.'

O'Neill and McGuire's days at Norwich were a mixture of good times and bad, and ironically, that 1982/83 promotion season was not one of the better ones for either. It was a struggle neither was to survive: McGuire moved, and O'Neill eventually headed back to Nottingham to sign for another former Forest team-mate, Larry Lloyd, then manager of Notts County in the First Division under the direction of the extraordinary Jimmy Sirrel. 'Martin played well enough,' McGuire recalled, 'but we struggled. We didn't quite have enough quality to start with and it took us time to bed in. The system was changing. I got left out of the team over the Christmas period and had left by March after a big fall-out with Ken Brown. My last game was against Martin's old team, and John Robertson scored the winning goal with his head. At our Christmas party Martin said to me, "You played very well against Forest." The following week we went down to Ipswich and the manager left me out. Martin said, "Micky, I can't believe it," but we won 3–2 so it was justified, wasn't it?'

Current Newcastle manager Glenn Roeder first met O'Neill when he spent a month with him at Notts County on loan from Queens Park Rangers. 'I was getting over an injury at Rangers and was out of the side,' he recalled. 'When you're 27 or 28 you want to be playing first-team football, and I was one of those "have boots will travel" type of players. Rangers were going for promotion and County were struggling in what was then the First Division. Jimmy Sirrel came in for me, and Terry Venables, then in charge at Loftus Road, let me go on loan. Strangely, I then went from one club nicknamed the Magpies to its namesake in Newcastle soon afterwards. But Notts County had their money's worth: what with League Cup games, I made seven appearances for them.

'There was a good team spirit, but it would be fair to say that, Martin excluded, they were a little short of genuine quality. Martin was captain and the senior professional. He was very respected in the game. Everyone knew him. He was what I would call an intelligent footballer, the type I prefer to have around me. Some players talk a lot of nonsense, and as a manager you sit there shaking your head. Martin always spoke sense. He was good in the dressing room talking to the lads.

'I spent a lot of time with Martin that month. I had a few afternoons to kill and used to go round his house. He was a hyperactive person, as he is now. He was always on the go. In those days he had a couple of betting shops in mining villages outside Nottingham and I can remember that after every single race he used to ring both shops. "Have we won or have we lost?" he would ask. He was very much the bookie rather than the punter. He must have learned early on in life that bookies drive Rollers and punters ride bicycles. He wanted a Roller.'

McGuire, whose observations are always pertinent and kindly considered, also appreciated that side of O'Neill. 'He was very astute, and it wasn't just horse racing, he was a great football punter, too. I think he once won a seven-selection accumulator, predicting homes and aways. He was interesting to listen to. He could always work the odds out. Like all the gambling lads, he had a gut feeling for it – that's why he goes for it on the pitch sometimes. He'll take a chance, but he's not a chancer. He's got such massive belief. If you had to win 7–0 to go up, he'd go out there believing we could do it, or rather making damn sure every other bastard thought we could.'

However, O'Neill's supreme confidence is only the public part of the man's character, according to McGuire's unbiased assessment of the Irishman's qualities. He can overwhelm you with it, but there is another side to him verging on the downright diffident. 'He is the most humble of men,' McGuire observed. 'He used to do himself down as a player. If he'd beaten three men and crossed the ball for someone to score, he would say he'd stumbled and how he'd got there he didn't know. He always said he couldn't pass, couldn't shoot, but I'm sure he felt he could. He wasn't searching for a compliment, that was just the way he was. But he would never give anyone out there the impression that he is anything other than supremely confident. Humble, yes, always balanced. That was his way. I think he has misgivings and reservations and concerns, but he's also got mental strength, a bit like the Rudyard Kipling poem: "When all about you are losing their heads . . ."'

'Martin could be very appreciative of anyone who played well against him; he always took a balanced view and was totally principled in his ways, in that if he'd promised a player something, in writing or not, he would see they got it. It was a point I learned about him when he went to Leicester. But he'd never been found wanting for outward confidence. That is what really endeared him to the players around him.'

The greatest quality O'Neill possessed was his belief that if he played he would have to win, even if it meant overcoming his or his team's deficiencies. He might not have passed the ball as well as some, but he would find his man; he might not have been able to beat a man with the ease of some, but he would go past opponents. And so on. 'He had a trick,' McGuire remarked. 'It wasn't a stepover like everyone else, it was a sort of half-stepover; a drop of the shoulder and he'd go the other way. As a passer, he wasn't in my class [laughs]. You wouldn't say he was a very clean hitter of the ball like David Thompson at Blackburn. You wouldn't say he was a finisher, either, and you wouldn't say he could win the ball like a Souness. You wouldn't say he was an astute passer who could thread the ball through. He couldn't head it, by his own admission.'

So how could he have won two European Cups?

'What Brian Clough had a habit of doing – it's unfair to say he made stars out of players with low ability, because they all had ability, but he got something out of them that no one else could. Martin had such belief when he went out there. He would go past players, although not at a glide like Robbo did. He would score you a goal that bobbled in. He would thread a ball through so brilliantly you'd think, "Wow! Why doesn't he do that all the time?" He would always produce the sublime at the right moment.

'Martin was effective in all areas, rather than elite. There was not one area that you would say he was elite in. You wouldn't say he was an elite passer, you wouldn't say he was an elite finisher; he wouldn't say he was elite at winning the ball. In fact he used to laugh at himself when he tried to tackle, but if the chips were down, one on one, the other player wouldn't get past. Whenever it mattered, whatever was needed – a tackle, a 25-yard shot, even a headed goal – he just put himself about, geed up everyone around him, wanted as many touches as he could, losing the ball and not worrying but getting it back and having another go – that was what he did. He was a match winner, the sort of player he wants and gets today.'

Under his three managers at the club on the other side of the River Trent from Forest – Larry Lloyd, Ritchie Barker, who replaced him, and that gnarled old warrior Jimmy Sirrel, who eventually assumed temporary charge of operations – O'Neill played some 64 League matches and scored five goals, including one on his debut on 27 August 1983 in a 4–0 victory over Leicester. But it was to be a sad ending for him at Meadow Lane. Against Shrewsbury at home on 2 February 1985, in front of over four thousand fans, O'Neill was carried off on a stretcher with a knee so badly injured there would be no possibility of it withstanding the physical demands of even lower League football. He had passed the age when he could shrug off such injuries. There was no alternative: he would have to finish his playing career and look for new ways to keep his family. He has never forgotten that things came to an end with a free transfer, this man who had won trophies with Nottingham Forest including a European Cup winners' medal, but who limped out of the game on crutches and with a disability pension of just £85 a fortnight. Many insurance policies were flogged and some media work was undertaken before he re-emerged at Grantham – and then yet again, in a managerial capacity, at Carrow Road.

Before he left in the mid-1990s, Norwich chairman Robert Chase was fiercely criticised by supporters and has remained silent about accusations that in 1995 he refused O'Neill finances to push the club forward, but he remained bullish. 'During my ten years there – and I'm not boasting, just being factual – we finished third, fourth and fifth in the top flight, reached two FA Cup semi-finals, and during one season stayed at the top of the First Division longer than any other club. Rarely does a club as small as Norwich hold the top spot for so long. I can't see that being repeated. We also qualified for Europe on three occasions, but unfortunately, because of the English ban, we only had the opportunity to play in the competition once. That was crowned by a trip to Bayern Munich when we beat them on their own soil. We built three new stands and a magnificent new training ground. We invested heavily in buying eight acres of land around the ground, which were a derelict mill and a car park. It's now worth fifteen times more than we paid for it. There was also a lot of modernisation at the ground.

'All this was due to David Stringer, a manager I held in the highest possible regard, and Mike Walker who followed him. After Mike Walker left John Deehan took over briefly, and then Gary Megson [in April 1995]. I still think Gary has the qualities to become a great manager, but there was no doubt he didn't have the support of the fans or the unanimous backing of the board. He didn't do quite well enough to keep us in the Premiership, but I remember him with fondness.

'At that time, there was one man out there the whole board agreed they would like, and that was O'Neill, already rated as one of the brightest young managers in the game after transforming Wycombe Wanderers over the previous five years. We had been down to Wycombe for a cup game when Martin was manager and we were all very impressed with the ground, the way things were organised and, of course, the team's performance. Martin had done exceptionally well and you could see his influence had extended to all quarters of the club, not just the playing side. He was obviously the driving force and the main man. He stamped his authority on the club. We beat them, but we came away thinking how well Wycombe was managed.

'We knew Martin had been linked with several top jobs, but when our vacancy came up we did make some enquiries and it was whispered to us that he was someone who might be ready to move if the proper steps and procedures were followed. So we contacted Wycombe to see if they would allow us to talk to him. Fifty or so names had been put forward, but Martin had the support of the entire board.

'All was done within the laws of the game and an agreement was reached between the two clubs that should Martin decide to come to Norwich we would pay Wycombe £200,000 compensation. The door was open for us to talk to him formally, and we met at the Post House at Heathrow, where we had hired a meeting room, at eight o'clock in the morning, which suited Martin because he could go on to training afterwards. He was waiting for us, drinking coffee, when we arrived.

'We got on exceptionally well. We talked around the job. We really went on a fishing trip for this first meeting to see what he wanted and the sort of terms he might be prepared to accept. We took on board what he had in mind. He wanted to bring two coaches with him from Wycombe, Paul Franklin and Steve Walford, told us the terms he wanted for them, and hoped we would accept them. He left no room for discussion. He said he thought they were fair. A few days later we made him a formal offer in the same room at the same hotel. We left him with concrete proposals and he read through them. There was no great haggling over anything.'

Yet O'Neill must have been aware of the financial restraints at Norwich because the night before he took the job Deehan, whom he officially replaced although Megson had been in charge temporarily (as player-manager for just five matches at the end of the 1994/95 season), had spoken to him on the phone. 'I told him I had a contract which stipulated that I had to notify the board of any offer of £1 million or more for any of our players,' Deehan revealed. 'I had generated £11 million for the club. I also told him we had some good young players. So he was aware of the situation and that this appeared to be a club prepared to sell its best players, and with little cash to spend. But then Martin was a strong character.'

Chase was able to officially announce O'Neill's appointment a few days later, in June 1995. 'Martin drove up and met us at the Norwich training ground,' he said. 'He was there before the groundsman and had gone before anyone arrived. By mentioning that, I'm saying he was a man who did not sit back and court publicity or talk about the move. He later attended a very quick press conference and then went off to Portugal on holiday, taking with him a bundle of video tapes of Norwich games. He wanted to think about things, about tactics and so on, while he was away. He was also very particular about wanting uncut videos of matches. I don't know how many he watched in Portugal, but knowing him, it was probably the lot.

'There was one thing he did specifically ask for, and that was his own little room close to the changing rooms at Carrow Road. And we provided him with that. It was a little office, no more than twelve foot square, with a fridge, a drinks cabinet and a few armchairs. I think it was fair to say that after games he would much rather be with his own friends than socialise with directors and visitors.

'Contrary to what some like to believe, I never got involved in the football side. Martin had his office at the training ground, and I only went there once, when there was an open day for the media and some VIPs so everyone had the opportunity to meet and talk to him. I simply introduced him and he addressed everyone and told them of his aims. He spoke very well indeed. That was my only involvement at the training ground in the short period he was with us.

'We were delighted to get him in front of bigger clubs and thought he was the best vehicle for us to move back into the Premiership. His appointment was a big gamble, but he was obviously a highly rated man capable of doing so much. We were pleased, and, we thought, very fortunate, to have obtained his services. I don't think we perhaps had the success on the field that we had hoped for, but he had always stressed it was not a five-minute job.'

O'Neill quit six months after arriving, just before Christmas, to take over at Leicester amid talk that he had been starved of finances at Carrow Road. Chase's version of events is more complicated and gives an insight into why O'Neill, who didn't move his family to East Anglia, never really settled in Norfolk. 'I think it was always difficult for him,' he stressed. 'He had been living in the London area. Within minutes you could be on a motorway and be in the Midlands relatively quickly. He had big clubs all around him. This is not a criticism, but he did find it difficult sometimes making a three-hour drive from his home to Norfolk. At that time there was only a very limited stretch of dual carriageway. After a long day, the journey back was a long, long trip.

'He had decided to keep his family back at Wycombe even though the club had put in his agreement that we would find him a home and assist him in its purchase so that he could relocate. But Martin never went about it with the same resolve and determination as the two colleagues he brought with him. To be fair, his children were at a difficult age as far as education was concerned, an important age. I'm not sure, but I think they went to a particularly selective school. Martin made it clear it was an important part of his life. Perhaps there was not the same choice of schools in Norfolk. I think that moving to Norwich was a much greater wrench than moving to another London club, or where he eventually went. Leicester was only an hour away on a good day. Once you start for the east coast you have single-lane traffic with heavy industrial vehicles on the road, and it was sometimes, certainly in those days, quite bad.

'Martin worked exceptionally hard though, and made a terrific effort. And while the travelling was a burden, he never once complained or grumbled about it. He just got on with the job in a very efficient and businesslike way. But I do think that relocation was a personal problem for him and the travelling a physical problem he had not experienced before. He stayed in a hotel at first, and we then rented accommodation for him, but there is nothing like your own home. I'm not trying to make this an excuse for what happened, but it was a burden, and one neither of us had considered at the time. He did do a great job for Norwich and we were all bitterly disappointed when he decided to go.'

The availability of the Leicester job influenced his decision to quit, although others suggest the trigger was the fact that Norwich lacked his ambition. Chase, however, is adamant that this was not mentioned to him as a reason. 'I was driving up to Leicester, who we were playing the next day, when he telephoned me in the car,' he recalled. 'He asked if I could come and see him. I turned around and drove to the training ground. He said he had made up his mind that he would like to leave and could I approach someone else to take charge of the squad that was playing the next day. I asked if there was anything I could do or say to persuade him to stay. He replied that there wasn't. It was a disappointment, but he acted professionally. No voices were raised. It was very much what you expected from Martin.'

On reflection, Chase feels that the campaign against him had not helped O'Neill. 'I was getting a lot of stick as chairman of the club,' he admits. 'I think he found that disruptive – although it was nothing to do with me.' But did Chase hold on to the purse strings too tightly, as some have claimed? Did O'Neill feel he was being held up by not being given more cash to spend in the transfer market? O'Neill was certainly unhappy at Norwich's failure to buy Dean Windass, then a highly rated and powerful young forward with Hull City who went on to play for Aberdeen, Oxford, Bradford, Middlesbrough and Sheffield United. For the first time, Chase gave his side of the story. 'I think that our funds, like most clubs', were limited,' he conceded. 'Martin asked for two players, who we bought, but then there was the problem with Hull. We talked terms for Windass, but when we agreed a fee they suddenly changed their minds. We took the view that you either do a deal or you don't. I think we were offering £600,000, and I think that was a good deal. Then there was a change of heart at their end and our offer was turned down. There was always the impression that they thought if they hung on they could get more money from us or another club. We had a clear policy, rightly or wrongly, that once you have made an offer it was either accepted or rejected. We didn't get involved in Dutch auctions.

'Martin had of course told us he wanted him, which is why we made the offer. Martin was very much involved in that decision, and we made the offer he recommended. Of course he was disappointed that Dean Windass didn't come, that he didn't get his man. Perhaps we could have shown more flexibility, but I don't think that tipped the scales for Martin wanting to leave. He was too big-hearted a man to allow one decision not going his way to disrupt his career. He was a much, much more principled man than that. He would have rolled up his sleeves and said, "Well, I didn't win this one but I'm going to win the next."

'Asking him to come to Norwich was a calculated risk. It was a gamble on the fact that he was going to stay a long time with a small club. But we were prepared to take the risk. He had been with the club as a player and was popular with everyone. I think the fact that we didn't have substantial resources in itself didn't have any impact on Martin at all. He never asked what funds would be available to him. He never said he would leave if he couldn't have this or that, and I don't think he would ever say he left Norwich because there were insufficient resources. I don't think he would ever say he left Norwich because of its location, or the city, or the education and welfare of his family either. I think it was a combination of things. He brought with him a host of ideas on how the game should be played, and on management. He had a unique style. He always spoke exceptionally highly of Brian Clough. In fact, I never heard him say anything critical about anyone. He was a good guy, there is no doubt about that. He took a chance coming to us, but it never clicked, never sparked. I don't think that if we had vast sums of money to spend it would have resolved some of the problems he had.

'The location and education of his children, for instance, were mostly resolved by moving to Leicester. It no longer caused him family problems. They just didn't help while he was at Norwich. He was very much a family man. His wife attended all the games at Norwich, and she'd also been very involved at Wycombe. I remember that from the time we visited.

'I remember Martin with a great deal of affection and a great deal of respect as a football man. I was pleased to have the opportunity of knowing him, and I don't feel any bitterness at all about leaving Norwich. I had ten fantastic years at the club, and some of my best moments in that time were with Martin. I just regret that the move didn't really come off for either of us. But that's life.

'I have never said anything controversial about him, and I think, to be fair, he has never said anything controversial or critical about Norwich. What I remember is a man who had the ability to come to the point clearly, precisely and quickly. He was a thinking man, and a man, perhaps like Brian Clough to some extent, who would do the unexpected. He might be late, keeping everyone waiting on the coach after an away game, and then sometimes he would be first on it. It was one of the qualities of his management. It was a way of letting everyone know that he was in charge. It kept everyone on their toes. But he was also a man who told us to the day when he wanted to go on holiday, and the day on which he would be back, and he kept to it. As far as a business relationship is concerned, he was first class. He was a man who knew exactly what he wanted and exactly where he was going.'

By the time O'Neill left for Leicester, Chase had become a hate figure for many supporters, who wanted former manager Mike Walker, out of work but still living locally, back in charge. Megson took over from O'Neill, but when Chase finally sold out, Walker returned in the early summer of 1996. Walker had gone public with his criticism of Chase, accusing him of a lack of ambition, and of wanting to sell his best players rather than speculate on the transfer market. In contrast to Chase's view, Walker claimed, 'Martin was no mug. He did the same as I did: he walked away. There was no way I was going back to the club while Chase was still there. What I did, in leaving Norwich and going to Everton, was reinforced by what happened to Martin. His record speaks for itself with what he did at Leicester and Celtic. If he had been given money he would have brought success to Norwich.

'The feeling among the players about Martin was mixed from what I heard. Some didn't like his style of management, but the more sensible ones said he got the job done, and that they had worked hard for him. But I don't think he bothered whether he was popular or not. He would sometimes not appear at training for a couple of days, then he would suddenly appear. Very much like Brian Clough used to do at Forest. It was that unpredictability. He was his own man. Some might not have liked his methods, but he had a knack of building team spirit. What I liked about him whenever I had any dealings with him was that he was always straight and open. He told you what he thought.'

13. LEICESTER – WINNING THE WAR

O'Neill's choice of associates has been crucial to sustaining his success as a manager, and, who knows, at the same time maybe his sanity. Steve Walford, O'Neill's coach from Wycombe onwards, is an old friend of Mick McGuire. They used to get changed next to each other at Norwich, and their wives still correspond. McGuire explained why the Londoner's straightforward approach to coaching is so valued by O'Neill. 'Wally makes him laugh. What he likes to do is the little bit of organising and coaching Martin doesn't want to do. He's very knowledgeable, too. You don't play the games he's played, for Arsenal, Tottenham, West Ham and Norwich, without becoming knowledgeable. He was teaching PE at a private school when Martin came and plucked him for Wycombe. He said he was spending six hours a day in the bloody swimming pool, his legs were shrinking, and he couldn't wait to get out. Martin had always told him he would bring him along. He couldn't at Grantham, but he did at Wycombe, and the rest is history.

'I would think what Martin likes is that Steve doesn't massively overelaborate. He knows what he's doing – I think he's got his full badges – and he gives Martin that little bit of organisation for set-pieces, and generally more of a coaching approach. Martin could do it, but he doesn't want to. When I've been with him he's been more inclined to put a tracksuit on and just go and mess around in the warm-up. He needs someone to organise it, to practise free-kicks for half an hour after training. I'd imagine he's invaluable in assessing his own team and opponents.'

Walford had played an essential right-hand-man role for O'Neill as he built his reputation at Wycombe, and O'Neill took him to Leicester City where the Irishman proved conclusively that he had the calibre to be a manager of distinction. Leicester was his triumph, but it was not a painless journey. He was well equipped intellectually to cope with the intensity of the intrigue and the boardroom politics, but the dirty fight waged by those opposed to him at the club stalked him until the day he decided to accept Celtic's offer to become their manager, a decision that allowed him to fulfil one of his ambitions and also released him from the mayhem emanating from the Filbert Street boardroom.

Wounds were opened from the very outset of O'Neill's appointment at Leicester; they have not healed, and probably never will. The animosity increased over the years, despite the success his management brought to the club. It is a shocking indictment of a group of men who essentially were his employers, to be so unforgiving as to maintain a state of war against their manager long after peace was justified and should have been declared. But when O'Neill realised he would have to fight his corner politically to survive, he did so with a determination and a venom that initially would surprise his enemies and cast them out of the club. He was up for the fight, as they say.

Leicester had been forced to find a new manager when Mark McGhee walked out on the job after just one season to join Wolverhampton Wanderers. The resignation was sudden and therefore shocking to the club, though some had seen it coming. The official reason from McGhee was his exasperation at his failure to extract the cash needed not only for what he considered essential new players, but for development within the club, particularly to improve training facilities that were pathetically inadequate for the modern game. Whether that was an excuse or not, a convenient get-out in order for him to take up a good offer from Wolves, was a suspicion at the time; nevertheless, a replacement for McGhee had to be found, and urgently. There was accord on who the successor should be: Mike Walker, the former Norwich and Everton manager and father of goalkeeper Ian, who ironically signed for Leicester from Tottenham some years later. In December 1995, Walker was odds-on to be confirmed as manager.

O'Neill's name had been on the list of possible candidates, and initially it had been a straight choice between going for an experienced manager who would stabilise the club or a young, energetic type who would bring in modern ideas and rejuvenate the set-up with his enthusiasm. But one man was preparing to challenge the appointment of Walker – chairman Martin George, re-elected as chairman in April 2002 after an absence that corresponded with Leicester's latest dip out of the Premiership. George, wealthy but no Rothschild, was powerful enough for his will to prevail. Even so, Walker was considered installed to the point of being introduced to the supporters' club.

Leicester, coincidentally, were due to face Martin O'Neill's Norwich City at Filbert Street on 17 December 1995. Walker was in town working as a summariser for Anglia TV when two things happened that destroyed his chances: on the eve of the match, O'Neill walked out on Norwich after only a few months in charge; at the same time, Norwich chairman Robert Chase was being entertained by Martin George as part of George's official duties as FA councillor for the area. George began to quiz Chase about O'Neill, who had been Leicester's first choice when Brian Little departed only for him to turn down the vacancy that was filled instead by McGhee. The key question posed to Chase was this: who was the best man to be Leicester's manager, Mike Walker or Martin O'Neill?

Now, Chase did not, outwardly, have the easiest of relationships with O'Neill. They had rowed, and he had just walked out six months after joining them from Wycombe. But he was also being criticised by Walker in his regular column in the local Norwich paper. Could this be used as an opportunity to even the score? If so, which gladiator would receive the emperor's thumbs down? Chase was a businessman of substance, and decisions like that had to be taken. He was not going to avoid the issue. Chase replied with admirable frankness, though doubtless Walker would be disgusted by his words: O'Neill, he told George, would be a better manager for Leicester than Walker. Chase's regard for O'Neill was considerable, as already stated, both as a player and manager for the Norfolk club. The endorsement was all George needed to hear. He went to his board, who were ready to announce officially the Walker appointment, to tell them that he wanted O'Neill. Points were made, and George won the argument; for the sake of propriety the board was, shall we say, convinced by its strength, and O'Neill was installed. But the seeds of resentment were sown. Because of that one decision against them, the 'Gang of Four' Leicester directors – Roy Parker, local bus company owner Gilbert Kinch, Phil Smith and chief executive Barrie Pierpoint – was established, though they were self-defeating in the end and their antagonism towards O'Neill had no apparent impact on his ability to manage with flair and success. Still, to say the vendetta had no effect on him as a person would be nonsense. To highlight the depth of feeling against O'Neill, one of the Four was heard to say in the club's foyer, 'Martin O'Neill will be manager of Leicester City over my dead body.'

Walker, a thoroughly pleasant man, was bewildered by the about-turn. It was particularly upsetting because he had to assume that those who had led him to believe it was a done deal must have changed their minds, willingly or not.

Walker had no option but to suffer the indignity of it all and return home to Norfolk. From this situation sprang all the problems, the in-fighting and the bad feelings O'Neill would have to live with as he took Leicester back to the top league, into three League Cup finals (they won two of them) and back into Europe, and established them as a Premier League club of repute.

Ian Silvester, then Leicester's secretary and until 2005 a director and club secretary at Leeds United, recalled the events surrounding Mark McGhee's departure. 'Mark walked out on a Thursday night after a long meeting,' he said. 'He just said no to the suggestions made, and that was it – he was off to Wolves. I believe the board was split between going for someone with experience, because we wanted to get back into the Premiership, and what was deemed to be the next talented young manager on the managerial roll. It was definitely a decision between Mike Walker and Martin O'Neill. I actually took Mike around the ground when he came for his interview, and I think at that time the majority wanted him.'

Cliff Ginnetta, chairman of the Leicester City supporters club and a fan of 40 years, was in no doubt about who the next manager was going to be: Mike Walker, of course. Ginnetta explained, 'After the Norwich match we had a meeting at our club, a supporters thing, and they were actually showing Mike Walker round and we were introduced to him and told, "This is the new manager of Leicester City." It was directors telling us that. When I spoke to a couple of them not long afterwards and asked what had happened, they were not too pleased. They weren't at all happy with the chairman, but Martin George was funding the club at the time so he had the final say.'

O'Neill's was, of course, to be nothing less than an historic appointment, and George would be entitled to a certain smugness that his intuition about the Irishman, rubber-stamped by Chase, had been so brilliantly accurate. George's pursuit of O'Neill had covered a number of years and included a close study of his progress in non-League football – and he had interviewed him before. 'Long after I had been appointed chairman in 1991,' said George, 'we met because I had a business in High Wycombe. I knew very well that wasn't the time I could appoint him, but I'd watched what he'd been doing prior to that. It was to be four years before I interviewed him again, but I remember telling him that having had Brian Hamilton as manager the last thing I was going to do was appoint another fast-talking Irishman. Then, when Brian Little left, I interviewed him again while he was at Wycombe and he was quite anxious to complete another promotion, so after a lot of thinking and a lot of talking he came to my house one day, rather than ring me up, to say that he'd decided he was going to stay with Wycombe. That's when I appointed Mark McGhee.

'One of the jobs of the chairman, in my view, is to know who your next manager's going to be. For one reason or another managers move, so I've always made it my business to know who my next one will be. Martin had been near the top of all the lists I'd compiled from the time I was appointed.' Mainly because O'Neill possessed all the attributes George wanted. His age and his lack of managerial experience at the top was a plus, not a minus, for the Leicester chairman, who confirmed, 'I didn't really want somebody who had been there and done it. In other words, I wanted somebody who had shown a degree of success lower down, who had an understanding of the economics of football, certainly at a lower level, had balanced the books and produced a decent team. Martin had certainly done that. It had to be somebody who wanted to get to the top, indeed that's the first thing, and he definitely fulfilled that criterion.

'Martin is substantially more intelligent than most football people, privately educated in Northern Ireland. He's a good thinker about matters other than the game, but a particularly good thinker about the game. He will spend the club's money as though it was his own, so he would never spend the last bit of the budget. There are those with perhaps less strong chairmen who will go out and spend the contingency every year, never mind the budget, but he would never come into that category. He had what I thought would be excellent attributes for the club. Our finances were tight at the time and I was guaranteeing money through my bank. I had to pay for a player on one occasion when the bank wouldn't, so he and I, if you like, understood each other. When my successor took over he was much more of a supporter of the club and eager to sign the best players. In that situation Martin would probably be the one who kept it balanced. That's why he was appointed. I was "replaced" when I got them into the Premier League for the second time, which is an odd time to do it. But anyway, that's what happened.'

George had pointed out to the rest of the board the dire consequences of appointing Walker should he lose his first series of matches. 'The only way I got it through to them was to say that if their man was appointed and he lost five matches between now and February 1996, they'd all be out. They settled for that and thought they had better have my man. Martin knew that, and he also knew there were factions on the board that would say something was black if I said it was white. They'd treat Martin the same. Unfortunately, if you have non-football people in a football boardroom you are going to have that attitude.

'We had been quite successful through that period with Little and McGhee so I think they began to believe anybody could do it. They were absolutely itching to have a go. When it appeared unlikely we'd qualify for the play-offs by April 1996, they were loving it. They wrote this damning report about how Leicester City was being run, and then all of a sudden we were promoted. They had very little ground to stand on then.'

Leicester's promotion to the Premiership was the first of O'Neill's triumphs, and enough, you would have thought, to suggest to his opponents that this was a battle they might never win. They managed to force Martin George to stand down as chairman in that summer of 1996, but O'Neill's position was strengthened with every match. He had in a short time become untouchable as far as the Leicester public were concerned, yet the Gang of Four persisted in sniping and would do so right to the moment they 'resigned', which they did before O'Neill had decided to move on to Scotland.

O'Neill had been quick to organise his own gang: there was John Robertson, Steve Walford and reserve-team coach Paul Franklin, plus secretary Ian Silvester and Paul Mace, the club's press officer. All of them diligently performed the jobs they were employed to do, and all of them worked closely with the manager. Mace's job meant he had to be in daily, hourly if necessary, contact with the manager. O'Neill had no need to worry about the loyalty of either Silvester or Mace. He had won over the players, too – not difficult when you show them how to win their way back into the Premier League. Yet again he had proved his expertise at finding players others barely used or witheringly dismissed as 'good pros, but . . .' O'Neill used to joke that he was so ashamed of the Filbert Street facilities when he tried to sign a new player that he would back them out of the tunnel in the hope they wouldn't be disheartened by their first sight of the east stand, the double-decker and the family enclosure, but those players invariably signed and fitted into a system that would be perfected by the likes of Neil Lennon and Muzzy Izzet, salvaged from Chelsea's reserves, Matt Elliott from Oxford, Robbie Savage from Crewe, Steve Guppy from Port Vale and striker Steve Claridge. The common denominator in these signings was gratitude, without it developing into an upstairs, downstairs subservience. O'Neill had plucked them from anonymity and made them Premier League performers; he had them starring in Wembley finals, playing in European competitions, making the sort of money that can allow you to retire in your thirties, if not before. He was building reputations.

It was head-spinning stuff, and it was all down to the manager and a system based on power, speed and directness. It was criticised, inevitably, as the long-ball game, but any suggestion of that would enrage O'Neill. He would not change, and why should he? 'You could argue that Martin made spontaneous decisions on all sorts of matters relating to the team and the club,' Martin George reflected, 'but it wasn't done on a wing and a prayer. Everything had been well thought out. Because of our position initially it was very important to put things together quickly, so we needed somebody who could do that and go running with it. I mean, we weren't in a bad position in the table, we were in a play-off position in that first December, but with McGhee saying, "Oh well, you know, there are better clubs in the Midlands than Leicester, therefore I'm moving," it was important for somebody with a bit of personality to get hold of it. Martin did that. I was just so impressed with the way he applied himself to the job. He wasn't a boardroom manager; he worked through the chairman, and that was me to start with. If he had to turn up to a board meeting he didn't mind doing so, but that wasn't his forte. He didn't really want or need to explain to too many people what he was doing.' O'Neill saw himself as the boss of the club; if he was not the most important individual, his players as a unit were, and he was in charge of them. George agreed with O'Neill's philosophy. 'Where the manager works through the chairman, it is best. I don't think you can have more than one person from the board directly responsible for football matters, and that has to be the chairman.'

The fans are invariably perceptive observers of changes within 'their' club. The only thing they are interested in is success, maximising the talents of whatever players are available, and like George's fellow directors they were concerned initially that the wrong man had been handed the job. So in this sense as well it was a more than difficult start for O'Neill – traumatic wouldn't be an overstatement, according to outsiders' description of events, and it became even worse as he struggled to produce a result, any sort of result, good enough to calm his detractors in the boardroom and on the terraces. At this point the relationship between the manager and the Leicester fans was crucial, and it was deteriorating from a starting point that was low. O'Neill had to win them over with a series of performances that would inspire confidence in him and his ability to produce a winning team, and soon. Promotion to the Premiership was the target, but as game after game came and went without a win and the pressure built up on O'Neill and the board, the Premiership looked to be an impossible target.

It took O'Neill eight attempts to win his first match, though it was a particularly satisfying one when it came, on 21 February 1996: former City boss McGhee and his Wolves side had to swallow a 3–2 defeat after his new team had been 2–0 in front. An up-and-coming young striker by the name of Emile Heskey scored two of Leicester's goals, and went on from there to play a considerable role in Leicester's success over the next few years before switching to Liverpool and developing his international career with England. His goals at Molineux that day helped Leicester to climb into position for the nerve-jangling play-offs.

But if that brightened the Leicester scene, it was only temporary relief. The fans' disillusionment at the appointment of O'Neill and disgust at results, Wolves apart, soon turned into an abusive, dangerous assault and attempted break-in at Filbert Street. It was ignited by a 2–0 defeat at the hands of Sheffield United on 30 March, as a result of which Leicester were left ninth in the table and as good as out of the play-offs. So frustrated were the supporters that about three thousand stayed behind in protest. A few of the unruliest tried to break into the dressing-room area. The police asked O'Neill to help out by talking to a delegation of fans, provided that the rest dispersed, which they did.

'They turned on Martin in a big way,' Silvester recalled. 'Promotion looked hopeless and the crowd went mad. They tried to break into the stadium at the end, and I had to hold on to the door of the changing rooms to stop them trying to batter their way in. It was distressing then, and depressing to think about now. They were demanding to talk to someone. They were gathered at the main entrance and the players' entrance. We had to shut all the doors. It was about six p.m. and the police advised us to do something about these people because they weren't going to move. We were told, "Someone will have to come out and talk to them." I think a few people went out and asked them to select a dozen or so supporters and come round into the office where Martin would talk to them with members of the board. He would tell them what the club was planning and listen to what they had to say. All the rest had to do was go home.

'The select few were brought round the pitch and put into the press interview room at the side of the tunnel. Martin sat down with them and was very full and frank. "I accept things aren't going well," he said, "but you haven't given me a chance. I've only been here three months, there is very little money, but I promise that I will turn it around." It was impressive, and the fans, I'm sure, admired him for that, but he never forgot the day they went for him. He never tired of reminding them, in his way, of the abuse they gave him.

'On the Tuesday after the trouble we travelled to London to play Charlton, and then Crystal Palace on the Saturday. Leicester's record in London was abysmal, we hardly ever got a result. No matter who we played, we would lose. But we won that game against Charlton and went on to beat Palace with the same 1–0 scoreline.'

Alan Birchenall has been involved with Leicester City for decades as club co-ordinator, a post that has put him in the unique position of having worked with every department at Leicester, involving the players, the commercial side and the supporters. In his time he has introduced nine new managers to the fans, and he recognised the problems O'Neill faced. 'I know what people were saying,' he said, 'I know they didn't think he was going to be good enough. Martin realised that, too. When you work with the man you quickly accept how intelligent he is. The club was in the doldrums when he joined and he was a former Forest player, which made it worse for Leicester City supporters. He'd had his success up the road and he came and joined us, and I remember during his first week I took him to my pub in the village. He knew the area, but every new manager and player comes out for a chat; they want to get to know the background.

'Leicester's a great club, but for the first few matches he didn't think it was so great. He suffered from the previous season's bad results – and then came the Sheffield game. I wouldn't call it a riot, but there were skirmishes and things looked black. It was bad, but it was also the turning point. From that moment on we looked up, not down. It was all hands to the pumps. It was as low as the club could get, as low as Martin's career at this club was. They had gone so long without a win. They'd had a few draws, but Sheffield United was the final straw for our fans. Martin wasn't the target, but that didn't make it any easier for him. The affection grew from there.'

Was the demonstration seized on by certain directors as a way of weakening Martin George's position – the chairman was not at the match because of a business engagement – by ingratiating themselves with the fans and also maintaining the plot against O'Neill? It is a perfectly reasonable question to ask. Indeed, things went further than that. Mike Walker was actually contacted around this time, and it was suggested to him that he should not take up another appointment as the presumed failure to qualify for the play-offs meant that O'Neill, and hopefully George, would be forced out and the job would be his.

Ginnetta gave the supporters' view of the run of poor results that culminated in the demonstration. 'We know McGhee hadn't left a good team. Although they played some fantasy football at times, they just weren't consistent. So Martin walked into a barrage of criticism. Being ex-Nottingham Forest didn't go down too well with the

Leicester fans for a start. There are people in both camps: people who are Leicester v. Derby and people who are Leicester v. Forest, and who care about both games equally. It depends on what part of the county you live in: there are a lot of Forest fans in the Loughborough area, then a bit further round you've got Ashby de la Zouch which is virtually Derbyshire. If you've played for one club or the other, you don't really go and manage one of the others, so there was a lot of hostility towards him. He had a run of games when he couldn't buy a win. It was terrible. Things picked up a bit for a short while, but then it started going wrong again.

'It came to a head during that Sheffield United match at Filbert Street. They didn't just want O'Neill out, they wanted the board out. We'd lost Brian Little and Mark McGhee in quick succession and we weren't making any headway in terms of getting back into the Premiership after dropping out the year before. It was one of the most famous days in the history of Leicester City.

'Full marks to Martin, then. He did tackle the fans after the game, speaking to some of them in the offices, on the Kop and in the car park afterwards, as far as the police would let him. He tried to explain what had gone wrong. He was just saying, "Give me time." To be perfectly honest, the way things had developed he couldn't expect much time.

'Martin can say what he wants, but his style of football was a bit long-ball, and after a year of good football with McGhee – some of the best football Leicester have ever played came during McGhee's reign – it wasn't very pretty to watch. The only time Martin and I spoke about it was when he criticised something I'd said in the paper about the Sheffield United game. I said people weren't going to put up with this for ever when they were paying hard-earned money for tickets. Martin had a right go at me about that, said we'd have to give him more time. He took it that I was trying to get him out of the job. Another time, I was praising him for how well we'd done, and I had to say that this long-ball game suited some of the players. He took the real hump about that, too, and had a real go at me, claiming that he didn't play the long-ball game. He was the only one in Leicester who thought we didn't. But that's Martin. He wasn't devoid of tactics, but I still don't think he is the greatest tactician ever. He knows how to hold a team together, though.

'We were never great mates, but we spoke together from time to time and sometimes, as I've said, he'd have a go at me for something I'd said. He's very shy, actually. I know he does these things on telly, and some things he has to do that he doesn't want to do, but any little bit of criticism, he's very sensitive to that. But that's the case with a lot of football managers. He's just more sensitive than most.'

Those results in London against Charlton Athletic and Crystal Palace relaunched Leicester's push for promotion and rehabilitated O'Neill, but the memory of the letters pouring in and the phone-ins crackling with vitriol was still fresh. The lowest point professionally for O'Neill was the 3–1 defeat at Oldham in February. One official with the party at the time described it as 'garbage, absolute garbage'. Leicester had missed a penalty and had had a man sent off – two incidents that added to O'Neill's anger. This was to be an early example for Leicester folk of the flip side to O'Neill's shy sensitivity. An eyewitness explained: 'We travelled back on the M62 in an horrendous snow storm. We were nearly stuck on the motorway and the atmosphere was awful. A couple of players had decided to play chess rather than cards on the return, and that is when Martin flipped. "They're not playing chess, they're not doing anything after that!" It was the worst coach ride imaginable, certainly the worst I have experienced with the team.'

Silvester also remembered how it was best to stand back when the O'Neill touchpaper was lit. 'If he was angry, then there would be a good reason. The majority of the time I found him very calm, well within himself, always in control. But he demanded respect. That initial five-month period was when things were very difficult for him at both boardroom and staffroom level – and I am talking about ordinary members of staff who'd think, "Who's this Martin O'Neill? He's done nothing. He didn't do anything at Norwich and walked out after six months." It was that kind of attitude, and very few people stuck by him. I did. I saw it as my role as secretary. It was very strong stuff, too. The main argument was that Martin couldn't manage. From that point on, though, I think we only lost one more match for the rest of the season, and we made the play-offs. It was a sweet moment for the club, but particularly for Martin, as you can imagine.'

Having reached the play-offs, Leicester faced Stoke at Filbert Street, and that suited O'Neill, who always prefers a home match first in a two-legged tie. His philosophy was simple: if the other team do not score, all you have to do is win 1–0 or draw 1–1 at their place. In theory, the advantage should be yours. In the event, a 0–0 draw at Leicester was followed by a 1–0 away win. It had been an amazing run of results, with Wembley and a final against Crystal Palace still to come.

After the Sheffield United rumpus O'Neill had managed to wrench some money from the board, and he'd bought Steve Claridge for a reported £1.2 million from Birmingham City. It was a masterstroke. Claridge scored the goal at Charlton that spawned the revival, and it was his goal that sent Leicester into the Premiership, his extraordinary winner against Crystal Palace coming seconds from the end. The goal on its own was worth millions. It transformed Leicester and gave Martin O'Neill the opportunity to take on England's top clubs in what is vigorously championed as the world's most competitive league (which is different from calling it the world's best). O'Neill had achieved his ambition; if questions were still being asked about his managerial ability, they were fewer in number, and none now emanated from a Leicester crowd who had taken him to their hearts.

But he would never forget the abuse they'd hurled at him when he was struggling to survive. He actually considered giving the Leicester fans the V sign when he collected the play-off trophy at Wembley. The alternative was to stick out his tongue at them, which he did, but so subtly that few noticed. O'Neill is not an automaton, which means he is sensitive to criticism, although given his chosen profession perhaps on occasions too sensitive. He had been told by apologetic fans that they were campaigning against the board, not him, but O'Neill's reply to that was always the same: 'It was my name they were shouting.'

He has never found it easy to relate to directors, not so much individually as to their boardroom mentality, which is alien to him. He sees himself as the boss-man and will not accept what he considers interference from directors, indeed expects their co-operation when required. It was he and his players who had taken the club to Wembley and determined whether they would win promotion or not. It had little to do with the directors, a number of whom, of course, would happily and summarily have driven him out had a good opportunity presented itself. These were the same people, the Gang of Four, who didn't think O'Neill was good enough for the job. Their dumbness isn't quite in the league of the agent who turned down the Beatles, but it is up there in the misjudgement stakes. They compounded their error by continuing to refuse to acknowledge their mistake and persisting in their niggling condemnations of him, those he supported and those who supported him.

In truth, this was all wrapped up in the struggle for overall power at the club. The first target was Martin George, and O'Neill's appointment was a symbol, as they saw it, of his overbearing chairmanship. There was some substance to their initial argument over O'Neill. They had wanted Walker's experience, having previously gone for the relative inexperience of Little and McGhee, only to see them use Leicester City as a stepping stone to the next level, Little to Aston Villa and McGhee to the Sir Jack Haywardfinanced Wolves. Neither was to gain fulfilment in these new jobs. But the argument against O'Neill's appointment could not be sustained because he was so successful. It would surely have been better for them had they forgiven and forgotten.

As for O'Neill, he had joined Leicester after failing to acquire the funding he needed for new players at Norwich, so it was crucial that this move was successful for him. Failure, a row and another walkout, for instance, would mark him as unemployable in the eyes of the major outfits. Silvester, who developed a good working and social friendship with O'Neill, confirmed that the Irishman, as a result, had been 'up for it, up for the job' when he arrived. He added, 'I remember the first time I met Martin, at a reserve game in early December [1995]. There were some boxes at Leicester behind the old north stand with orange seats. We sat in a box up there, Martin George, Martin O'Neill and myself. I remember his first comment was, "My God, the pitch is shit here, isn't it?" It was true, because we had a terrible pitch. He said again, "The pitch, look at the pitch." I said it was a problem, that we would have to get it sorted out next season. That was my first impression of him, and I liked the guy, I must admit, from the word go. From my position, if I don't get on with the manager then there is not much point in me working. You have to get on with the manager, and thankfully I have got on with all the managers I've worked for.'

O'Neill not only had to confront directors and supporters in those pre-promotion months; most disturbingly, a group of his players were also against his appointment. Steve Walsh, Leicester's veteran captain, saw himself as a candidate, and there was a measure of support for him to become player-manager. That, too, was a difficult one for O'Neill to accept, though it is unclear exactly how much he knew about this players' revolt. If it concerned him, as it must have done, then it did not check his stride. He stood by his beliefs and continued to build a team in the image he desired. But these were not pleasant days.

Concerns had been aired inside Filbert Street, for example, that Geraldine, O'Neill's wife, was being treated less than courteously, certainly not in a way befitting the manager's wife. One source said he was 'appalled' by the treatment she received. Basically, as those who knew her saw it, she was not brought into the boardroom fold; instead, she was to be settled into a side room with some other wives, when the more appropriate action, given the tensions during that early period, would have been some attention, some corporate tender, loving care.

Still, with John Robertson, Steve Walford and Paul Franklin by his side, with those first months behind him and the 1996/97 Premiership campaign in front of him, and with the zero tolerance of his regime restricted to a few soured directors immersed in a battle for control of the club, O'Neill was ready to move forward at a bewildering pace. But there was one act he had to perform at the end of that promotion season. He had stored every letter sent to him at the club not merely criticising him but calling him everything from useless to the unprintable. Now was the time to reply, in his own special way.

'There was no doubt he could be idiosyncratic,' Silvester observed. 'He very rarely replied to mail. He got lots of crank letters, and they can be irritating if you let them get to you, but clubs try to respond to them, even if it is simply an acknowledgement. But Martin would just keep these letters, and if they really were having a go at him, he would leave them in a drawer or in a file.

'I remember we were having a chat about the year ahead in the Premiership and as we sat in his office he opened a drawer, took some letters out and rang the people up. "Is that John Smith?" – "Yes." – "Martin O'Neill here." There would be a silence, and Martin would say, "You wrote me a letter and you called me this and that and said I couldn't do this job, so I thought I'd ring you and ask what your thoughts are now." I thought it was great – what a satisfying way to embarrass someone or get your point across! It is the way he got back at people. He would always refer to it in conversation, you know, hark back to the difficult days. There was one guy who kept digging him up on Radio Leicester. No, he didn't dig him up, he slaughtered him. But after the promotion, whenever he got the opportunity, he would say he was sure that "Glen in Littleover" or wherever it was would be delighted they'd gone up. Martin lifted the club. I hope these people who went for him without justification have a guilty conscience.'

Over his five seasons at Filbert Street, the plaudits were fully deserved. The three League Cup finals – they beat Middlesbrough in 1997 after a replay, lost to Spurs in 1999 and beat Tranmere in 2000 – were superb achievements. Again, O'Neill's critics will say he only succeeded in that competition because it had lost its appeal so far as the major clubs such as Manchester United, Arsenal and Liverpool were concerned. It's true all of them saw the competition as a nuisance; the big boys could instead depend on multiple admissions to European Cup competitions, to the European League for Non Champions as the cynics have tagged it, which they have devalued with their greed and the need to pay top performers massive salaries. But there were plenty of other good clubs above and below Leicester who regarded the League Cup as both prestigious and a potential money earner. For the supporters it was a joyful day out, as enjoyable for the participants as the FA Cup final – an opportunity to take part in the climax of what is still a national event.

O'Neill, too, enjoyed these finals as pure football events that kept the club in the limelight, raised their profile, gave the players confidence and was a route to European football in the form of the UEFA Cup. The first of them was relatively trouble-free, Claridge scoring the only goal of the replay against Bryan Robson's Middlesbrough at Hillsborough. The final against Tottenham had bad vibes about it even before the day of the match, when O'Neill had to discipline Frank Sinclair, one of his key players, when he got back late to the team hotel after a night out.

O'Neill can turn away from confrontation with his players if he feels their indiscretion is small enough to be ignored, but he was infuriated by Sinclair's crass stupidity before such an important match. Even if he hadn't exactly put his fitness in doubt, his commitment could be considered suspect. O'Neill would have seen Sinclair's behaviour as a slight against him, and that he will not tolerate, even at the expense of losing a player who could be the difference between winning and losing (Sinclair did not play in the final). O'Neill had himself offended some 'purists' two years earlier with his decision to use Pontus Kamark to man-mark Boro's Juninho in both the final and the replay. But why would anyone think the little Brazilian should be allowed the freedom to express his talent unhindered? It's just plain humbug. O'Neill's prime motivation is always to win, and to make sure his team develops a taste for this good habit.

Unfortunately, it deserted them against George Graham's Tottenham in March 1999. The final ended in bad feeling after Robbie Savage overreacted to a Justin Edinburgh challenge that got the Spurs player red-carded. Savage had the honesty to admit his behaviour had caused the referee to send off a fellow professional, but his conduct was not appreciated. Nor was the defeat. When they returned a year later to face Tranmere Rovers, as expected they came out on top, though it was a lot closer than anticipated, skipper Matt Elliott scoring both Leicester goals in a 2–1 win with the winner coming nine minutes from time. Three cup finals in five seasons is better than good, but it was Leicester's Premier League form that was most impressive: four top-ten finishes in the four seasons since promotion. That was the O'Neill legacy which, alas, was squandered as soon as he turned his back on the club for Celtic.

By the end of O'Neill's first eighteen months, following that first League Cup win, Leicester City had already zoomed from distraught to delirious. O'Neill's 'fan cred' was up there with the gods, as Ginnetta confirmed. 'The fans were totally and utterly behind him and believed in the guy and the players he had. Neil Lennon was great, and Izzet, the way he was playing at the time, should have picked up caps for England, although he eventually chose to play for Turkey. Steve Guppy was doing it on the left since he'd come in. We'd never seen a team like it. We'd had good, even great teams at Filbert Street, but never as good as that.

'And Martin – he was just getting bigger and bigger. They say no one's bigger than the club, but he was getting that way. I don't think he ever intentionally rubbed people up the wrong way. He was always Joe Blunt, saying the first thing that came into his head sometimes. He never liked being compared to Cloughie, but he was a Cloughie and is a Cloughie. He doesn't spend a lot of time on the training ground, that was all left to Robbo and his coaches. The players had such a respect for him. He really liked the closeness of it all, everyone together.'

But the supporters, perceptive as ever, also recognised the split that had developed within the club as a result of the warring factions. 'There was this drift,' Ginnetta added, 'with all the playing staff spending all their time down at the training ground at Beaver Drive. We'd had this huge Carling Stand built before Martin came. All the corporate things were in there and there was no room for footballers. There were two changing rooms that were dead basic, a couple of breezeblock rooms, and the rest was for business people. Martin, even when he first came to the club, remarked that it wasn't like a football club, and he was right. That's where the split came, as we saw it. There was the chairman and corporate people at Filbert Street and all the football people at Beaver Drive.' In the view of the highly observant Ginnetta, maybe Martin's personal team, naively perhaps, had helped to widen the gap. 'Some of the people round Martin who should have known better always made the point, when the press asked what was happening at Filbert Street, of saying, "We don't know, we're not part of that, no one tells us anything." Instead of uniting the club, some people, more than Martin, made this split even worse. More and more was leaked. Someone should have had a word with Martin, who had a lot going on in the background with the moves towards making the club a plc, which Martin didn't fancy. A lot of traditional football people didn't like the idea of Leicester City turning into a plc.'

The comparison between what was happening at Leicester and what had happened up the M1 at Nottingham in the 1970s was inescapable. There are so many similarities between the experiences of these humble Midlands clubs coming from nowhere, from promotion to prominence. But whereas Brian Clough was able to see it through to a League and two European titles, O'Neill found himself combating both the changes in the national game, which were making the rich and powerful clubs even more rich and powerful, and the boardroom squabbling that would soon become psychologically exhausting, with the factions spending more time than was good for the club at one another's throats.

The club had, as Ginnetta remarked, literally been split in two: on the one side there was O'Neill, his players and staff plus vice-chairman, then chairman John Elsom and Martin George; on the other, the Gang of Four – Parker, Kinch, Smith and chief executive Pierpoint, who was given the chance to put forward his side of the story here, but politely declined. Pierpoint had joined the club as director of marketing and had come to see himself as Top Cat at the club. He was doubtless successful and was in charge of planning the new stand in the Filbert Street stadium, now defunct and replaced by the Walkers Stadium. The appointment of O'Neill and the success he was to bring pushed the imperious Pierpoint from centrestage to a point somewhere in one of the wings. The commercial side of the business, Pierpoint's main responsibility, employed 150 full-time non-footballing staff. That suggests, even to someone who could not crunch a figure to save his life, a bizarre imbalance. A prominent insider said, 'Mr Pierpoint didn't quite understand that a football club runs around the football team and not how many dinner dances you have in a year.' His battles might not have been waged exclusively against O'Neill, but when they involved the manager, he responded.

So much of it was petty. Take the row after the then (short-lived) chairman Tom Smeaton told everybody to have a new suit on the club after their first Wembley League Cup final appearance. Pierpoint tried to stop secretary Ian Silvester and the club physio from being part of this, and it needed an intervention by O'Neill to sort it out. 'Martin was good for that,' Silvester said. 'He looked after everyone and he cared about everyone. He cared about the lady in the laundry, the kit man, the cleaner, all of those who weren't on big salaries. It doesn't happen now, but it did in those days. You know about the way they did it at Tottenham? They'd fine a player £500 and say go and give it to the lady in the laundry room. It was brilliant. There is at least one occasion when Martin handed a laundry lady £100 straight after fining a player. I had a lot of time for that. Martin always made sure that those at the lower end of the scale who did a good job for the club were looked after. He treated them as part of the team. We knew he'd sign people on. One of them was the coach driver who had a heart attack. Obviously he worked for the coach company, but next thing the board knew this coach driver was working down at Beaver Drive as the second kit man. They were saying, "Why do we need two kit men?" They found out that the players were basically paying his wages.

'I know Martin enjoyed being manager of Leicester, but things did get difficult behind the scenes. Barrie Pierpoint will deny it. I read an article he wrote where he said it wasn't him, it was other people. I don't accept that. It was all down to him. It was a clash. He was a person who thought he could have whatever he wanted as managing director. In my opinion he knew nothing about the game, but still started to interfere on the football side.'

Pierpoint wanted to set up a Football Committee chaired by director Phil Smith, but the thought of Martin O'Neill being just one voice in a committee of five (deciding what, exactly?) is laughable. It exposed the Gang's lack of knowledge and understanding of how a top football manager operates. The *Leicester Mercury* ran a story by chief football writer Bill Anderson detailing the plan and opposition to it under the headline THINK AGAIN OR ELSE. The next line, OR I QUIT, was pulled at O'Neill's request.

The interference from Pierpoint and the other three Gang members ranged from the absurd to the serious. One day O'Neill and the rest of his staff were asked to pay for their own mobile telephones in return for a £30-per-head monthly allowance. This apparently penny-pinching move that threatened lines of communication within the club irritated O'Neill when he was alerted to it, and he had a pow-wow with various staff members on how best to deal with it. In the end, O'Neill called in every member of his staff, ordered them to put their mobiles in a bin liner, carried all 30 phones to Pierpoint's office and dumped them on his desk, saying, 'Now, get on with my job.' Pierpoint rang O'Neill in the manager's office almost immediately, telling him it wasn't his idea but the chairman's, John Elsom, and that it was about cutting costs. He urged O'Neill not to be hasty, not to do something daft. By the end of the day every one of the phones had been returned to their owners.

Far more serious was the determination to undermine O'Neill with stories about pre-match drinking to excess, as hinted at by board members after an end-of-season match in 1998 at West Ham. At the time, Leicester were in with a chance of qualifying for Europe. A win and a couple of other results going their way could secure them a place in the UEFA Cup. They had travelled down on Saturday for the Sunday game, which is normal, but it was always a problem for the Leicester board who thought overnight stays were an extravagance that should be stopped. Leicester were 3–0 down by half-time, and Europe was soon out of the question.

It was then that club secretary Ian Silvester was questioned by Pierpoint and another director, Terry Shipman. When did the team travel? Why travel on Saturday for a Sunday kick-off? They were told it was because you have to make sure you get to the game on time and with London traffic that can be difficult. Pierpoint stunned Silvester by accusing O'Neill, who knew nothing about the grilling, and the rest of the travelling staff of drinking. Silvester was told Pierpoint had studied all the hotel bills and the amount drunk. Silvester asked him to confirm that he was accusing the players of drinking before a match. The reply was that they must have been, the team was a shambles on the day.

O'Neill had to be told. To have him criticised so severely behind his back after such an impressive season disgusted Silvester. O'Neill sensed something wasn't right, then Silvester told him exactly what had occurred, that he was being rubbished by two directors over the travel arrangements. Those who witnessed his reaction say O'Neill seemed ready to quit on the spot, and was muttering, 'I've had enough of this.'

At the time, Everton were looking for a new boss. O'Neill grabbed Silvester and dragged him upstairs to confront Pierpoint. He stormed into the boardroom shouting, 'Where's that Pierpoint?' The chief executive wasn't present, but Terry Shipman was. O'Neill fumed, 'Don't you ever question the way I run my football teams again behind my back. Leave that to me, keep your nose out of my affairs.' As he flew out of the private room he saw Pierpoint and Roy Parker, who had always seemed like blood brothers. This time witnesses heard Parker saying, 'Martin, Martin, Martin.' O'Neill turned round and told him what he thought of him and demanded a meeting to sort it out. He then dashed on to the team coach to thank the players for their efforts in what was a great season that hadn't quite worked out. He thanked Silvester for putting his professional life on the line to advise him about what was going on, and added, 'We are going back to the hotel. You will go to the bar and you will order what you want.'

At the bar, Silvester was approached and asked if it was possible that the players could stay that night in London. O'Neill agreed, if the rooms were available, and they went into London for an end-of-season party. So, if the directors hadn't unjustly complained the team would have returned to Leicester on Sunday night with a £5,000 hotel bill instead of returning on the Monday with a bill for £10,000.

Silvester was expecting to be sacked for telling O'Neill about his conversation with Pierpoint. But two days later, the chairman John Elsom departed and was replaced by Phil Smith – there had been a boardroom coup. Smith contacted Silvester and told him he wanted him to remain as club secretary. Both Silvester and Mace, the media man, were still on edge though, certain they would be asked to leave if O'Neill quit. To protect them, O'Neill arranged for them to have pay rises and one-year contracts. Silvester left voluntarily a short while later for his post at Leeds United.

Club co-ordinator Alan Birchenall was extremely impressed by the way in which O'Neill swept aside the problems associated with the job without directly involving his players or affecting the performance of the team. Birchenall has been round the block more than once and has yet to meet the perfect manager. He doesn't believe O'Neill is that, but he credits the Irishman in particular with special man-management skills. 'You can't put your finger on what he's got, not exactly, but I put it down to man management. He knows when to be seen out on the training pitch, he knows when to keep out of the way, he knows when to let the players have their head, he knows when to give them a going over, he knows when they need to be brave. All these, for me, are attributes that make a good manager.

'Martin's shrewd, too. He's shrewd with his buys, though every one's not a winner. He makes mistakes, but I would say a large percentage of the time he gets it right. It's about being able to handle players, I'm totally convinced about that. I've studied managers here, and Martin is for me the ultimate man manager. When you've got thirty, forty individuals and about a quarter of them with egos as big as dustbin lids with the wages they're on, you've got to handle them. If you can do that and gain the respect of your lowest YTS lad, which Martin did and not through fear, it's quite an achievement. He's unique. He came back at the end of [one] season for the game with Celtic and stood there for a good ten minutes, acknowledging the crowd.

'I've seen nine managers come and go at this club in my time here. I've introduced nine managers on the pitch, and they've all had their different ways of doing things, but he is certainly head and shoulders above everybody – with all due respect to Micky Adams, who is, I think, like a young O'Neill. Martin was so quick-witted, banter wise. The players knew not to cross the line with him. He was clever enough to gain their respect and put together a well-balanced side, and he had John Robertson and Steve Walford, completely different characters to him, whom he needed. It was the good guy and the bad guy thing. It was a team thing that turned it round.

'People say it was just lucky, but it wasn't luck. He moulded that side together and it became a unit; even when we played badly. There was a sign in the dressing room, THE GRINDERS, and we used to grind out results. Sometimes they weren't pretty. Don't get the illusion that Martin O'Neill's regime here at Leicester was all fancy football. No, they would grind them out. It produced results, and it all kicked off for us. There were times when I would say, "Oh, dear, this is not, you know, a real quality Leicester City," but it won, we were promoted, and the rest is history. He seems to pick a style of play where everybody knows what he's doing. Everybody slots in; if they don't, he lets them know. He's very uncompromising, yet in a way he's as soft as jelly. But his authority is total.'

John Robertson agreed with Birchenall's assessment, but claimed that the only similarity with the old Brian Clough/

Peter Taylor partnership they'd played for in the old days was the players' attitude to training whenever the boss arrived. They'd be going through the motions, but as soon as Cloughie appeared they would sharpen up. You could sense the difference in attitude, even though his appearances on the training ground were rare. He didn't need to say anything to have an effect.

It has to be said, however, that O'Neill sometimes left himself ridiculously exposed to possible trouble from his players by always flying in for tours the day after the team. It is not the wisest policy, and it blew up in his face on a pre-Wembley break in February 2000 at the La Manga complex in Spain. The players had flown in to relax before the League Cup final against Tranmere, but they ended up too relaxed; in fact, some of them were so relaxed they were comatose. Those who could move unassisted headed for a fire extinguisher, the weapon of choice for extremely relaxed English football club stars. The honour fell to Stan Collymore, undoubtedly O'Neill's most controversial signing, to set it off. The hotel management at La Manga was not impressed, and the whole squad was ejected. At one stage there was the possibility of O'Neill arriving just in time to see his squad head back in the other direction. Robertson, supposedly in charge of the party, was, however, forgiven. And we know what happened to Tranmere at Wembley.

The boardroom fever had reached its peak a few months earlier, just before Christmas 1999 at the club's infamous EGM, with O'Neill publicly backing Elsom and Martin George against the Gang of Four. Ginnetta, on behalf of the supporters club, was so concerned he tried to act as peacemaker with Gilbert Kinch. The fans believed the rowing would not only rip the club apart but sicken O'Neill to the point where he would quit. Chairman of Leicester City plc Sir Rodney Walker and Elsom were off the board, and they denied they had resigned; it was evident to everyone that the Four were going to lose. The whole messy business had been a waste of resources and time. Ginnetta actually rang Gilbert Kinch to advise a retreat. 'Don't do this, I said to him. You can't win this argument with Martin George, you can't take the whole of Leicester on. Even if you're right, it doesn't matter that you're right. Swallow your pride, let the other two come back. But they were having none of this, and it got nasty. The press were going to stand by Martin, right or wrong. The Four, even though they were running the club by then, would have to go because Martin was staying. There were these massive protests at the ground. Anyone else would have walked away, saying, "I don't need this." But out of loyalty to Elsom and George, his preferred ticket, Martin O'Neill stayed and backed them. The Gang of Four too, if they'd been normal people, would have left, but they fought it.

'We had this fabled EGM. Martin was meeting groups of fans and telling us exactly what was going on. No matter what anybody else said, they were going to believe Martin because he was king. There was talk of Brian Kidd being put on standby if Martin O'Neill left, but I don't think any of the fans were worried because they knew the Four would be out at the EGM, and that's what happened. A lot of the votes came in by proxy, so the day before the EGM three of them resigned. Pierpoint had to go to the EGM because he was the chief executive. He was big enough to come over and shake my hand even though I'd done as much to get him the sack as anybody else. "It's not personal, it's business," he said, "and I hope we can remain friends." And we have.

'But we all knew that day that Martin's time was coming to an end. We knew he didn't need to stick this, and perhaps the next time a good job came up, he'd be off. The fact that Martin kept the players away from all that is testimony to what a great manager he is. It was amazing what they achieved. It was the best team in Leicester's history.'

Ginnetta was right: the end for O'Neill was nigh. Drained by the political infighting but still driven by ambition, he needed a new challenge. He'd negotiated a get-out clause in his contract two years earlier after being outmanoeuvred by the then chairman Elsom when Leeds United came calling for the first recorded time. O'Neill had been sickened by Elsom's refusal to acknowledge what O'Neill believed was a gentleman's agreement between them allowing him to talk to other interested clubs when approached. Everton was another club who had shown more than a passing interest in inviting O'Neill to join them, but he was clearly very interested in what Leeds might wish to say to him as they searched for a replacement for George Graham. O'Neill has never sought to hide his feelings, and he was at his most cutting when he sliced through Elsom at a press conference called to confirm he was remaining at Filbert Street. He said, 'The phrase "gentleman's agreement" will disappear from my vocabulary. I've been denied the opportunity to go and speak to a club and it rankles with me. Foolish me, who once studied law for a living. I should've realised an unwritten agreement is precisely that. What it has forced me to do is to get things written down and try to understand English. The fact is that had I been given the opportunity it would have been a *fait accompli*. Leeds United might not have offered me the job at the end of it, though I would have been disappointed if that had happened. I am going to insert about 194 clauses into the new contract, get them written down and get them sorted. If you ask me if I would go out for dinner with him [Elsom] again, as I did a few times before this, then the answer is no.'

So the ground rules had not only been set, but were now legally binding. When Celtic moved for him he was able to talk to the Scottish club and then join them. The disappointment in Leicester was immense and genuine, and it didn't meet with the approval of the board or staff members who had put their own positions in jeopardy by supporting him during the boardroom battles, but for O'Neill, with his background, managing Celtic was as good as a duty. At least he could argue he wasn't doing it for the money but for the honour, having taken a reduced salary to join Celtic. It was O'Neill's determination that eventually helped create real change at the club and produced the climate that inspired the Gary Lineker/Jon Holmes takeover. And they love him still.

14. NOT ALL HE SEEMS

There are so many sides to Martin O'Neill. One-dimensional he is not. The most popular image of him derives from his antics on the touchline. A fertile mind once described him as the Michael Flatley of the bench, and there is certainly an athletic quality to O'Neill's performances during matches that remind you of Flatley's onstage dance routines, if only for the energy expended. O'Neill will spin, turn, gesticulate, agonise and celebrate in an amazing public display. It is a source of irritation for opposition managers, but O'Neill's supporters love it. After all, doesn't it prove how much he cares? If you asked him, he would really prefer to watch from the terraces surrounded by a group of true fans like himself, the only true believers. There are those who see method in his mania, see him working the crowd like one of the better stage comedians. When he prances around, occasionally swigging comfortably from a water bottle, when he looks increasingly demented to a point when we expect the men in white coats to emerge from the tunnel and lead him away, he is telling everyone he is there with them, living every moment of a 90-minute experience. Yet within minutes of a match finishing he will be on television explaining victory or defeat with the hushed tones of a cleric and the clarity of a don.

These are the only clues to O'Neill's nature the vast majority of the football public can have. They will have admired his success, justifiably, and his support of issues during the political furore at Leicester when he alone scattered what he saw as the destructive Gang of Four before they could take over the club from directors he trusted. Above all, he is seen as a winner, and what else matters to supporters? But the other sides to this complex man are fascinating too, and are experienced only by a much smaller audience: his family, his closest associates, club staff and, to a lesser degree, reporters in print and on radio and television.

Martin Hugh Michael O'Neill is a hyperactive contradiction: manic and wild-eyed one moment, mild and almost doleful the next. He can be rude and brusque, kind and caring; he can be helpful or dismissive, arrogant or humble, super-confident or totally lacking in confidence; he can be quick-witted and slow to respond; he can be shy and diffident, yet capable of incredible exuberance in company; he's a loner who likes people close to him, a demander of loyalty who has not always been considered loyal; he's also highly ambitious, but even people who know him are not convinced he wanted to be a manager at the outset.

His most impressive quality as a player was commitment, a need to win that separates the professional from the herd. It can manifest itself at inappropriate times, too, when it is less of an asset and more an embarrassment. There was just such an occasion on a pre-season tour with Celtic in Austria, after the 2002 World Cup finals at a time when the Leeds United saga and his link with the post vacated by David O'Leary had settled down. There are reporters who enjoy a Press v. Club football match and the opportunity it provides for a 25-year-old, say, to be shown up as a talentless, wheezing, unco-ordinated, unathletic misfit by a 50-year-old former international player. With someone like O'Neill still a stranger in town, it was also a way for both sides to do a bit of bonding, to get to know each other as friendly opponents. What happened on that July day and on a subsequent day had the merit of being informative: it was the day the press saw an entirely different O'Neill. They knew about 'Manic' O'Neill and 'Mad Eyes' O'Neill, but this was a league on from that.

There are those convinced that the change in O'Neill's attitude from wary to positively aggressive stemmed from a confrontation he had with a 'news hound' at Bisham Abbey outside London where Celtic were training before leaving for Austria. The big question that remained unanswered then was when he was going to sign a new contract. Now, O'Neill, in the opinion of most media men, had fashioned a good enough working relationship with them; there were to be no exclusive interviews and that offered a line of protection for both manager and reporter, but as compensation there would be regular press conferences, and some had a mobile phone number for use if required. He was not going to be out of touch. The incident that weakened this link came when the reporter jumped out at him from behind a bush with a photographer in an attempt to secure an exclusive story. The only exclusive his paper achieved was a picture of a startled-looking O'Neill. The Celtic manager was furious, and worried that the press would continue to deal with him in this disrespectful way. For the expectation of a story that was never going to materialise under that sort of pressure, the reporter and the publication that encouraged him had effectively threatened the relationship between the Celtic manager and the rest of the press corps.

O'Neill's experience in working with the media had developed over a number of years and had involved major events as a player and manager in England and internationally, but he had never before experienced the intensity of demand that existed at Celtic, with its constant requirement to feed the media beast. At Leicester, daily contact had come in the form of the *Mercury*'s Bill Anderson in the first place, plus the nationals' Midlands-based reporters. There would be agency calls to deal with, or to parry, but it was controllable compared to what was expected of him in Glasgow, and even there the Scottish media weren't ecstatic about their access arrangements. It was difficult, but he was coping – until the 'snatch' incident at Bisham.

The Press v. Club match in Austria was therefore an opportunity to repair broken trust. The result was unimportant: the press team was taken apart and lost eight goals to a Celtic side comprising O'Neill, John Robertson, Steve Walford, John Clark, a couple of Celtic TV people and a couple of kit men. It was just about par for the course in these matches. Interestingly, though, it was noticed that the second half had far exceeded the original pre-arranged twenty minutes each way. O'Neill happened to be referee and timekeeper as well as player; he scored his first goal of the match in the 26th minute then blew for time. 'So what?' said the reporters. 'It was good enough fun.'

Later that evening, Celtic phoned the journalists with a challenge to play another match next morning. There was some bartering: the press wanted a goal start, they wanted a reasonable pitch size and they had to agree the number of players in each team (they settled on eight) before the game went ahead. There was even talk from Celtic about the losers paying out £10 for every goal conceded. These are vital points to be agreed in matches at this level. The game was on, but it was to turn out to be a bizarre and unpleasant encounter.

O'Neill was in a weird mood from the start, and by the time the game ended he had lost control of himself in the most dramatic way. The press wanted to use an Austrian ringer because they had barely enough players to field a team, but when O'Neill saw him he asked who he was. The situation was explained to him, but he would not accept it and demanded that the Austrian leave the field. Things were already heated by the time Celtic scored their opening goal. It was then noticed that Celtic had nine men on the field, and when the pressmen protested it was the spark that ignited an O'Neill tantrum that stunned onlookers. The

European Cup winner, World Cup star and now manager of one of the most famous clubs in world football flew into a shouting and swearing rage that went on and on. His venom was directed at one particular reporter, but all were shocked by what they were witnessing. As if it mattered, the Celtic goal was allowed to stand, O'Neill still refusing to accept that his team had cheated by using nine men. The goodwill disappeared fast, but it was still an enlightening experience for the reporters. They saw O'Neill the bully, the control freak, the man who must be obeyed, the man who must win at all costs. It was noted that neither Robertson nor Walford interfered while the boss was raging.

This was not the Irishman who is charm itself, so unassuming, as one of the BBC's analysts. The pressmen had never seen O'Neill so demented, they couldn't even believe it possible under the circumstances, and he was not joking with them. It made them realise exactly how powerful his personality was, and what an influence he must be on the Celtic players over important issues. It also explained why he'd been ordered from the bench twice during Celtic's European ties. Bench rage, even allowing for poor refereeing and unjust decisions against his players, is inexcusable.

When O'Neill was once asked outright if he thought of himself as potty, he gave a perfectly lucid answer: 'When you look at the way I behave on matchdays I suppose I am. I don't want to be, but I have to say that when I see myself on television replays I am terribly embarrassed. I just don't realise what I am doing out there.

'Managers have different ways of watching a game and thinking at the same time. I believe being constantly on the move, totally involved with every kick, header, throw-in and tackle, helps me think more clearly. I might look frantic, but I can still see a pattern of play and the things I need to do. Maybe if I was calmer, more dispassionate, it wouldn't be as effective. I need to be part of what's going on. I'm driven by the desire to win trophies. I remember the

League championship and European Cup triumphs at Forest. There is no feeling to compare – things you never dreamed of. My wife, Geraldine, says my ego will always be bigger than my bank balance, but that's the way I am. To win a title, to conquer Europe – that would be the ultimate.'

O'Neill's loyalty to those he likes is total, but he is capable of making decisions that anger others, and in the case of Leicester City that left a number of staff wondering why they had come out so strongly in support of him when as soon as the battle against Barrie Pierpoint et al had been won the leader quit to join Celtic. A top Premiership director was in touch with Leicester throughout the saga, close enough to the then Filbert Street hierarchy to realise why they regarded O'Neill as a political animal who tried to create a power struggle to show he was the strongest. In their opinion, he wanted to be dictator and was therefore not interested in a democracy prevailing at the club. A biased view, but one that would reinforce the argument that he always wanted to be in complete control. It also fits with his determination, his concentration and his commitment to whatever cause he happened to be championing. The Leicester directors at the time accepted his success and were grudgingly but realistically aware of his popularity. They knew he would win conclusively if he continued to target them as the opposition. On the day that Smith, Parker and Kinch stood down as directors, O'Neill was accused of stoking the fire that had engulfed them. It was an extraordinary declaration to make about a football manager, but in this case it had a broad base of truth.

'I think,' Smith announced, 'that he [Martin O'Neill] has used the situation to manipulate the outcome. He is a fine manager and has done a fantastic job for the club. But we are disappointed that having given him our support he should have been so unreasonable. He left no one in any doubt as to his position and the possible consequences if we won the vote, yet at no time has he given us any concrete reasons why he is not able to work with us. On the other hand we have continually shown our willingness to work with him. Our board made Martin one of the highest-paid managers in British football, and we have, on many occasions, provided funds to break the club's record transfer fee, the latest of which was only last week when we signed off £3 million to buy Darren Eadie. Does this demonstrate any lack of support for the manager? Our departure should offer comfort to the fans and shareholders, and ensure, after his strong support for [Rodney] Walker and [John] Elsom, that Martin O'Neill will not leave the club at least until the end of his contract in June 2002, irrespective of the break clauses he insisted were within it. We would now expect at least that of him.' We can deduce from this statement that the Four had no confidence in O'Neill's staying. It was their last barb, the one thing we can safely say they were accurate about.

O'Neill's ruthlessness had done for them. He felt he had been messed about by Pierpoint, and if the other three, none of whom had had any great relationship with him, were aligned to the chief executive then they would be opposed too. It was as simple as that. In victory, and it was a considerable one, there was no sympathy for the defeated – quite the opposite. O'Neill said, 'They have brought this on themselves. They misunderstood the whole situation and brought trials and tribulations upon this football club as a result of what has been going on politically for so many weeks. I found my energies being sidetracked, but now we can get on with concentrating on the football and achieving the target of qualifying for Europe in either the Premiership or one of the cup competitions. I am under no illusions that if I have five or six bad results I will still be threatened with the boot. Whatever support I have given Sir Rodney [Walker] and John Elsom will not prevent me losing my job eventually. That is the way football is.'

Some thought it was almost a matter of satisfying the ambition his father Leo had for him, but for many at Leicester the mystery remained as to why O'Neill accepted the offer to manage Celtic. Cliff Ginnetta said that the club's supporters could not believe it was Celtic who enticed their man away. 'I'd never heard him mention being the Irishman who always wanted to go to Celtic,' Ginnetta said. 'Neil Lennon, yes. Martin, no. We all understood that Martin was a Sunderland fan, that he'd supported them as a kid and had always wanted to manage them. When the Celtic job came up, that was the one time I thought, "He won't go there." I went off to Norfolk and took some calls from press guys who said he's going to Celtic, and I said, "He can't be." I couldn't believe it. I was amazed, knowing how passionate he was about football, how he loves to win, why he wanted to go there.

'I can't believe Martin and Robbo are happy playing in that standard of football, even though they came and beat Blackburn in the UEFA Cup [in November 2002]. To pit your wits against the best every week is what Martin O'Neill, I would imagine, or any manager, would want to do. I can understand players because it must be an easy life: you've got four hard games a season. Yes, I was bitterly disappointed that he did that. Perhaps one day he will say why. Perhaps he really was a lifelong Celtic fan. Why anyone would want to deal with so many journeymen I can't understand, not when there are jobs going down here like Leeds, even the Leicester job or the Sunderland job. If Leeds had had money to pay the compensation of £2.5 million or £3 million, they would have paid it.

'I had a run-in with the press up there, threatened never to go to Scotland on holiday. I received some nasty letters. The Scottish *Sun* rang me back after the treble and I had to eat humble pie. Neil Lennon took a pay cut to go, but Muzzy Izzet didn't go, nor did Matt Elliott. He didn't want to play in that standard of football, and he knows about it because he plays for Scotland.'

It is unlikely O'Neill will consider any of the career decisions he has made as in any way disloyal, but it is up to those affected by what he has done to decide on that. And you can be certain that many weren't happy. But O'Neill never forgets the kindnesses extended to him by former team-mates – no problem about loyalty there. When he was a youngster at Distillery he was watched over by older team-mate Alan McCarrol, who remembers Martin's first day at the club and being given the instruction to look after him. Three decades later they keep in touch. McCarrol and his family were guests of O'Neill's at Filbert Street. McCarrol also received a phone call on the night of the Belfast Sportsman of the Year Awards in the summer of 2000 and was invited by O'Neill to come to the hotel for a chat. They sat up talking until early the following morning, and it was then he first heard of the Celtic offer. McCarrol said he must take it, and forecast that if he did he'd win the treble.

O'Neill needs to make money, likes making money, and is not afraid to spend it when he feels it is important to do so. When he found he wouldn't be available to attend a reunion of the Distillery Irish Cup-winning side scheduled for Belfast, he arranged for the team to fly to Glasgow for a night out with him. He goes out of his way to meet old friends and former team-mates. He tells of the 1982 World Cup reunion when he was approached by a Glasgow Rangers fan who asked him to sign an autograph and then told him, 'Jeez, you didn't half make my life a misery.' He was talking about Celtic's clean sweep for the treble. O'Neill enjoyed that.

It was O'Neill who made the arrangements for the coach driver at Leicester to be looked after when the man had recovered from a heart attack. It was O'Neill who intervened and sorted out the contracts of his allies Ian Silvester and Paul Mace when their support of him suggested their future at Leicester was balanced between bleak and non-existent. It was O'Neill who handed over fines to people far less well remunerated but whom he considered part of the chain of success at the club. Every year, O'Neill arranged for a Christmas night out for the staff, the coaching staff, the laundry staff and all the other backroom people. He would pay for them to have dinner and go to the theatre in London. At the end of the season he would take them out to a local restaurant. O'Neill recognised it wasn't just about him or John Robertson or Steve Walford or Silvester or Mace; there was far more to Leicester's success than that. It depended on so many others, and he wanted them to know they were appreciated.

O'Neill may be thought of as one of the smartest kids on the block, but not too smart (or too proud) in the early years that he couldn't phone more experienced managers for advice. He had a list of those he thought were responsible people in the game. He didn't pester them, but would contact them when required to tap their knowledge, mainly on matters concerning transfers. Eventually he joined clubs that could instruct their own lawyers, but before that he relied on the help of his fellow managers.

There is a stern exterior to O'Neill that doesn't always reflect his mood, a mood that can change in an instant. What he will not tolerate in his players is misery – unless as a reaction to defeat. As he explained, 'I refuse to have a drab dressing room, a sullen atmosphere. It is possible to mix fun with business. I want my players to feel the pain of defeat as much as I do and the sheer joy of winning. You ask if I am potty. Well, if I ever heard one of my players laughing on the coach half an hour after losing, that would drive me insane.'

It is only a question of time before O'Neill will have satisfied his own club ambitions, and if he is as potty as he seems to think it may well be that he'll take charge of the Northern Ireland international squad. On current form, however, it will be quite a few years before that happens. He has been asked before: he was favourite for the job when it became vacant in the summer of 1999, but he declined and Englishman Lawrie McMenemy stepped in. The former England assistant made a point of inviting O'Neill to join him in a part-time capacity. McMenemy said, 'I was aware I was the first Englishman to manage Northern Ireland and it was vital I maintained the Irish link. I spoke to Martin. He would have been delighted to work with the national side again, but there were far too many commitments at Leicester for him to consider even a part-time role. Northern Ireland needed a strong character like Martin and we were lucky to convince Pat Jennings to work with us, to have Joe Jordan as the coach, and to have Chris Nicholl on board. Martin O'Neill is very impressive. It takes a strong character to play for Brian Clough. If he can stand up to Brian then I can see why he would be a success as a manager.'

O'Neill has had to cope with sectarian abuse from time to time. There have been moments when he's been greatly concerned by it. The abuse has had nothing to do with religion as such, more with his well-known background in Irish nationalism. Some of the worst O'Neill has had to endure was when his teams played in the British Army garrison town of Colchester. He was prepared for blasts of sectarianism from Glasgow Rangers fans, but hadn't expected aggression from Colchester's supporters. O'Neill remarked after one particularly bad experience when he was Wycombe manager, 'The Colchester mob gave me dog's abuse. That is one time I wish I hadn't been Irish. I've had my games since I came to Celtic when I've had dog's abuse, and there were occasions before that. But when the Colchester mob take over the stand you know all about it.' O'Neill has never hidden or tried to disguise his Irishness from his team-mates, but not one of them ever felt his tub-thumping to be aggressive or offensive.

Billy Bingham, his old Northern Ireland mentor, said, 'You have to find your forte. Most of my managerial life was in national management. I had found my forte. You have to know where you are going, what you are good at and where you want to be. I managed the Greek national team, I managed the Saudi Arabian team and Northern Ireland twice. So I found my forte and I blossomed. The day-to-day running of a club is an entirely different matter.

I think in time there will be a place for both of them in an England set-up because it will be forced to change. Martin has gone to Celtic because that's the love in his heart from way back. I am absolutely certain of that. Most of Northern Ireland's Catholics will follow Celtic, and the Northern Ireland Protestants follow Rangers. They go over to Glasgow with their union jacks and their tricolours, they sing their songs and they are happy. Martin was brought up in that atmosphere, and for him to go to Celtic was great. It was something I think he had to do. He may feel he still has something to fulfil in England, but he has done the Leicesters. He needed Leicester because he wanted to prove himself there, and he did, tremendously. So then he went with his heart, to Celtic. Now, what more can he do?'

There were those convinced that O'Neill's ambition would force him out of Celtic. There was a counter view, now discredited, that his role in Glasgow would satisfy him if Celtic could provide the financial backing to buy players to keep improving the side, to make them into a team capable not of a UEFA Cup Final, achieved, but, given time and added resources, to appear again in the final of the European Cup, now the Champions League. Celtic would have been happy to meet these requirements as far as possible, but the belief among Celtic's directors and fans was the near certainty O'Neill would move on. What they did not envisage was the ill health of Geraldine being the reason. O'Neill retreated to the family home in Buckinghamshire in May 2005 where he was pursued by a number of Premiership clubs anxious to secure what they saw as his guarantee of success. Only Aston Villa were able to persuade him to make a comeback and you can be certain O'Neill's decision was taken with the full backing of Geraldine and their two daughters, Aisling and Alana – the driving force in his life.

FACT FILE

Full Name: Martin Hugh Michael O'Neill MBE
Born: 1 March 1952; Kilrea NI

PLAYING CAREER

Schools: St Columb's, Londonderry (Gaelic football)
         St Malachy's College, Belfast (Gaelic football)
Youth: Rosario Youth Club, Belfast

PROFESSIONAL CLUBS

August 1969–October 1971	Distillery (Irish League)
October 1971–February 1981	Nottingham Forest (£15,000)
February 1981–June 1981	Norwich City (250,000)
June 1981–January 1982	Manchester City (£275,000)
January 1982–August 1983	Norwich City (£150,000)
August 1983–May 1985	Notts County (Free)
	Retired due to injury

INTERNATIONALS

Northern Ireland (1971–84) 64 appearances (58 + 6 sub) 9 goals

PLAYING HONOURS AND CAREER HIGHLIGHTS

1971   Won Irish Cup with DISTILLERY beating Derry City in final
       Appeared in European Cup Winners Cup v. FC Barcelona (aged
       19)

1977 Helped NOTTINGHAM FOREST gain promotion to 'top flight'
      (in third place)
      Won Anglo Scottish Cup
1978 Won League Championship with NOTTINGHAM FOREST
      Won League Cup beating Liverpool in final at Wembley
      Won Charity Shield beating Ipswich Town at Wembley
1979 Helped NOTTINGHAM FOREST win European Cup (did not
      play in final) beating Malmo
      Won League Cup beating Southampton in final at Wembley
1980 Won European Cup for second year running beating SV Hamburg
      in final
      Won European Super Cup beating FC Barcelona
      Runners-up in League Championship
      League Cup finalists losing to Wolves in final at Wembley
      Won World Club Championship beating Nacional
1981 Lost European Super Cup to Valencia
1982 Helped NORWICH CITY gain promotion to 'top flight' (in third
      place)
      Captained NORTHERN IRELAND in World Cup finals in Spain

PERSONAL HONOURS

1982 Awarded MBE for services to football

MANAGERIAL CAREER

July 1987–July 1989	GRANTHAM TOWN (Southern League – Midland Division)
July 1989–September 1989	SHEPSHED CHARTERHOUSE (Northern Premier League – Premier Division)
July 1990–June 1995	WYCOMBE WANDERERS (Football Conference 1990–93; Football League 1993–95)
June 1995–December 1995	NORWICH CITY (Football League Division 1)
December 1995–June 2000	LEICESTER CITY (Football League Division 1 1995–96; FA Premier League 1996–2000)
July 2000–May 2005	CELTIC (Scottish Premier League)
August 2006 to date of publication	ASTON VILLA (FA Premier League)

MANAGERIAL HONOURS AND CAREER HIGHLIGHTS

1991 Won FA Trophy with WYCOMBE WANDERERS beating Kidderminster at Wembley

1992 Won Bob Lord Trophy (for Conference Clubs) beating Runcorn

1993 Won Football Conference with WYCOMBE WANDERERS (gaining automatic promotion to the Football League)
Won FA Trophy again, beating Runcorn at Wembley

1994 Steers WYCOMBE WANDERERS to promotion to Division 2 in club's first ever League season; Preston North End beaten in Divisonal play-off at Wembley

1996 Guides LEICESTER CITY to promotion to FA Premier League in his first season at Filbert Street; Crystal Palace beaten in Divisonal play-off at Wembley

1997 Won League Cup with LEICESTER CITY beating Middlesbrough at Hillsborough
Takes the club into Europe for first time since 1961, in the UEFA Cup

1999 LEICESTER CITY are League Cup finalists, losing to Tottenham Hotspur at Wembley

2000 Won League Cup again, beating Tranmere Rovers at Wembley

2001 Won Scottish domestic 'treble' with CELTIC in his first season:
– Scottish Premier League champions
– Scottish FA Cup winners beating Hibernian at Hampden Park
– Scottish League Cup winners beating Kilmarnock at Hampden Park

2002 Won Scottish Premier League (second year running) with a record 103 points. Losing finalists in Scottish FA Cup going down to Rangers at Hampden Park. O'Neill appears in European Champions League for the first time, CELTIC going out at the end of the First Group stage. Celtic 'drop into' the UEFA Cup competition, immediately losing to Valencia

2003 UEFA Cup finalists – losing to Porto

2004 Won the Scottish Premier League and Scottish FA Cup Double. CELTIC go out of the 2003/04 Champions League competition after the first round and eventually lose to Villarreal in the UEFA Cup.

2005 Won the Scottish FA Cup, CELTIC's sole trophy when they beat Dundee United 1–0 at Hampden having lost the Scottish Premier League title to Rangers on the last day of the league campaign six days earlier.

INDEX